# The Surprising Joy
## OF EXPLORING GOD'S HEART

A Daily Adventure with 365 of His Names

# GAYLYN R. WILLIAMS

www.RelationshipResources.org

# Table of Contents

**To get a free copy of the following books in PDF go to www.rrbooks.org/free-e-books:**
- *De-Stress Your Life*
- *Reconcilable Differences*
- *Unlocking Your Joy*

# Dedication

This book is dedicated to all the intercessory missionaries at the Jericho Center and around the world with Every Home for Christ. I have been so blessed by you and your worship. Thank you. I pray God will show Himself more and more real to you as you continue to get to know Him and worship Him.

# What's in a Name?

**Foreword by Dick Eastman**

We all agree—one's name is important!

A name, according to Webster's dictionary, is "a word or phrase that constitutes the distinctive designation of a person or thing." In our lives, the unique ability to give "distinctive designation" to people and things, through a name, helps us order our very existence. When we hear the name of a friend or loved one, we immediately conjure up images of that person and his or her characteristics.

One of the first jobs Adam was given in the garden was to name all the animals. From the beginning, God made humans with the ability to organize their life and identify things around them through naming. But often we forget just how important a name can actually be. Imagine using only generic terms when speaking to those around us? Hey, you! Or, hey person with the brown hair! Imagine shouting to a child in one's family: "Come here, short person with the freckles." Life would be sadly generic and sometimes even confusing. What if two of one's children were short and both had freckles?

The reality in life is that each of us was given a name by our parents, and this name is one of the primary means of preserving our identity in a world of seven billion-plus people. Names, in our western culture, often represent decades or sometimes centuries of family heritage. What comes to your mind when you hear the name Winston Churchill, Dwight David Eisenhower or Mother Theresa? Likewise, names often carry special meaning or ascribe particular attributes to us.

Names can represent societal trends and therefore identify someone with a specific era in history. In some unique instances in the Bible what a child was named was so important that angels would actually come to earth and tell expecting parents what to name their coming child. For example, an angel told Zachariah (see Luke chapter one) to name their son John. We would know him for generations to come as John the Baptist. Joseph, likewise, was told in a dream to name Mary's baby boy "Jesus," a name that literally means "God saves." Clearly, what we are called by those around us is significant. Names have always been a big deal to God.

Throughout time, God has been gracious enough to reveal His own name in multiple ways to humankind. Starting with Adam and progressing until today, in various times and in various ways, God has revealed His identity to people using phrases that one might view as His names. Today, we're more accustomed to hearing the various names attributed to our Lord. Can you imagine what it was like when the first prophet learned that our Lord was "the God of angel armies?" Undoubtedly there was a sense of awe and wonder. Even today, I am filled with that same awe and wonder when I hear many of the names of our Lord. What an amazing privilege that God has actually told us Who He is by revealing His vast variety of names in so many ways throughout His Word!

Over my years of following Jesus, I have found tremendous confidence and strength from regularly considering the names of the Lord in prayer. For decades I have compiled my own personal list of the Lord's names, drawing these names from numerous translations of Scripture. From these lists, I have written into each day's entry in my journal one of those names, claiming the fullness of that name for that specific day. Often I allow that name to become a song that I sing in my devotional time for that day.

As I meditate, speak, and pray the names of the Lord over the situations of my life, I have found that what I'm actually doing is inserting God's very identity into those situations. When I proclaim a biblical name of our Lord, I'm making a statement of faith—God is Who He said He is! The knowledge of God's name literally transforms the way we live by infusing faith into our prayers! Of course, certain passages of Scripture fortify this reality. The Psalmist sang:

> *Hallelujah! Thank God! Pray to him by name! Tell everyone you meet what he has done…Honor his holy name with Hallelujahs, you who seek God…Keep your eyes open for God, watch for his works*
> Psalm 105:1, 3-4 The Message Bible

On an earlier occasion the psalmist declared:

> *All day we parade God's praise—*
> *we thank you by name over and over*
> Psalm 44:8 The Message Bible

All these thoughts lead me to highlight this wonderful collection of Names of our Lord that you hold in your hand. They have been compiled by a special friend of my wife and me, Gaylyn Williams. Like me, years ago Gaylyn began compiling descriptive phrases that define and describe our Lord. My list contains almost 700 such names, but Gaylyn's goes far beyond that. You will find literally hundreds and hundreds of such descriptive expressions in Scripture in the pages that follow. Indeed, the author of this helpful guide has saved you countless hours in searching out these cherished expressions describing the nature and character of our Lord.

My suggestion to you is this: Pray these names daily—and sing them, memorize them and (most of all) live them. You'll soon discover a personal Jesus that you've never known before. Further, you'll find practical ways to apply these names. A famous credit card commercial once saturated their advertising with the phrase—"Don't leave home without it!" May I suggest that you start each day with a fresh Name of our Lord from this list and that you "don't leave home without it!" Carry Christ's Name into your day! You will never regret it.

**—Dick Eastman,**
International President of Every Home for Christ

# *Acknowledgements*

I am deeply indebted to many people who made this book possible. Rubin Paxton spent tireless hours fixing the format, inputting changes into the manuscript and helping with all the details of getting the book finalized. Thank you. You kept my sanity.

Thank you to all the people who read through the book and gave me their insights and found typos: Steve and Evelyn Sherwood, Ken Williams, Lori Kenzel, Linda Harris, Paulette Harris, Megan Whalin and Amy Hartman.

A special thanks to Gordon and Dian Bredvick. I have gotten so much motivation and writing done at your lovely cabin.

I appreciate all the encouragement and support from friends, family and those who read my daily blog: www.365NamesOfGod.com.

Finally, thank you to my sons, Jonathan and Timothy. Both of you have been such an encouragement to me as I've worked through this book. Jonathan helped with getting the book in order. Timothy gave much needed professional advice on the design. Thank you.

*Discovering Joy in Intimacy with God*

## Thoughts from the Author

I began my adventure exploring God's names when my second son, Daniel, was three months old. After being in and out of the hospital—mostly in—his whole life, the doctor had just told me Daniel had six to twelve months left to live.

What had been a time of grief, sadness and questioning turned into a surprisingly joyful experience. After six surgeries and seeing twenty-five pediatric specialists, I finally realized the doctors couldn't do anything to save Daniel. God was his only hope.

The previous three months, I had focused on my problems and became more and more depressed. The day the doctor delivered my son's "death sentence," I knew I had a choice. I could be sad and miserable, or I could choose to focus on God and trust Him.

Daily I cared for my three-year-old son Jonathan, along with juggling Daniel's numerous doctor appointments and high levels of oxygen. During those difficult months, I started a list of God's names from the Word. Every day I chose to take time to focus on God, even though it was not easy.

Daniel's health slid downhill, until he went into a three-day coma when he was almost six months old. He woke up briefly just before he went to be with Jesus. At that moment, I experienced an unexpected joy, because I knew God had healed him—not as I hoped, but he was now completely whole and healthy.[1]

I discovered that when I focus on my problems, they seem to get bigger and more overwhelming. However, when I focus on God, my problems seem to shrink compared to how great He is. And I experience amazing joy and peace.

That adventure started 25 years ago and I'm still on it, although I took a break for a few years. And guess what? During those years when I stopped focusing on God—because I was fixated on my problems—I experienced less peace and joy, as well as depression and hopelessness.

I now have over 1800 names of God from the Word and I'm still finding more. I'm constantly astonished at all of God's names. The more I study them, the more joy, peace and excitement God is giving me with life. Our God is so great. I'm sure no matter how much we learn about Him, we'll never know everything.

Studying God's names and getting to know Him better through them has been one of the greatest adventures of my life. I pray you too will be surprised by incredible joy and peace as you study His names and as you get to know Him better with all the various facets of Who He is.

**Blessings on you,**

*Gaylyn Williams*

To get a free digital copy of my latest book, *All Stressed Up and Everywhere to Go!: Solutions to De-Stressing Your Life and Recovering Your Sanity*, email me at Free@365NamesofGod.com.

# How to Use This Book

The purpose of this devotional is to reveal more of Who God is and empower you to experience a deeper intimacy with Him. It is not meant to be me sharing all *my* wisdom. It is designed to help you dig deeper to discover more about God for yourself and grow in your relationship with Him.

Each day has a Scripture, questions to ponder and a short prayer related to the name. You can use them as a springboard to a deeper prayer time and study. There is space to journal on most days; however, you might want to keep a separate journal beside you to add more. I briefly share some of my stories so you can see how God's names have affected my life. I share both victories and defeats in my adventure to know God better.

**You Can Use This Book in the Following Ways:**

- in your personal devotions, drawing you into deeper intimacy with God

- as a couples devotional, growing in your relationship with each other and God

- with your children, helping them gain a bigger view of God

- in a small group, sharing your insights together

If you don't yet have a personal relationship with God, you've come to the right place. You can explore more of who God is in a relaxed way. If you want to know more, go to page 369.

In this book, I use different translations of the Bible, which show variations and nuances of God's names. You might want to check other translations to see how they depict our awesome God. The abbreviations for the Bible translations are on the copyright page. All unmarked verses are from the New International Version.

Throughout the book I encourage you to memorize Bible verses. When you have the Word in your heart, you'll be amazed at the times God will bring it back to you—just when you need it. I've been memorizing Scripture since I was a child. Often during the night, when I wake up and can't go back to sleep, I'll begin meditating on a verse.

I had a missionary friend, Chet Bitterman, who was captured by terrorists in Colombia in the 1980s. Although he had no Bible, he the

Word in his heart and mind. He had just finished memorizing the book of 1 Peter. His letters to his wife were filled with Scripture. If you were suddenly without your Bible, how much of it would you have in you? For help on memorizing verses, go to www.365NamesofGod.com.

At the back of the book are lists where you can find help for specific situations. For example, if you are feeling sad, you can go to page 22, where you can find comfort in God's name "My Exceeding Joy." If you need hope, go to page 13.

**Hebrew and Greek Words:**

I include many of God's names in the original languages. However, I am not a Hebrew or Greek scholar. I only include that information to add to your understanding. I don't pretend to fully comprehend them. I'm a fellow adventurer, longing to continue to know God more intimately.

About spelling: I write the Hebrew and Greek words so they are easy to pronounce (I'm sure there are other ways to spell them).

About pronouns: When a name of God starts with a pronoun, such as my or your, I only show the Hebrew root, not the pronoun. The pronoun is a suffix on the noun.

About capitalization on Greek and Hebrew words: When the word is always and only used for God, it is capitalized, as well as full names of God. Other Hebrew and Greek words are left lowercase.

The Hebrew Word, *Sh'ma,* on the front cover is the first word in Deuteronomy 6:4, "Hear, O Israel: the LORD our God, the LORD is one." It means hear, listen in order to obey the Name (God's Name). The ancient Hebrew symbols in *Sh'ma* were a picture of an eye and a picture representing "name," meaning "See the Name." This book is all about seeing and hearing God's Name(s). *Sh'ma* is also written *Shema* or *Shma.*

## January 1

### The Beginning and the End

Arkhay Kai Telos (Greek)

*I am the Alpha and the Omega, the First and the Last,*
**the Beginning and the End.**
Revelation 22:13 (ESV)

**Steps on Your Journey to Know God More Intimately:**

- *Arkhay* means beginning or principality. *Telos* means end, ending and finally.

- Happy New Year. Just think: this is a new year, an opportunity to begin fresh. As we end one year and begin a new one, it's a great time to focus on the Lord being the Beginning and the End.

- Think about this name. What does it mean to you?

- How does this name affect your life today? This year?

- How did last year begin, what was different at the end?

- As I begin this year, I choose to let go of the difficult things from this last year and begin fresh. I encourage you to do the same.

- Take some time today to reflect on all the good things God did in your life this last year. Thank Him for His blessings (even if things were not as positive as you would have liked).

- Talk to the Lord about this coming year. What do you want to be different this year? Remember, He is the Beginning. He can bring you new beginnings.

**A Prayer for You:**

*Thank You, Lord, that You are the Beginning and the End. Thank You for all the great things You did in my life last year. I'm looking forward to seeing what You have for me this coming year. Thank You that I can start over fresh with You, the Beginning.*

# Him Who Is from the Beginning

Ton Apo Arkhay (Greek)

*I am writing to you, fathers, because you know*
**him who is from the beginning.**
1 John 2:13 (ESV)

**Steps on Your Journey to Know God More Intimately:**

- *Ton* means he, one, the and that. *Apo* means from, of and out of. *Arkhay* means beginning.

- Meditate on this name.[2] What does it mean to you today that God is from the beginning?

- How does it affect your life knowing He has always been there? He has no beginning … or end. If you're like me, it's hard to really comprehend that He has no beginning. Ask the Lord to reveal to you what that means.

- Spend some time praising the Lord using this name.

**A Prayer for You:**

*Lord, I praise You that You have always existed and You always will. Open my mind to be able to comprehend this truth that You are Him Who Is from the Beginning. Please show me what this name means to me personally.*

## January 3

### *God*

Elohim (Hebrew); Theos (Greek)

*In the beginning **God** created the heavens and the earth.*
Genesis 1:1 (NKJV)

**Steps on Your Journey to Know God More Intimately:**

- Deuteronomy 10:17 says, "The LORD your God is God of gods, and Lord of lords. He is the great God, the mighty and awesome God, who shows no partiality and cannot be bribed" (NLT).

- This is the very first of God's names that He gives us, in the first verse of the Bible. These verses use *Elohim*, which means Almighty God, the Creator. It is also the word that is used of any god, not just the One True God. *Elohim* is plural of God, revealing the first hint of the Trinity, one God in three persons. *Theos* means the supreme deity.

- Each word for God and gods is exactly the same word in the Old Testament verses above.

- Ephesians 2:4-5 says, "But because of his great love for us, God, who is rich in mercy, made us alive with Christ even when we were dead in transgressions—it is by grace you have been saved.

- I grew up in a little village high in the mountains of Guatemala, where my parents were missionaries with Wycliffe Bible Translators. I saw the Mayans worshipping all their gods, burning their incense and candles in front of the Catholic Church.

- Meditate on this name. Ask God to reveal more of Himself to you today.

- What does the name God mean to you?

**A Prayer for You:**

*God, I praise You that You are the God of gods and Lord of lords. Thank You that You are the mighty and awesome God, that You are the Creator. Please open my eyes, ears and heart to know You more and more intimately.*

3

## January 4

### *My Faithful God*

*Into your hands I commit my spirit;*
*deliver me, Lord, **my faithful God**.*
Psalm 31:5

**Steps on Your Journey to Know God More Intimately:**

- When Jesus was hanging on the cross, He quoted part of this verse in Luke 23:46: "Jesus called out with a loud voice, 'Father, into your hands I commit my spirit.'"

- The Hebrew word for faithful is *emeth* and means certainty, truth, trustworthiness, establishment, faithful, right, sure and true. Some versions translate this name as "The God of Truth." *El* is the singular for *Elohim*.

- Merriam-Webster[3] defines faithful as, "steadfast in affection or allegiance; firm in adherence to promises or in observance of duty; given with strong assurance; true to the facts, to a standard or to an original." Think about these definitions. What does it mean to you that God is *your* faithful God?

- I have seen God's faithfulness in my life so many times. One example is in how He has provided for all of my needs, sometimes in a miraculous way. As a young single mom, I was so poor that I was turned down for the indigent health care. Why? Because I didn't make enough money. That is a true story! However, even though many months I didn't have enough to pay my bills, yet I always paid them—from my own checkbook. I can't explain it, except for God's faithfulness. He is faithful to you too.

- Because He is faithful, we can depend on Him for anything and everything. Often we can't depend on people to remain faithful to us, but we can stake our lives on the fact that God won't ever change.

**A Prayer for You:**

*Thank You, My Faithful God, for always being faithful to me. I praise You that You are trustworthy, truthful and dependable. Teach me to trust You more and rely on You for every area of my life.*

## January 5

### LORD

YHWH or Yahweh (Hebrew)

*Take delight in the **Lord**,*
*and he will give you your heart's desires.*
Psalm 37:4 (NLT)

**Steps on Your Journey to Know God More Intimately:**

- This is the Hebrew word, *YHWH, Yahweh* or *Jehovah*. It means the Self-Existent One, the Covenant-Keeping God, the Unchangeable and Intimate God. In many English versions, it is written with small capital letters. We'll look at the name "Lord" (with lower case letters) later.

- Proverbs 3:5-6: "Trust in the Lord with all your heart; do not depend on your own understanding. Seek his will in all you do, and he will show you which path to take" (NLT).

- This was such a sacred name of God, that the Israelites would not even say it. Yet often people in our culture use God's name in vain. Ask the Lord to show you if you need to change anything you say. If you have misused His name, ask for His forgiveness and decide that you will no longer do it. I'm so glad our God is a forgiving God. Aren't you?

- This name is used thousands of times in the Old Testament. Meditate on it today, asking the Lord to reveal more of Himself through it.

**A Prayer for You:**

*Thank You, Lord, that You are a personal, intimate God, even though You are holy. Thank You for being trustworthy, because You are a covenant-keeping God. Help me to learn to trust You and delight in You more and more.*

## January 6

### *Everlasting God*

*Have you never heard? Have you never understood?*
*The Lord is the **everlasting God**, the Creator of all the earth.*
*He never grows weak or weary.*
*No one can measure the depths of his understanding.*
Isaiah 40:28 (NLT)

**Steps on Your Journey to Know God More Intimately:**

- This name is *Olam Yahweh* in Hebrew. *Olam* means everlasting, ancient, old and evermore. *Yahweh* means Self-Existent or Eternal One. Think about what it means that your God is the Everlasting God. What does that mean to you? Talk to Him about this name today.

- Does it comfort you to know that He will never grow tired or weary? At times I get exhausted, but I know I can depend on the Lord (and so can you), because He never will get tired. Wow! How encouraging. And when I need wisdom and understanding, I can go to Him, because His understanding is more than I (or you or anyone else) can even begin to fathom. Again I say, "Wow!"

- I love the whole chapter of Isaiah 40. It is so powerful. I memorized it when I was in high school. I'd encourage you to read it. We'll look at this verse again tomorrow.

**A Prayer for You:**

*Thank You, Everlasting God, that You never get tired or weary and You have limitless understanding. I praise You because You are so amazing. Such an awesome God! Help me learn to lean on You more.*

# January 7

## Creator of the Ends of the Earth

*Have you not known? Have you not heard?*
*The Lord is the everlasting God, the **Creator of the ends of the earth**.*
*He does not faint or grow weary; his understanding is unsearchable.*
Isaiah 40:28 (ESV)

**Steps on Your Journey to Know God More Intimately:**

- This name is *Bara Katsa Erets* in Hebrew. *Bara* means create, creator and make. *Katsa* means end. *Erets* means land, earth and world.

- As I look out my window and see Pikes Peak (over 14,000 feet high) and the whole mountain range, I'm amazed at how huge and majestic it is. Yet our God is much greater. He created all the way to the ends of the earth. Think about how big the whole earth is.

- Now, imagine how much fun God must have had creating everything—the mountains, valleys, lakes, rivers, oceans, trees, birds, fish, animals, people, bugs and so much more.

- Since God is the Creator of the Ends of the Earth (as well as of the whole universe), don't you think He is big enough to handle whatever difficult situations you may have? I often remind myself that since God created the universe, I know He can handle whatever may come into my life and yours.

- Meditate on this name. Ask God what He wants to show you through it.

**A Prayer for You:**

*Creator of the Ends of the Earth, I praise You and thank You for Your remarkable creativity that I can see all around me. Help me to become more aware of Your presence when I am in nature.*

## January 8

# He Who Brings Out the Starry Host One By One,
### and Calls Them Each By Name

*Lift your eyes and look to the heavens: Who created all these?*
***He who brings out the starry host one by one, and calls them each by
name.*** *Because of his great power, not one of them is missing.*
Isaiah 40:26

**Steps on Your Journey to Know God More Intimately:**

- NASA estimates the number of stars just in the *known* universe to be 1,000,000,000,000,000,000,000,000! Just try to imagine how many that is! I wonder how many stars are still not seen by us yet.

- Consider how great our God is, that He takes care of each one of the stars, and calls them each by name. That's *a lot* of names! Imagine trying to keep track of all those names.

- Praise Him for His greatness and that He calls you by name also. Isaiah 43:1 says, "Fear not, for I have redeemed you; I have summoned you by name; you are mine."

- When I was a missionary in Guatemala, I began learning Cakchiquel, a Mayan language, in a little village high in the mountains. There were no lights for miles around. We could see so many stars. I couldn't begin to count them, if I wanted to. Yet, they were only a few of the stars and God knows each one's name.

- Think about this name. Ask the Lord to show you more of Himself through it.

**A Prayer for You:**

*Lord, You are so amazing. My mind can't even begin to comprehend how great and awesome You are. Thank You that You call me by name, but You also call every one of the stars by name. You are a personal God. I'm so blessed to be Your child. Thank You.*

8

## King-God

*Listen, God! Please, pay attention!*
*Can you make sense of these ramblings, my groans and cries?*
***King-God****, I need your help. Every morning you'll hear me at it again.*
Psalm 5:2 (MSG)

**Steps on Your Journey to Know God More Intimately:**

- This name is *Melek Elohim* in Hebrew. *Melek* means king or royal. *Elohim* means God, judge, great and mighty.

- God is the King of the universe and yet He is a God we can talk to and who listens to us. How has God answered your prayers recently?

- In what areas do you need help? King-God is listening, waiting for you to call. Talk to Him today.

- Have you ever met a king? I haven't, although I did meet the President of Guatemala. I even got a hug from him at church one Sunday. It was such an honor to meet him, yet it is much more of an honor to know the King-God.

- In this verse, King David is asking God to make sense of his ramblings, his groans and his cries. Can you relate to that? Anytime you are having a hard time making sense of how you're feeling and even your ramblings, you can ask God to help you figure it out.

- David says that every morning he talks to God. I believe it is important to start every day by spending time with the Lord, talking to Him as well as letting Him talk to you through His Word.

- What a privilege to talk to our God and King every day.

**A Prayer for You:**

*King-God, I'm so grateful that You aren't too busy to listen to my prayers. Thank You that even though You are the King of kings, You care about the things that are happening in my life. (Take some time now to tell King-God what your concerns are.)*

## January 10

### Lord God

*David said to Solomon his son, "Be strong and courageous,
and do the work. Do not be afraid or discouraged,
for the **Lord God,** my God, is with you."*
1 Chronicles 28:20

**Steps on Your Journey to Know God More Intimately:**

- Genesis 2:4 says, "This is the history of the heavens and the earth when they were created, in the day that the Lord God made the earth and the heavens" (NKJV).

- This is the second name God is called in the Bible. Genesis 1 only calls Him God. In Genesis 2-3, He is called Lord God, *Yahweh Elohim* in Hebrew. Then in Genesis 4, He is called Lord. I wonder why He is called Lord God before He is called Lord. Lord God is the name He was called as He was creating Adam and Eve and then when they fell.

- What does it mean to you that He is the Lord God? How is that reflected in your life?

- Look what 1 Chronicles 28:20 tells us to do and not to do. Why can we be strong and courageous, not afraid or discouraged?

- It is so comforting for me to know that the Lord my God is with me, no matter where I am or what I'm doing. There have been things I've had to do that looked overwhelming or I didn't want to do them. This verse, when I would remember it (which wasn't always) gave me the courage I needed to be strong and bold. Meditate on it today.

**A Prayer for You:**

*Lord God, thank You that because You are with me, I don't have to be afraid or discouraged. Because I know You will always be here, I can be strong, courageous and do whatever work You have given me. Please remind me not to be afraid or discouraged, but instead trust You in every area of my life.*

# January 11

## *Spirit*

Ruah (Hebrew); Pneuma (Greek)

*I will pour my **Spirit** upon your offspring,*
*and my blessing on your descendants.*
Isaiah 44:3 (ESV)

**Steps on Your Journey to Know God More Intimately:**

- Romans 8:26 says, "In the same way, the Spirit helps us in our weakness. We do not know what we ought to pray for, but the Spirit himself intercedes for us with groans that words cannot express."

- The Hebrew word for Spirit is *ruah*. The Greek word is *pneuma*. Both words mean spirit, breath or wind. Ask the Lord to show you how His Spirit is like breath or wind. What does that mean to you?

- The Holy Spirit longs to bear His fruit in you—of love, joy, peace, patience, kindness, goodness, faithfulness, gentleness and self-control (Galatians 5:22-23). As you go through the day, ask Him to bear His fruit in you—especially when you're tempted not to live out these qualities.

- As we'll see later, the Holy Spirit has many, many other names.

- Read the verses above again. Look at what they say the Spirit does for us. I appreciate that the Spirit helps me in my weaknesses, because I have a lot of them. Over the years, I've learned to be grateful for my weaknesses, because when I am weak then I am strong in the Lord (2 Corinthians 12:9).

**A Prayer for You:**

*Spirit of God, thank You that You help me in my weaknesses and You pray for me. Help me get to know You in new ways and learn to rely on You more each day. Reveal more of Yourself to me today.*

# Lord of Heaven's Armies

## Yahweh Tsaba (Hebrew)

*Holy, holy, holy is the **Lord of Heaven's Armies!***
*The whole earth is filled with his glory!*
Isaiah 6:3 (NLT)

**Steps on Your Journey to Know God More Intimately:**

- Isaiah 54:5 says, "For your Creator will be your husband; the Lord of Heaven's Armies is his name! He is your Redeemer, the Holy One of Israel, the God of all the earth" (NLT).

- This name combination shows God's personal side (*Yahweh*), along with His great power and authority (*Tsaba*). This name is also translated: Lord of Hosts; Lord Almighty and God-of-the-Angel-Armies.

- We don't know how many angels there are. Daniel 7:10 refers to ten thousand times ten thousand angels. Matthew 26:53 talks about more than twelve legions of angels. In Jesus' time a legion was 6000. Hebrews 12:22 speaks of an innumerable company of angels. While we don't know the exact number of angels, we know there are an incredible amount.

- Jeremiah 32:27 says, "I am the Lord, the God of all mankind. Is anything too hard for me?" Think about this, if God is great enough to rule Heaven's armies, don't you think He is strong enough to handle whatever may come into your life? Talk to Him today about whatever you are facing.

**A Prayer for You:**

*Thank You, Lord of Heaven's Armies, that nothing is too hard for You. Since You are big enough to lead all the angels, I know You are big enough and strong enough to handle my problems. I praise You that the whole earth is filled with Your glory. Open my eyes to see more of Your glory, Lord.*

# God of Hope

Theos Elpis (Greek)

*May the **God of hope** fill you with all joy and peace as you trust in him,
so that you may overflow with hope by the power of the Holy Spirit.*
Romans 15:13

## Steps on Your Journey to Know God More Intimately:

- *Theos* is the Greek word for God, meaning a deity and the supreme divinity. *Elpis* means hope, expectation, anticipation and confidence. Hope is not wishful thinking. Instead it is a confidence and an expectation that what we desire *will* happen. Think about what it means that God is the God of Hope.

- How does God, being the God of Hope, impact your life today?

- In what areas do you need more hope?

- Ask the Lord to reveal more of Himself to you today as you focus on Him.

- After my fiancé was killed on his motorcycle, I lost hope. Up until I met him, most of my life had been difficult. Then finally I had something to anticipate. When he died, I gave up. I didn't want to keep living. Over time, God showed me that He was my hope and I could rely on Him. The tears kept falling, but I was no longer sobbing uncontrollably.

- So many people around us are lacking hope in their lives. How can you bring hope to others? One way is to give examples of times when you had lost hope and God answered you in an unusual way.

## A Prayer for You:

*God of Hope, thank You for the hope You bring to my life, when all around me people have very little hope. Help me to know You more and as a result discover more hope in my life and spread it to those around me.*

# January 14

## God Who Gives Endurance and Encouragement

*May the* **God who gives endurance and encouragement**
*give you a spirit of unity among yourselves as you follow Christ Jesus,
so that with one heart and mouth you may glorify
the God and Father of our Lord Jesus Christ.*
Romans 15:5-6

**Steps on Your Journey to Know God More Intimately:**

- Meditate on this name. What does it mean to you that God gives endurance and encouragement?

- When I first became a single mom, I often wondered how could I possibly raise my four and ten-year-old sons alone. Growing up I only had sisters, so boys were foreign to me. When I tried to do it on my own, I got overwhelmed and discouraged. It was too hard. But when I turned to the Lord, He gave me endurance and encouragement. He always knew just what I needed.

- In what ways do you need endurance and encouragement today? Ask the Lord to give them to you.

- Write this verse, or at least the name, on a card or paper. Put it someplace where you'll see it often. Throughout the day meditate on how God gives you endurance and encouragement. Be on the lookout for what He is doing. I'm sure we miss what He's doing so often because we are too focused on ourselves and our problems.

**A Prayer for You:**

*Father God, I need Your endurance and encouragement in my life. (Talk to Him about specific areas you need God's help.) Thank You that You are the God Who Gives Endurance and Encouragement. I want to know You more and find all I need in You.*

## January 15

# *LORD is Peace*

Yahweh-Shalom (Hebrew)

*And Gideon built an altar to the Lord there
and named it **Yahweh-Shalom** (which means "the **Lord is peace**").*
Judges 6:24 (NLT)

**Steps on Your Journey to Know God More Intimately:**

- Peace in Hebrew is *shalom*, meaning peace, wellness, prosperity, health and welfare. Peace in Greek is *eiraynay* meaning: peace, rest and quietness.

- Look at the following verses in ESV to discover more about peace.

    o Philippians 4:9: "Whatever you have learned or received or heard from me, or seen in me—put it into practice. And the God of peace will be with you."

    o Romans 16:20: "The God of peace will soon crush Satan under your feet. The grace of our Lord Jesus Christ be with you."

    o Philippians 4:6-7: "Do not be anxious about anything, but in everything by prayer and supplication with thanksgiving let your requests be made known to God. And the peace of God, which surpasses all understanding, will guard your hearts and your minds in Christ Jesus." See also Romans 15:33.

- In what areas of your life do you need more peace?

- After my fiancé died, I often struggled at night to catch my breath because of my sobbing. The Lord often reminded me of verses about peace. Over and over He said to me "Peace I leave with you, my peace I give to you…" (John 14:27). Eventually I fell asleep wrapped in His arms.

- Meditate on this name today. Ask God to show you how to allow Him to be your peace.

**A Prayer for You:**

*God of Peace, teach me how to rest in You more and allow You to be my peace. Give me quietness and rest. Thank You for being my peace (Ephesians 2:14).*

15

## January 16

### *I Am*

Haya (Hebrew)

*God replied to Moses, "**I Am** Who **I Am**.
Say this to the people of Israel: **I Am** has sent me to you."*
Exodus 3:14 (NLT)

**Steps on Your Journey to Know God More Intimately:**

- The Hebrew for I am is *haya*, meaning to exist, to be or become, the One Who Is or the Self-Existent One.

- John 8:58 : Jesus answered, "I tell you the truth, before Abraham was born, I am!" (NLT).

- Think about this name. Ask God to reveal more of Himself to you through it. Why would He use this name?

- In John 8:58, by using this name, Jesus showed that He is God and has always existed as God. The Jews understood what He was saying and wanted to stone Him, because that phrase only referred to the eternal God.

- How do you want or need God to reveal Himself to you as the I Am?

**A Prayer for You:**

*Lord, I praise You that You are the One who has always existed. Please reveal more of who You are to me through this name. Help me to see You as the God who is the same today as You were before Abraham was born.*

## Eternal God

Qedem Elohim (Hebrew)

*The **eternal God** is your refuge,
and underneath are the everlasting arms.*
Deuteronomy 33:27 (NKJV)

**Steps on Your Journey to Know God More Intimately:**

- *Qedem* is translated eternal, old, east and ancient. Think about what it means that God is eternal—He has no beginning or ending. He has always existed. Think about this: how can God have no beginning? Ask God to show you what that might look like.

- When you think of Him today, remind yourself that "The eternal God is your refuge." He is the One you can depend on.

- In what ways do you need to know God as the Eternal God?

- We'll look at other names in this verse over the next couple of days.

**A Prayer for You:**

*Eternal God, please draw me close to Yourself and help me to grow to know You more. I praise You that You have always existed and You will never end, so I know I can depend on You.*

## January 18

## *Your Refuge*

Mehona (Hebrew)

*The eternal God is **your refuge**,*
*and underneath are the everlasting arms.*
Deuteronomy 33:27 (NKJV)

**Steps on Your Journey to Know God More Intimately:**

- *Mehona* means den, habitation, dwelling place and refuge.

- Ask the Lord to show you how He is your refuge or your dwelling place. What does that look like to you?

- In Isaiah 32:1-2 we see the Lord as our "refuge from the storm" and in Psalm 59:16, He is our "refuge in times of trouble." How do these verses add to your view of God as your refuge?

- Do you have a place you go to for refuge, when you need to get away from the stresses and pain of life? Could the Lord be that place of refuge for you?

- If God is not already your refuge, what might you need to do to find your refuge in Him? If you're not sure, ask Him. He'll show you.

**A Prayer for You:**

*Lord, thank You that You are my refuge. You are the place I can find shelter from all the storms of life. Teach me to live in You—in Your refuge.*

## Everlasting Arms

### Olam Zeroa (Hebrew)

*The eternal God is your refuge,
and underneath are the **everlasting arms**.*
Deuteronomy 33:27 (NKJV)

**Steps on Your Journey to Know God More Intimately:**

- *Olam* means eternity, perpetual, always and continuance. *Zeroa* means arm, strength and power. God's strength and power are always with us.

- This is one of my favorite verses. When I'm going through a tough time, it helps me to remember that when I hit the bottom, I'm resting on God's everlasting arms. That is so comforting.

- Right now, imagine yourself resting in God's arms.

- Meditate on God's everlasting arms. Ask Him to show you what they look like and feel like to you.

- Write this verse and put it somewhere you can see when you need comfort and encouragement. It is short enough you could easily memorize it.[4]

**A Prayer for You:**

*Thank You, Lord for Your everlasting arms that are always underneath me. Help me to learn to feel Your arms around me and under me during the easier times in my life, so I can recognize them quicker when times get harder.*

## Spirit of Justice

### Ruah Mishpat (Hebrew)

*He will be a **spirit of justice** to him who sits in judgment,*
*a source of strength to those who turn back the battle at the gate.*
*Isaiah 28:6*

**Steps on Your Journey to Know God More Intimately:**

- *Ruah* means spirit, wind and breath. *Mishpat* means judgment, justice, manner or right.

- God is the one who brings justice to us. When people judge you, ask the Spirit of Justice to come to your defense.

- Meditate on what kind of justice God brings.

- What does it mean to you today that your God is the Spirit of Justice?

- In what areas do you need fairness? Ask the Spirit of Justice to bring it to you.

**A Prayer for You:**

*Spirit of Justice, thank You that You bring justice for me. I invite You to surround me with Your presence and Your protection.*

# January 21

## Source of Strength

### Gebura (Hebrew)

*He will be a spirit of justice to him who sits in judgment,
a **source of strength** to those who turn back the battle at the gate.*
Isaiah 28:6

**Steps on Your Journey to Know God More Intimately:**

- *Gebura* means might, strength, victory and power.

- We are in a battle against the enemy (Ephesians 6:10-18). God is our source of strength when we are in the middle of the battle. He is the first one we should turn to when we need help.

- In what ways do you need the Lord to be your source of strength today? When you need strength, ask Him. He is faithful.

- The Lord should be our first and primary source of strength, not just one of our sources that we go to after we have exhausted all of the others. In Him is all the strength we need for each day. Do you believe that? If not, talk to the Lord about this issue. I admit that too often I try to handle things on my own and only turn to God when all else fails. I want to learn to go to Him *first* for strength—not last.

- Ephesians 6:10 says, "Be strong in the Lord and in his mighty power." I've been meditating on that almost every day lately before I put on the armor of God. It's when we are *in* Him that we can be strong.

**A Prayer for You:**

*Thank You, Lord, that You are my Source of Strength. I want You to be my first and primary source of strength each day. I choose to be strong in You and in Your mighty power, rather than in my own strength or in other people's.*

# My Exceeding Joy

## Simha Gil (Hebrew)

*Then I will go to the altar of God, to God **my exceeding joy**,
and I will praise you with the lyre, O God, my God.*
Psalm 43:4 (ESV)

**Steps on Your Journey to Know God More Intimately:**

- *Simha* means joy, gladness and rejoice. *Gil* means rejoice and joy.

- Think about this name. The God of gods is your joy. And He doesn't want to be just a small amount of joy. He is your *exceeding* joy. He *wants* to overwhelm you with His joy. So why don't you always feel that joy? Ask the Lord to show you. Here's one thought, but definitely not the only reason. Just like any of His names, I have a choice to let Him be all that He wants to be in my life. He's not going to force me or you to have joy.

- In John 15:11, Jesus said, "I have told you this so that my joy may be in you and that your joy may be complete." Jesus wants us to have His joy *and* that it will be complete. Ask the Lord to show you what that looks like for you.

- Let the Lord be your exceeding joy today. If you don't feel it, ask Him to show you what might be standing in your way of receiving it. But don't forget to wait for Him to answer and show you. I'm convinced there are times that I don't experience His joy because I'm too busy— even doing good things for God or just talking to him, but I don't take the time to listen—really listen. What about you?

- I co-wrote a book called *The Door to Joy* about discovering deeper joy in life.[1]

**A Prayer for You:**

*Lord, I praise You that You are my Exceeding Joy. Thank You that when I focus on You and get to know You more intimately, I experience more of Your joy. I'm ready for You to overwhelm me with Your joy.*

## My Delight

*Then will I go to the altar of God, to God, my joy and **my delight**.*
*I will praise you with the harp, O God, my God.*
Psalm 43:4

**Steps on Your Journey to Know God More Intimately:**

- Is God your delight? What does that look like to you?

- Psalm 37:4 tells us "Delight yourself in the LORD and he will give you the desires of your heart." How do you delight *in* the Lord? I'm sure there are many ways to do it. Ask the Lord to show you. When I meditate on who He is and all the things He's done, I find great joy and delight in Him.

- Think about delight. What or who do you delight in? What does it look like? How does the other person know that you delight in him or her? I don't think that delight is supposed to be serious business. Do you find you are usually serious with the Lord?

- Go ahead—have some fun. Laugh. Dance. Sing. Shout. Smile. How would the humans you delight in know they are your delight if you are always serious with them? Do they like you to show it? I think God also wants us to show our delight in Him. Okay, so… what are you waiting for? Let God be your delight. If you're not sure, ask God to show you how to do that.

**A Prayer for You:**

*God, my Delight, show me how to delight in You more and what that might look like. Thank You that You are my Delight. Teach me to understand more of what that means.*

# He Who Gives You the Ability to Produce Wealth

*Remember the Lord your God,*
*for it is **he who gives you the ability to produce wealth**.*
Deuteronomy 8:18

**Steps on Your Journey to Know God More Intimately:**

- Today and in the coming days, let's remember the Lord and all He has done for us. It's so easy for us to forget who He is and what He's done. We need to make a choice to remember.

- Think about this name today. Let's look at each part of this name:

  o He who gives—The Lord is the one who gives us everything. He gives freely. Our God is not a stingy God.

  o You—God gives what you need. It's not just for other people.

  o The ability—Sometimes God pours out wealth on us, but sometimes, God gives us the ability to do something ourselves. What abilities has God given you? Are you using them? Do you recognize that they come from God or do you take credit for them yourself?

  o To produce wealth—God gives us the ability to produce wealth. What does wealth look like to you? Are you using your abilities to produce wealth? If not, why not?

- Why does God give us wealth? Ephesians 4:28 gives one reason, "Let him who stole steal no longer, but rather let him labor… *that He may have something to give him who has need*" (NLT, italics added). What are other reasons?

- If you don't feel wealthy, talk to the Lord about it.

**A Prayer for You:**

*Thank You, Lord, that You are the One who gives me the ability to produce wealth. Teach me what that means and how to know You more in this way.*

# He Who Formed You

*But now, this is what the Lord says—he who created you, Jacob,*
**he who formed you**, *Israel: "Do not fear, for I have redeemed you;*
*I have summoned you by name; you are mine."*
Isaiah 43:1

**Steps on Your Journey to Know God More Intimately:**

- *Yatsar* is the Hebrew word meaning form, potter, fashion and maker.

- Today, consider God's unimaginable attention to the smallest detail when He formed you. Your complete set of DNA contains about 3 billion base pairs of chromosomes and the total length of your DNA equals nearly 70 trips from the earth to the sun and back! Isn't it amazing how He formed you? Thank God for creating your unique DNA.

- Look at what the One Who Formed You says to you (at the end of the verse): He redeemed you, called you by name and made you His own. How could this keep you from being fearful?

- When I was a child at boarding school, I didn't like who I was. I thought I was ugly and stupid. I couldn't seem to make better than C's. But when I got to high school and college A's were easy. Over the years, God showed me that He made me just the way I am. Since He made me, I need to accept myself, otherwise I'm saying God made a mistake.

- Meditate on this whole verse today. Share it with someone who struggles with fear or a negative self-image.

**A Prayer for You:**

*Lord, thank You that You formed me just the way I am. You not only formed my external features, but You cared about the tiniest cells in my body. Help me to never insult what You created.*

## January 26

### *My Redeemer*

Gaal (Hebrew)

*Let the words of my mouth and the meditation of my heart
be acceptable in your sight, O Lord, my rock and* **my redeemer**.
Psalm 19:14

**Steps on Your Journey to Know God More Intimately:**

- *Gaal* means redeemer, kinsman and avenger.

- Isaiah 43:14, 18-19: "This is what the LORD says—your Redeemer, the Holy One of Israel: "Forget the former things; do not dwell on the past. See, I am doing a new thing! Now it springs up; do you not perceive it? I am making a way in the wilderness and streams in the wasteland."

- We're going to spend the next few days looking at God's names in Isaiah 43. As we look at who He is, we want to also focus on verses 18 and 19—forgetting the past and looking ahead to the new things God wants to do.

- Meditate on this name: My Redeemer. To redeem means to deliver, pay our ransom, to recover ownership by paying a price or to buy— especially of buying a slave to give him his freedom.

- Jesus is our Redeemer. He paid the ransom for our sins. He bought us to give us freedom from slavery to sin and Satan. That is something to get excited about. Think about that! God bought your freedom. It definitely was not cheap for Him. Your freedom cost Jesus His life.

- Because He is our Redeemer, we can forget the past and watch the new thing He is going to do in our lives. He can, and will, redeem our past, if we ask Him. What is it that you need the Lord to redeem for you?

**A Prayer for You:**

*My Redeemer, thank You for what You have already done for me and how You redeemed me from my sin and its consequences. Help me to forget the past and watch the new thing You want to do in my life.*

# Holy One of Israel

## Qadosh Yisrael (Hebrew)

*This is what the Lord says— your Redeemer, the **Holy One of Israel**:
"Forget the former things; do not dwell on the past."*
Isaiah 43:14, 18

**Steps on Your Journey to Know God More Intimately:**

- *Qadosh* means holy, Holy One and saint. *Yisrael* means Israel.

- Holy means pure, devoted, separated from evil and set apart. Our God is absolutely holy and set apart from evil.

- What does it mean to you that God is holy?

- Our God is the Holy One of Israel and the Holy One of the nation where you live. Think about this: is He treated as the Holy One in your nation? Take some time today to pray for your nation that God will be honored and respected. It's easy to complain about what our leaders are doing, but that doesn't do any good. Every time we are tempted to complain and put our leaders down, let's remember to stop and pray for them. Pray they will have the fear of the Lord and will recognize that God is Holy and He must punish anything that is unholy.

- I am part of the National Day of Prayer Task Force, because I know the United States needs God and prayer is the answer. We also pray for Israel.

- Aren't you glad that Jesus' blood made you holy?

- If you don't yet know Jesus personally, go to page 369 to learn more.

**A Prayer for You:**

*Holy One, I praise You that You are not like other gods. You are set apart from evil. You are pure. Teach me to honor and respect You more and to live my life in a holy, pure way.*

# Your Holy One

## Qadosh (Hebrew)

*I am the Lord, **your Holy One**, Israel's Creator and King.*
Isaiah 43:15 (NLT)

**Steps on Your Journey to Know God More Intimately:**

- Merriam-Webster defines holy as: exalted or worthy of complete devotion as one perfect in goodness and righteousness.

- Proverbs 9:10 and Revelation 16:5 both call God the "Holy One."

- In Isaiah 43:15, we see a personal side of God's holiness. How are you affected today by God being *your* Holy One? Do you need to change anything about your life because He is your Holy One? Do you need to confess anything?

- Worship Him as your Holy One, by focusing on Who He is and how great He is.

- Matthew Ward wrote a beautiful song called "The Holy One is Here." I often fall asleep listening to it. Then I find myself singing it as I go about my day, reminding me of God's presence.[5]

**A Prayer for You:**

*Lord, thank You that You are holy and You are my Holy One. I don't have to be afraid of You, because You are a personal God who cares about me. Help me to live a holy life to bring You praise.*

# January 29

## *Israel's Creator*

Yisrael Bara (Hebrew)

*I am the Lord, your Holy One, **Israel's Creator**, your King.*
Isaiah 43:15

**Steps on Your Journey to Know God More Intimately:**

- *Bara* means to create, do or make.

- God created you, your body and soul, as well as the whole earth. He also creates nations. He created Israel as well as the nation where you live.

- Many people today are against Israel, *Yisrael.* Think about this: God chose Israel to be His special people and He created them. Plus, our Savior was a Jew. Ask the Lord to reveal truth to you about Israel and how He wants you to react to them.

- Today, let's pray for Israel and pray for our own nations. Recognize the Lord as your nation's Creator and pray that as a nation you'll recognize Him as your creator.

- Someone recently sent me an email with the preambles to the constitutions for every state in the United States of America. It's interesting. Some people are trying so hard to take God out of our nation, yet the preambles for every state begin by talking about God. Our founding fathers had such hope for this nation, our country has fallen so far from their ideals.

**A Prayer for You:**

*Lord God, I praise You for Your creativity, not only in creating the universe, but also in creating nations. Please remind me to pray for my nation, as well as for Israel.*

# Your King

Melek (Hebrew)

*I am the Lord, your Holy One, Israel's Creator, **your King**.*
Isaiah 43:15

**Steps on Your Journey to Know God More Intimately:**

- *Melek* means king or royalty. It has a pronominal suffix on it showing that He is *your* King.

- Matthew 21:4-5 says, "This took place to fulfill what was spoken through the prophet: "Say to the Daughter of Zion, 'See, your king comes to you, gentle and riding on a donkey, on a colt, the foal of a donkey.'"

- What is a king's role? What does he do?

- How are a king's subjects supposed to act toward their king?

- Meditate on God as *your* King. How is He your King?

- How do you need Him to be your King?

- How does your life reveal that God is your King? If it doesn't, you might want to talk to God and ask Him how you can honor Him as your King. What might you need to confess and change in your life?

- I sometimes close my eyes and imagine I'm going into the throne room of Heaven. My King is seated on His throne. The massive room is filled with people on their knees worshipping Him. I, too, fall on my knees before Him. Worship the Lord as your King today.

**A Prayer for You:**

*Lord, I choose to praise, worship and serve You as my King. Thank You that You are a loving, just and righteous King. Forgive me for the times I don't honor You as my King. Teach me how to act toward You.*

# He Who Made A Way through the Sea

*This is what the Lord says—**he who made a way through the sea**,*
*a path through the mighty waters.*
*"Forget the former things; do not dwell on the past.*
*See, I am doing a new thing! Now it springs up; do you not perceive it?*
Isaiah 43:16, 18-19

**Steps on Your Journey to Know God More Intimately:**

- The beginning of the passage, above, describes who this God is that is talking. The last part is what the Lord says to them and to us.

- The first thing these verses say about God is that He is the One who makes a way through the sea, a path through mighty waters. He did that for the Israelites in Exodus 14. But He will also do the same for you today. What sea are you going through? Are you in deep waters? He will make a way through them. Ask Him right now to do that. Then thank and praise Him for what He has done and what He will do.

- Now look at what the One who made a way through the sea has to say to you: "Forget the former things; do not dwell on the past."

- What do you need to forget? There is a time to remember, and we need to remember the good things God has done for us. But there are other things we need to forget and stop dwelling on. Ask God to show you what you need to leave behind, so that He can do a new thing in your life this year.

**A Prayer for You:**

*God, thank You that You are the One who makes a way through the mighty waters in my life. I'm so glad I can trust and rely on You to take care of me, protect me and guide me. Show me what I need to forget so that I can see the new thing You want to do in my life.*

## February 1

## *He ... Who Drew out the Chariots and Horses*

*This is what the Lord says—*
**he ... who drew out the chariots and horses,**
*the army and reinforcements together, and they lay there,*
*never to rise again, extinguished, snuffed out like a wick.*
Isaiah 43:16-17

**Steps on Your Journey to Know God More Intimately:**

- God is bigger than our problems or our enemies. He can draw them out, destroy them, extinguish them and snuff them out like a wick, just like He did with Pharaoh's chariots and horses in Exodus 14.

- Who are our real enemies? I know sometimes it looks like people are our enemies, but they are not our true adversaries. See Ephesians 6:12. Satan and his demons are the primary opponents. Ask the Lord to snuff out your enemies. He can and will, but sometimes He waits for us to ask Him or to partner with Him. We have the authority to bind the enemy in Jesus' name.

- In Matthew 18:18 Jesus says, "I tell you the truth, whatever you bind on earth will be bound in Heaven, and whatever you loose on earth will be loosed in Heaven." Jesus gave you that authority. Use it! I've seen God do amazing things in my life and my family's life as I have learned to partner with Him in binding the enemy and loosing God's Spirit and His power.

**A Prayer for You:**

*Lord, I'm so glad You are bigger than any enemy I can ever face. Thank You that just as You defeated Israel's enemies, You will also defeat mine. Help me to learn to trust You more.*

February 2

## One Who Makes a Way in the Wilderness

*Behold, I am doing a new thing; now it springs forth,
do you not perceive it?
I will make **a way in the wilderness** and rivers in the desert.*
Isaiah 43:19 (ESV)

**Steps on Your Journey to Know God More Intimately:**

- This name today is extrapolated from what God does. God says He is making a way in the wilderness and rivers in the desert. Stop and meditate on what that means.

- Imagine you are trudging across the Sahara desert. You're hot, parched and about to faint because there is no water in sight. Has your life ever felt like that? God says He'll make rivers in the desert—in your desert.

- When my son Timothy was eleven years old, we rode a bus across the hot dry desert in Jordan, going to Israel. For miles and miles there was nothing but blowing sand. At times it was hard to see. Sometimes life can seem like that dry, blowing wilderness. It's those times I need to trust God to make a way through it. And so do you.

- Ask God to show you how He will make a way through whatever wilderness you are in. Trust Him today to create rivers in the desert of your life. Believe Him to do some impossible things in your life this year. Remember, nothing is impossible with God (Luke 1:37).

**A Prayer for You:**

*Thank You, Lord, that You make a way through every wilderness I encounter. Help me to trust You more during the hard times and learn to see the rivers You create in the deserts of my life.*

33

# He Who Blots Out Your Transgressions

## Hu Makhaw Pesha (Hebrew)

*I am **he who blots out your transgressions** for my own sake,
and I will not remember your sins.*
Isaiah 43:25 (ESV)

**Steps on Your Journey to Know God More Intimately:**

- *Hu* is he. *Makhaw* means to erase, wipe out, blot out or destroy. *Pesha* means a revolt, rebellion, sin or trespass. Sin means an offense and its penalty. How comforting to know that God has completely erased our sins—never to be remembered again! When you confess your sin, you can imagine God saying, "What sin?"

- Thank Him that He blots out your sins and never remembers them again. However, we don't want to presume on God's grace and forgiveness. Galatians 5:13 says, "You, my brothers, were called to be free. But do not use your freedom to indulge the sinful nature; rather, serve one another in love."

- Are there any sins you need to confess today? You might want to ask the Lord to reveal to you anything you need to confess.

**A Prayer for You:**

*Lord, I'm grateful that You wipe out my transgressions and will never remember them again. Thank You that You not only erase my sin, You traded Your righteousness for my sin as 2 Corinthians 5:21 says. I know I don't deserve it, but I'm so thankful.*

February 4

## Shield Around Me

Magen (Hebrew)

*But you, Lord, are a **shield around me**,*
*my glory, the One who lifts my head high.*
Psalm 3:3

**Steps on Your Journey to Know God More Intimately:**

- *Magen* means shield, buckler and armed.

- There are four names of God in this verse. We looked at the name Lord earlier. It is the name *YHWH*, *Yahweh* or *Jehovah*. We'll continue looking at this short verse the next few days. I want to encourage you to memorize it. Write it on a 3x5 card or a sticky note and put it where you'll see it every day.

- Meditate on this name today. Normally I think of a shield as being something a person holds in front of himself. But this verse says God is a shield *around* you. Think about that. I'm so glad to know that God is all around me shielding me from the enemy. What does that mean to you today?

- How has God been a shield around you?

- How do you need Him to be your protection?

**A Prayer for You:**

*Thank You, Lord, that You are a shield that is all around me. I don't have to be afraid of anyone or anything, because You are always there to protect me. Help me to learn to recognize Your presence and protection more each day.*

# My Glory

Kabod (Hebrew)

*But you, O Lord, are a shield for me,*
**My glory**, *the One who lifts up my head high.*
Psalm 3:3 (NKJV)

**Steps on Your Journey to Know God More Intimately:**

- *Kabod* means glory, honor, glorious and weighty.

- Merriam-Webster defines glory as: "praise, honor or distinction extended by common consent; worshipful praise, honor and thanksgiving; something that secures praise or renown; or a distinguished quality or asset."

- In the New Testament the word glory is also translated "boast." Therefore, as the Scriptures say, "If you want to boast, boast only about the Lord" (1 Corinthians 1:31).

- Consider this name. How is the Lord your glory? What does that mean to you?

- An older New International Version version translated this name, "The Glorious One." Meditate on this name today. Ask the Lord to reveal to you what He wants you to know today.

- 2 Corinthians 3:18 says, we "see and reflect the glory of the Lord" (NLT). How does this verse add to your understanding of this name?

**A Prayer for You:**

*Lord, thank You that You are both the Glorious One and My Glory. Help me to see Your glory around me and in me more and more. I want to reflect Your glory, bringing You glory through my life.*

# February 6

## One Who Lifts My Head High

Ramam Roshe (Hebrew)

*But you, Lord, are a shield around me,*
*my glory, the **One who lifts my head high**.*
Psalm 3:3

**Steps on Your Journey to Know God More Intimately:**

- *Ramam* means to lift, to hold up, exalt and high. *Roshe* means head, chief and top.

- The New Living Translation refers to God as "the one who holds my head high."

- I love this name. So many times I've meditated on this when my head is hanging down and I'm struggling with sadness or grief (as well as other emotions). When my best friend betrayed me in some devastating ways, I was hurt, sad, depressed and discouraged. The Lord reminded me of this verse. I had to choose to let Him lift my head. It wasn't easy and didn't happen immediately.

- The Lord is the One who will lift your head today, if you let Him. How do you need the Lord to lift your head today? Ask Him. He loves answering prayers.

- We've been looking at this same verse the last few days. Have you memorized this short verse? If not, I want to encourage you to do so. It's important to hide God's Word in our hearts, so we have it when we need it.

**A Prayer for You:**

*I praise You and thank You, Lord, that You are the One Who Lifts My Head High today. It is so comforting to me to know that You understand how I feel and You see when my head is bowed down in sadness. Thank You for caring enough to lift me up.*

February 7

*Majestic Name*

Adeer Shem (Hebrew)

*O Lord, our Lord, your **majestic name** fills the earth!*<br>
*Your glory is higher than the heavens.*<br>
Psalm 8:1 (NLT)

**Steps on Your Journey to Know God More Intimately:**

- *Adeer* means excellent, famous, glorious, lordly, mighty, noble, principal and worthy. *Shem* means name, renown, fame and famous. A name represents all of who a person is.

- One definition of majestic is having or showing impressive beauty or dignity. Every day I get to see 14,000-foot Pikes Peak out my bedroom window. It reminds me of God's majesty. Each day Pikes Peak looks different, depending on the clouds, light and sunshine. In the same way, our Majestic God has many faces.

- What do you see each day that show's God's majesty?

- Meditate on God's Majestic Name. Ask the Lord to reveal to you more about Himself through this name.

- What does the Lord want to show you today about His majesty?

**A Prayer for You:**

*Majestic Name, I want to know You more. I praise You for the beauty and dignity in Your name. Help me to see You in new ways today and in the days to come.*

38

## Helper of the Fatherless

*But you, God, see the trouble of the afflicted; you consider their grief
and take it in hand. The victims commit themselves to you;
you are the **helper of the fatherless**.*
Psalm 10:14

**Steps on Your Journey to Know God More Intimately:**

- *Azor Yatom* is this name in Hebrew. *Azor* means help or helper. *Yatom* means fatherless or fatherless child.

- Today there are so many who are fatherless and orphans. Some who have fathers may feel fatherless because their fathers are or were abusive or absent. If you are (or feel) fatherless, remember that God is your Father. He's the best Father you could ever desire. He loves you so much—more than any human father could ever love you. Bask in that love today. If you don't feel Father God's love, ask Him to reveal it to you.

- If you are a single mother, raising children, remember this name. As I raised my sons alone for so many years, I relied on this name, because I knew I didn't have the wisdom and strength to raise them on my own.

- In what ways do you need God to be your helper today?

**A Prayer for You:**

*Thank You, Father God, that You are my Father, whether or not I have an earthly father. You are the best Dad I could ever want. Thank You that I can depend on You to be my Helper, especially if I don't have an earthly father who loves me.*

February 9

*Christ*

*Now while the Pharisees were gathered together,*
*Jesus asked them a question, saying, "What do you think about the **Christ**?*
*Whose son is he?" They said to him, "The son of David."*
Matthew 22:41-42 (ESV)

**Steps on Your Journey to Know God More Intimately:**

- Christ comes from the Greek word, *Christos*, meaning Messiah or Anointed One. Any Jew in Jesus' time would know that the Christ referred to the Messiah. We'll look more in depth at Messiah next week.

- Christ is the name that refers to Jesus' deity, while Jesus refers to His humanity.

- Jesus asked the Pharisees two questions: "What do you think about the Christ? Whose son is he?" How would you answer those questions?

- Meditate on this name. Ask God to show you what it means to you today and how you should respond to it.

**A Prayer for You:**

*Christ, thank You that You are the Anointed One, the Messiah. Help me to believe in You and trust You more as the Christ. I don't ever want to be as the Pharisees who didn't believe in You. Open my heart and mind to understand and know You more.*

February 10

*Love*

Agape (Greek)

*Whoever does not love does not know God, because God is **love**.*
1 John 4:8

**Steps on Your Journey to Know God More Intimately:**

- *Agape* is unconditional love. Think about God's love. It is not just what He does. Love is who He is.

- Meditate on what the following verses say about God's love. What is God saying to you through them?

  o Psalm 57:10: "For great is your love, reaching to the heavens; your faithfulness reaches to the skies."

  o Psalm 107:21: "Let them give thanks to the LORD for his unfailing love and his wonderful deeds for mankind."

  o Psalm 103:11: "For as high as the heavens are above the earth, so great is his love for those who fear him."

- Think about how high the heavens are above the earth. How can you even measure the distance? That's how much God loves you.

- The Bible is filled with stories of His love for us. It is God's love story to us. I want to encourage you to take the time daily to read some of God's love story for you.

**A Prayer for You:**

*God, thank You that You **are** love. Thank You that I can depend on You, because You love me with an unfailing love. Thank You that Your love for me is so much greater than I can even begin to imagine. Teach me to understand and know Your amazing, great love for me.*

## One I Love

*I will seek the **one I love**.*
Song of Solomon 3:2 (NKJV)

**Steps on Your Journey to Know God More Intimately:**

- The book of Song of Solomon is a picture of our relationship with Jesus, our Lover. I'm just starting to study this book in greater depth. I challenge you to study God's love for you more.

- Is Jesus Christ the one you love? It's easy to let other people take that place. Remember, He is the One who will never fail you or leave you. His love is perfect.

- There have been periods of my life when I have let a human take God's place as the one I love. However, over recent years, I have fallen deeper and deeper in love with the Lord. I don't ever want to go back.

- If He is not the One your heart loves, talk to Him about that. What might you need to do to grow in your love with the Lover of your soul?

**A Prayer for You:**

*Jesus, I want You to always be the One I love. I want to learn to know Your love for me in greater ways so I can continue to fall deeper in love with You.*

# My Dearly Loved Son

Mou Huios Agapetos (Greek)

*And a voice from heaven said,*
*"This is **my dearly loved Son**, who brings me great joy."*
Matthew 3:17 (NLT)

**Steps on Your Journey to Know God More Intimately:**

- *Mou* is my. *Agapetos* means beloved or dearly beloved. *Huios* means son.

- 2 Peter 1:17 says, "The voice from the majestic glory of God said to him, 'This is my dearly loved Son, who brings me great joy'" (NLT).

- As we prepare to celebrate Valentine's Day in the United States, this week we are looking at God's names that have to do with His love for us and ours for Him. Human love is great and ordained by God. But God's love is so much greater than any human love ever could be.

- Meditate on the name that Father God has for Jesus, "My Dearly Loved Son."

- Think about how much the Father loves Jesus. Imagine how difficult it must have been for the Father to watch all Jesus had to endure when He was on earth. Visualize just standing by and watching one of your children be mistreated, knowing that you *wouldn't* do anything to help him or her, because you had a plan. I can't even begin to fathom how hard that must have been for the Father.

**A Prayer for You:**

*Thank You, Father God, for Your great love for Your Son, Jesus. Thank You too for how much You love me. Teach me more of Your love for me that You showed when You let Jesus go through so much suffering.*

# Him Who Loves Us

*To **him who loves us** and has freed us from our sins by his blood,
and has made us to be a kingdom and priests to serve his God and Father—
to him be glory and power for ever and ever! Amen.*
Revelation 1:5-6

**Steps on Your Journey to Know God More Intimately:**

- Meditate on this verse and on the God who loves us. He showed His love to us by freeing us from our sins by His blood. This name is specifically referring to Jesus, because it was His blood that freed us from our sins. What an incredible way for Him to show us His love.

- Thank Jesus today for loving you so much that He showed His love by being willing to shed His blood for you. I can't even begin to understand how much He loved us. It's more than I can comprehend, but I'm so grateful. How about you?

- Look at what verse 6 says. The One who loves us made us to be a kingdom and priests to serve His God. Ask the Lord to reveal to you what that means.

- In Ephesians 3:14-19, Paul prays that we will be able to grasp "the extravagant dimensions of Christ's love" (MSG). I've been studying and meditating on this whole passage in the past year. I'm amazed at all God keeps showing me. I encourage you to meditate on it too. It will change your life when you begin to understand God's great love for you.

**A Prayer for You:**

*Lord, I'm so grateful You loved me enough to bring me freedom from my sins by Your blood. That was a very high price to pay to show me Your love. Help me to begin to grasp the extravagant dimensions of Your love for me.*

## February 14

### *My Lover*

Dode (Hebrew)

*How handsome you are, **my lover**! Oh, how charming!*
Song of Solomon 1:16

**Steps on Your Journey to Know God More Intimately:**

- *Dode* means love or beloved, with a pronominal suffix meaning my. Jesus wants to be your Lover today. Do you believe that? What might that look like? Ask the Lord to show you.

- Song of Solomon 2:16 says, "My lover is mine and I am his" (NLT).

- Today is Valentine's Day in the United States. Spend some special, intimate time with your Lover, the Lover of your soul.

- While you're thinking about how to make your special someone feel loved, take some time to think about how you can make your heavenly Lover feel loved. If you're not sure, ask Him. He enjoys spending time alone with you, when you focus on Him (not always asking Him for things). Tell Him what you appreciate about Him.

- Sometimes Valentine's Day is a difficult time for those of us who are single. We see people who have a spouse or other person to be their lover. I'm so grateful that I have the greatest Lover I could ever have. He is the One who meets all my needs (although sometimes I confess I think I need a human to meet those needs). He really is enough. He is all I need. He's all you need. Whether you have someone who loves you deeply or not, take time today to spend with Jesus and grow in your love for Him.

**A Prayer for You:**

*My Lover, thank You for how much You love me. Thank You for all the ways You reveal Your love to me. (List some of them right now.) Help me to know You more intimately as My Lover.*

45

February 15

## *Most High*

Elyon (Hebrew)

*I will be filled with joy because of you.*
*I will sing praises to your name, O **Most High**.*
Psalm 9:2 (NLT)

**Steps on Your Journey to Know God More Intimately:**

- The Hebrew word, *Elyon*, means lofty or the Supreme One.

- Meditate on this name today. What does it mean to you that your God is the Most High?

- How awesome is the Lord Most High! Praise Him today for His greatness.

- In this verse, David proclaims that he will be filled with joy because of the Lord. Does God fill you with joy? Why or why not? How has He filled you with joy?

- This verse tells us to sing praises to God's name. Take some time today to sing your praises to the Most High. You might sing a song you already know, or it might be a new song that you make up as you go. Don't worry how you sound. The Most High doesn't care if you sing in perfect tune.

**A Prayer for You:**

*O Most High, I choose to sing praises to Your name today. Give me a new song I can sing to You. Show me more about this name and fill me with joy today because of You.*

46

## February 16

### *Messiah*

*Know therefore and understand, that from the going forth of the command
to restore and build Jerusalem until **Messiah** the Prince,
There shall be seven weeks and sixty-two weeks.*
Daniel 9:25 (NKJV)

**Steps on Your Journey to Know God More Intimately:**

- The Hebrew meaning of Messiah, *Mashiah*, is Anointed One. The root of the word means to anoint, to rub with oil and to consecrate. Messiah is only used two times in the Old Testament, in Daniel 9:25 and 26.

- Matthew 16:16: "Simon Peter said to Jesus, 'You are the **Messiah**, the Son of the living God.'"

- Merriam-Webster defines Messiah as "the expected king and deliverer of the Jews; Jesus." Think about these definitions of Messiah. He is your deliverer, whether or not you are a Jew.

- Talk to your Messiah about this name. What do you want to say to Him today? What does He have to say to you?

**A Prayer for You:**

*Messiah, I praise You today that You chose to come to earth to save us from our sins. Thank You that You are the Son of God who came as our Deliverer. Teach me more about who You are.*

# Son of the Living God

*Simon Peter answered [Jesus]*
*"You are the Messiah, the **Son of the living God**."*
Matthew 16:16 (NLT)

**Steps on Your Journey to Know God More Intimately:**

- Think about this name. Who is the Living God?

- What does it mean to you today that He is the *Living* God?

- Consider that Jesus is the Son of the Living God. What does that mean to you? It doesn't say He is "a" son, it says He is "the" Son of God.

- Would you be willing to make the same declaration Peter made with *your* friends and family? If not, why not? What would hold you back?

**A Prayer for You:**

*Son of the Living God, I praise You today for who You are. Thank You that You came to earth to show us Your Father. Help me to get to know You more and honor You as You deserve—as God's Son.*

## *Jesus*

Iesous (Greek)

*She will give birth to a son, and you are to give him the name **Jesus**, because he will save his people from their sins.*
Matthew 1:21

**Steps on Your Journey to Know God More Intimately:**

- The name Jesus comes from the Hebrew word for Joshua (*Yeshua*). It means "Jehovah is Salvation" or "the LORD saves."

- Consider who Jesus is. Jesus is the Son of the Living God, He is the King of Heaven, the Creator of the universe. And yet, He chose to come to earth as a tiny, helpless baby, born into a human family. He chose to leave Heaven, where He was the center of attention, to become a human, who would be despised, rejected, hated and crucified.

- Meditate on the name of Jesus. What does it mean to you today?

- Think about what He did and does for you.

- Thank Him for what He's done for you.

**A Prayer for You:**

*Jesus, thank You for leaving Heaven to come to earth as a helpless baby, because You loved us enough to want a relationship with us. Thank You for coming to save us from our sins. Help me to understand more about You and what You did for me.*

# The Way

### Hodos (Greek)

*Jesus answered, "I am **the way** and the truth and the life.
No one comes to the Father except through me."*
John 14:6

**Steps on Your Journey to Know God More Intimately:**

- *Hodos* means way, road or journey. Think about what it means that Jesus is the Way. What does it mean to you that Jesus is the Way, your access to the Father? Look at the following verses:

  o John 10:9: "I am the door. If anyone enters by me, he will be saved and will go in and out and find pasture" (ESV).

  o Romans 5:1: "Since we have been justified through faith, we have peace with God through our Lord Jesus Christ."

  o Ephesians 2:18: "For through him we both have access in one Spirit to the Father" (ESV).

  o Ephesians 3:12: "in whom [Christ] we have boldness and access with confidence through our faith in him" (ESV).

- In the next two days, we'll continue looking at John 14:6. I'd encourage you to memorize it. You'll be so blessed when you have God's Word hidden in your heart. Find a friend with whom you can share this verse. Ask him or her to memorize it with you, or at least to be willing to listen to you say it.[4]

**A Prayer for You:**

*Thank You, Jesus, that You are the Way to the Father. Thank You that I can follow You wherever You take me, knowing You will never lead me astray. I don't have to see and know the whole journey. I just need to follow You step by step. Teach me to trust You more and follow You without question.*

## The Truth

Aletheia (Greek)

*Jesus answered, "I am the way and **the truth** and the life.*
*No one comes to the Father except through me."*
John 14:6

**Steps on Your Journey to Know God More Intimately:**

- *Aletheia* means truth, true and truely. Meditate on this name. What does it mean that Jesus is the Truth?

- How has Jesus been the truth for you?

- Later we'll look at the Spirit of Truth and the God of Truth.

- Our enemy, Satan, is a liar and the father of lies (see John 8:44). We need to be connected to the Truth, so the enemy can't deceive us.

- What do the following verses say to you about Jesus being the truth?

  o John 1:14: "And the Word became flesh and dwelt among us, full of grace and truth; we have beheld his glory, glory as of the only Son from the Father" (RSV).

  o John 18:37: "Jesus answered (Pilate), "You say correctly that I am a king. For this I have been born, and for this I have come into the world, to bear witness to the truth. Everyone who is of the truth hears My voice" (NAS).

- Write John 14:6 on a card and read it several times today. Ask the Lord to help you memorize it.

**A Prayer for You:**

*Jesus, thank You that You are the Truth. I can trust You because You will never, ever lie to me. Show me more of what it means that You are the Truth. I long to know You more and more intimately.*

## February 21

### *The Life*

Zoe (Greek)

*Jesus answered, "I am the way and the truth and **the life**.
No one comes to the Father except through me."*
John 14:6

**Steps on Your Journey to Know God More Intimately:**

- *Zoe* means life. Meditate on Jesus as the Life. The closer you get to Him and the more time you spend with Him, the more you will experience Life as He meant for you to experience it.

- In John 10:10, Jesus says that He came that we might have a full life. Thank the Lord for how Jesus has made your life full. If you don't feel like you have a full, abundant life, ask the Lord to show you what you may need to do. Also, ask Him to give you abundant life.

- In John 11:25 Jesus says, "I am the resurrection and the life. Whoever believes in me, though he die, yet shall he live" (ESV). Think about that.

- Colossians 3:4 says, "Christ, who is our life." Note, it doesn't say, He "gives" you life, although He does that too. It says He *is* Your life. Wow. To me that's exciting! Consider how Christ is your life.

- Continue memorizing John 14:6. Can you say part or all of it without looking at it?

**A Prayer for You:**

*Jesus, thank You that You came to bring me a full life now as well as eternal life forever. Thank You that You **are** my life. You've taken care of my past, present and future. Thank You. Teach me to rely on You more to **be** my life so I can experience a full, abundant life.*

# Prophet from Nazareth in Galilee

*The crowds answered, This is*
*Jesus, the **prophet from Nazareth in Galilee**.*
Matthew 21:11

**Steps on Your Journey to Know God More Intimately:**

- Greek word for prophet is *profaytace*. It comes from two words: *pro,* meaning in front of or prior and *famee,* meaning to show or make known one's thoughts. A prophet is one who tells what will happen prior to it happening.

- What do you think the people were saying about Jesus when they used this name?

- In what ways was Jesus a prophet?

- Many of the people thought that Jesus was *only* a prophet. They could even tell you right where He was from—Nazareth in Galilee. What they said was true, but they were also trying to prove that they knew His hometown, therefore He couldn't have been more than a prophet.

- If Jesus was only a prophet, He would have been a liar, because of all He said about Himself. He said He was the Son of God

- Ask yourself if you recognize that Jesus is the Son of God, the Messiah, the Savior. Or do you also think He is only a prophet or a good man?

- What difference does it make to your life that Jesus is more than just a prophet?

**A Prayer for You:**

*Thank You, Jesus, that You were more than just a great prophet. You are the Son of God. You are God. Teach me to know You more, in all of Your roles and names. Help me to never put You in a little box, like the crowds did when You walked on earth.*

# True Vine

*I am the **true vine**, and my Father is the gardener.
I am the vine; you are the branches. If you remain in me and I in you,
you will bear much fruit; apart from me you can do nothing.*
John 15:1, 5

**Steps on Your Journey to Know God More Intimately:**

- *Alethinos* means true in Greek. *Ampelos* means vine. Picture a grapevine. How is Jesus like a vine? What does that mean?

- How are you like a branch?

- What happens to branches that are cut off from a vine or tree?

- What does this verse say will happen if we remain in the vine?

- Consider how you can remain in Jesus, the Vine.

- Why is He called the *True* Vine? Could there be a fake vine? Could it be something we depend on and look to for our strength, rather than Jesus? How can Jesus, the True Vine, impact your life today?

- When I was on the Island of Cypress, teaching missionaries, I saw many grapevines growing everywhere. They grew incredibly quickly and had luscious grapes hanging from them. But, the grapes only grew when they were attached to the vine.

- Think about the last part of the verse, "apart from me you can do nothing." What do you think that means? How does it affect your life?

**A Prayer for You:**

*True Vine, thank You for this picture of what my relationship to You can be. Teach me more of what it means to remain in You and let You remain in me. I want to bear fruit for You. Please remind me that I can't produce fruit on my own, but that as I remain in You, fruit will come automatically.*

## February 24

# My Father

Mou Pater (Greek)

*I am the true vine, and **my Father** is the vinedresser.*
John 15:1 (ESV)

**Steps on Your Journey to Know God More Intimately:**

- *Mou* is my. *Pater* is father.

- John 5:17 Jesus answered them, "My Father is working still, and I am working" (RSV).

- Jesus called God His Father. In John 5, the Jews wanted to kill Jesus because they knew He was calling God His Father.

- Meditate on this name. What does it mean that God was Jesus' Father?

- When Jesus was on the cross, He prayed to God saying, "Father, forgive them; for they do not know what they are doing" (Luke 23:34 NAS). How can we imitate Jesus?

- Ask the Lord to reveal more of Himself through this name.

**A Prayer for You:**

*Father, thank You that You are Jesus' Father, as well as being my Father. Thank You that no matter what my earthly father was like, You are the perfect Father. Teach me how to relate to You as Jesus related to You when He was on earth.*

55

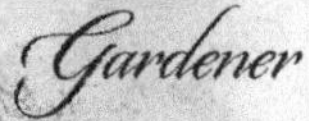



# Gardener

Gheoregos (Greek)

*I am the true grapevine, and my Father is the **gardener**.*
John 15:1 (NLT)

**Steps on Your Journey to Know God More Intimately:**

- *Gheoregos* means gardener, husbandman or farmer.

- What does a gardener do? Think about all the things involved in gardening, considering how Father God is like a gardener:
    - plowing the ground
    - preparing the soil
    - planting the seed
    - watering and fertilizing
    - weeding
    - pruning and trimming the dead leaves (and even live ones to make them grow better)
    - killing the pests
    - What else?

- In what ways do you need the Lord to be your Gardener?

**A Prayer for You:**

*Father, thank You that You are the Gardener. You know just what I need so I grow and produce the most and best fruit. Help me to understand You more as my Gardener. I choose to submit to You to allow You to do whatever You want with my life.*

## King Eternal, Immortal, Invisible

*Now to the **King eternal**, **immortal**, **invisible**, the only God,
be honor and glory for ever and ever. Amen.*
1 Timothy 1:17

**Steps on Your Journey to Know God More Intimately:**

- Meditate on this name today. What does it mean to you that the Lord is the King?

- Think about each part of this name:

  o The King

  o Eternal

  o Immortal. Immortal means living forever; never dying or decaying.

  o Invisible

- Talk to the Lord about each part of this name. Ask Him to reveal more of Himself to you through it.

- Worship your King.

**A Prayer for You:**

*Lord, I worship You today as the King Eternal, Immortal, Invisible. Reveal to me what that means. Teach me how to honor You as my King. Show me any ways that I don't treat You as I should. I want to bring You honor and glory forever and ever.*

## Only God

Monos Theos (Greek)

*Now to the King eternal, immortal, invisible,*
*the **only God**, be honor and glory for ever and ever. Amen.*
1 Timothy 1:17

**Steps on Your Journey to Know God More Intimately:**

- *Monos* means only or alone. *Theos* means God, deity or supreme divinity.

- Our God is the Only True God. People may worship other things and people as gods, but they are not the true God. Most of us don't have physical idols we worship, but many people treat money, power, status, people, etc. as more important than God. They make those things their gods.

- When I grew up in a little village in Guatemala, the Mayans worshipped many gods. When Catholicism came in, they converted, but still continued to worship their own gods, right in the Catholic church. How often do we do that? We say we are following the Only God, yet we continue to worship money, power or other things.

- Is there anything you worship (or make more important) in place of the Only God? If so, tell God you're sorry and choose to change your ways.

- Take some time to worship the Only God.

**A Prayer for You:**

*Lord, I honor You and worship You as the Only God. Nothing else in the whole world (or universe) begins to compare with You. Teach me more of what it means that You are the Only God. You deserve all praise, honor, glory and worship.*

# My Servant

### Ebed (Hebrew)

*See, **my servant** will act wisely;*
*he will be raised and lifted up and highly exalted.*
Isaiah 52:13

**Steps on Your Journey to Know God More Intimately:**

- *Ebed* means servant or bondservant.

- We're going to spend this coming month preparing for Easter. I want to encourage you to focus in on what the Lord did for us. We'll begin by looking at Isaiah 52:13 through chapter 53.

- Read Isaiah 52:13-15. Focus on how Jesus is described and what it says will happen to Him.

- Why do you think the Father calls the Messiah, Jesus, His Servant in Isaiah 52:13, rather than His Son or some other title?

- Philippians 2:7 says that Jesus took the very nature of a servant. Think about what a servant does and is.

- Since Jesus was God's servant, should we expect any different for ourselves?

**A Prayer for You:**

*Thank You, Jesus, that You were willing to come to earth as a Servant, rather than as a King. You chose to serve rather than to be served. Thank You for going through so much pain and heartache for me. Help me to know and understand You more through this name.*

# Choose Your Own Name

*Blessed be the name of the Lord*
*from this time forth and forevermore!*
Psalm 113:2 (ESV)

**Steps on Your Journey to Know God More Intimately:**

Since today is leap year, I want to do something different. Here are three options for you:

- You can read your Bible and search for God's names yourself. If you're not sure where to start, you could begin in the Psalms or in Isaiah. Actually, a majority of the Bible speaks of God's names (other than Esther).

- Review some, or all, of the names of God that we looked at in the past two months. Which of His names stand out to you?

- Think of a name you would call God today, based on what you need or how you have seen Him work in your life recently. That's what King David did hundreds of times. What name will you call the Lord today?

- Which option did you choose? I'd love to hear what you decided to do. You can post it on www.365NamesofGod.com.

**A Prayer for You:**

*Lord, You are such an amazing God. Show me more of Yourself today. I want to know You in new and fresh ways. Thank You that You love revealing Yourself to us.*

# Arm of the Lord

Zeroa Yahweh (Hebrew)

*Who has believed our message?*
*And to whom has the **arm of the Lord** been revealed?*
Isaiah 53:1 (NAS)

**Steps on Your Journey to Know God More Intimately:**

- *Zeroa* means arm, power and strength. When the Bible talks about God's arm, it is referring to His power. See Psalm 77:15, 98:1 and Acts 13:17.

- In the next ten days, we'll be looking at names of God from Isaiah 53. The whole chapter refers to the Messiah, Jesus Christ. Take some time to read this chapter today.

- In John 12:38, Jesus quotes this verse referring to Himself. I'd encourage you to look up the context.

- Meditate on this name today.

- Why is Jesus called the Arm of the Lord? How is He like God's Arm, reaching out to the world? To you?

- Praise the Lord today for how He reached down to reveal Himself to you.

**A Prayer for You:**

*Lord, thank You for revealing Your Arm to me through Jesus. Help me to understand You more through this name. Open my mind and heart to see You and know You in new ways.*

# Tender Shoot

*He grew up before him like a **tender shoot**, and like a root out of dry ground. He had no beauty or majesty to attract us to him, nothing in his appearance that we should desire him.*
Isaiah 53:2

**Steps on Your Journey to Know God More Intimately:**

- This name is one word in the Hebrew, *yonake*. This is the only time this word is used. It means a sucker, a twig of a felled tree or a tender plant.

- Other translations of this verse say tender green shoot, tender plant, delicate plant or a tender sapling. How do they add to your understanding of this name?

- Think about this name. Why do you think Jesus is referred to as a tender shoot?

- God protected this tender shoot for the task He had for Him. He can protect you for the tasks He has for you as well. May you truly know Yahweh in all His tenderness and love for you.

- Talk to the Lord about what He is showing you today.

**A Prayer for You:**

*I praise You, Lord, because You grew up as a tender, delicate plant. Reveal to me more of what this means and how You want me to relate to You differently. Teach me more about Yourself this month as I focus on You and what You did for me.*

## Root Out of Dry Ground

*He grew up before him like a tender shoot,*
*and like a **root out of dry ground**.*
*He had no beauty or majesty to attract us to him,*
*nothing in his appearance that we should desire him.*
Isaiah 53:2

**Steps on Your Journey to Know God More Intimately:**

- This name is similar to tender shoot that we looked at yesterday. Think about it. Why do you think the Messiah is called a Root Out of Dry Ground?

- A root growing up in dry ground would have to work extra hard. Could the dry ground refer to the hard hearts of the people around Him? Ask the Lord to show you what it means.

- This verse goes on to say that He had no beauty or majesty to attract us to Him. Are you attracted to roots? Interesting thought!

- He is the King of kings, yet He came as a *plain* human, leaving behind His majesty and beauty.

- Ask the Lord to reveal more of Himself to you today. Then thank and praise Him for what He shows you.

**A Prayer for You:**

*Jesus, thank You that You were willing to grow up like a Root Out of Dry Ground. Teach me what that means. I want to know You in new and fresh ways. I want to worship and praise You more.*

## Man of Sorrows

*He was despised and forsaken of men,*
*A **man of sorrows**, and acquainted with grief;*
*And like one from whom men hide their face,*
*He was despised, and we did not esteem Him.*
Isaiah 53:3 (NAS)

**Steps on Your Journey to Know God More Intimately:**

- The Hebrew name for Man of Sorrows is *Eesh Makob*. *Makob* means sorrow, grief, anguish, suffering, pain and affliction. *Eesh* is translated as man and husband.

- Think about this: Jesus is the King of the universe, yet He came to earth, knowing He would be despised and rejected, knowing He would go through terrible suffering, grief and pain. Yet He came anyway. What amazing love.

- Jesus experienced so much sorrow and stress for us. Think about all He went through.

- When I'm sad and grieving, it encourages me to know that Jesus understands my sadness. He went through it too.

- Thank the Lord that He was willing to endure all He did—suffering because of His great love for you.

**A Prayer for You:**

*Lord, I'm so grateful that You, the King of kings, were willing to become a Man of Sorrows. Thank You that You were acquainted with grief, so You understand when I'm sad. Thank You for all You were willing to go through for me, because You love me. Open my eyes and heart to understand Your love in new ways.*

# One from Whom People Hide Their Faces

*He was despised and rejected by men;
a man of sorrows, and acquainted with grief;
and as* **one from whom people hide their faces**
*he was despised, and we esteemed him not.*
Isaiah 53:3 (ESV)

**Steps on Your Journey to Know God More Intimately:**

• Jesus left Heaven, where He was worshipped, honored and praised to come to Earth where people hid their faces from Him. This verse also says He was despised, rejected and not esteemed. That is love. Amazing love. Take some time right now to thank the Lord for His incredible love for you.

• Why did people hide their faces from Jesus?

• Have you ever had people turn away from you? How did it feel?

• After my son Daniel was born with numerous problems, he was in and out of the hospital for almost six months, until he died. Many of the people who I thought were my closest friends were not there for me at all. They stayed away (hid their faces from me). It turned out that they didn't know what to say, so they figured it was better to not come around. That hurt deeply. Imagine how it hurt Jesus when His friends turned away from Him.

• Meditate on what this name means. Ask the Lord what He wants to show you from it.

**A Prayer for You:**

*Lord, thank You for Your wonderful love for me. Thank You for being willing to be despised, rejected and have men hide their faces from You. Help me to understand more of what this means, so I can know You and praise You more.*

## Savior of the World

*Then they said to the woman, "Now we believe,
not because of what you said, for we ourselves have heard Him
and we know that this is indeed the Christ, the **Savior of the world**."*
John 4:42 (NKJV)

**Steps on Your Journey to Know God More Intimately:**

- 1 John 4:14 says, "And we have seen and testify that the Father has sent his Son as the Savior of the world" (RSV).

- Father God sent Jesus to earth to be our Savior.

- Savior of the World is *Sotare Cosmos* in Greek. Savior, *Sotare*, comes from the Greek word *sozo*. It means "to save, heal, deliver and make whole." Jesus came to earth not just to save us from our sins, although He did that. He also came to bring healing to our bodies (as we'll see in a few days). He was sent to deliver us out of Satan's clutches and to make us whole.

- Meditate on this name. Think about all Jesus came to do for you and for the whole world.

- Since Jesus came as the Savior of the World, we should be out there sharing that good news with those who don't yet know Him. How can you do this in your sphere of influence?

**A Prayer for You:**

*Savior, I am so grateful for all You came to do for me (and the whole world). Thank You that You didn't just come to save my soul, but You also came to bring me healing, wholeness and deliverance. Teach me more about Yourself through this name. Show me how I can better share You with others around me.*

# God Our Savior, Who Daily Bears Our Burdens

*Praise be to the Lord, to **God our Savior, who daily bears our burdens**.*
Psalm 68:19

**Steps on Your Journey to Know God More Intimately:**

- Look what Isaiah 53:4 says Jesus did for us: "Surely he took up our pain and bore our suffering, yet we considered him punished by God, stricken by him, and afflicted." Jesus didn't just come to save us from our sins. He came to take our emotional and physical pain and suffering.

- Consider how Jesus bore your pain and suffering. How does this affect your daily life?

- If Jesus bore our suffering, why do we still suffer? Do you have any pain or heartache you need to give Him today?

- This name has given me so much strength and courage throughout the years. He is not only my Savior, He is also the One who bears my burdens.

- The New Living Translation translates this verse, "Praise the Lord; praise God our savior! For each day He carries us in His arms."

- Meditate on this name today and thank God your Savior that He does daily bear your burdens. You might want to thank Him for some specific ways He has done that.

- We don't have to bear our stress and burdens on our own. Isn't that great to know?! I pray that God will be your burden bearer.

**A Prayer for You:**

*Thank You, Lord, for daily bearing my burdens, pain and suffering. It is so comforting to know that I don't have to handle my problems and burdens on my own. Help me to remember You are always there for me and to trust You each day to carry me in Your arms.*

# March 8

## Lord, Your Healer

Yahweh Rapha (Hebrew)

*I am the **Lord, your healer**.*
Exodus 15:26b (ESV)

**Steps on Your Journey to Know God More Intimately:**

- "But he was pierced for our transgressions, he was crushed for our iniquities; the punishment that brought us peace was on him, and by his wounds we are healed" (Isaiah 53:5).

- Look at 1 Peter 2:24 to learn more about Jesus being our healer. "He himself bore our sins in his body on the tree, that we might die to sin and live to righteousness. By his wounds you have been healed" (ESV). See also Matthew 8:16-17.

- Notice that this is past tense: by his wounds we *are* healed. What does that say to you?

- How did Jesus' wounds heal us? If His wounds healed us, why do we still have disease? Talk to the Lord about that.

- Thank the Lord that He is your Healer.

- If you need a physical healing, claim this verse, saying out loud, "By Your wounds I am healed." I'm claiming this verse over my arthritis. It's not gone yet completely, but it is much better than it used to be. Yay, God! I also saw God heal me of a fast-growing pre-cancer and many other things.

**A Prayer for You:**

*Yahweh Rapha, thank You that You **are** my healer. Thank You that I am already healed because of Your wounds. Help me to learn to trust You more and believe in Your remarkable healing power. Increase my faith, Lord, and help my unbelief.*

## Atoning Sacrifice for our Sins

*He is the **atoning sacrifice for our sins**, and not only for ours
but also for the sins of the whole world.*
1 John 2:2

**Steps on Your Journey to Know God More Intimately:**

- Isaiah 53:6 says, "We all, like sheep, have gone astray, each of us has turned to our own way; and the LORD has laid on him the iniquity of us all."

- Think about this: God put all of your sin and mine on Jesus. But He also put the sins of the entire world on Him. I can't even imagine what that must have been like—the sinless Son of God with the enormous weight of all our sins on Him.

- 1 John 4:10 adds, "This is love: not that we loved God, but that he loved us and sent his Son as an atoning sacrifice for our sins." 1 John has the only two references in the Bible for "atoning sacrifice."

- Jesus being our atoning sacrifice or propitiation means that He completely satisfied God's just demands for judgment on our sin by His death on the cross. In other words, because we are sinners, we deserve hell. But because the Holy God loved us so much, He sent Jesus to take our place, to pay our debt, so we could have a relationship with Him. Wow!

- Meditate on Jesus being your atoning sacrifice. He paid your debt, to give you hope for the future, as well as intimacy with the God of the universe right now. Thank Him that He traded His love and eternal life for your sins and hell! I'd say you (and I) got an incredible deal!

**A Prayer for You:**

*Jesus, thank You for letting Father God put my sin on You. Thank You for becoming the atoning sacrifice for my sin. I deserved punishment, but You took it for me. Words can't even begin to tell You how grateful I am. Thank You for Your amazing love for me. Help me to understand it more.*

## Lamb to the Slaughter

*He was oppressed and afflicted, yet he did not open his mouth;*
*he was led like a **lamb to the slaughter**,*
*and as a sheep before its shearers is silent, so he did not open his mouth.*
Isaiah 53:7

**Steps on Your Journey to Know God More Intimately:**

- Lamb to the Slaughter is *Seh Tebakh* in Hebrew. *Seh* is lamb or sheep. *Tebakh* means slaughter.

- Picture a helpless lamb being led to the slaughter. Close your eyes and think about how Jesus was like a lamb led to be killed.

- How was He different than a lamb? (For one thing He knew exactly what would happen to Him, yet He went anyway. A lamb has no idea what's about to happen.) What are some other differences?

- Imagine how stressful it was for Jesus with all He went through.

- Ask the Lord to reveal more of Himself through this name. Thank Him for what He shows you.

**A Prayer for You:**

*Lord, thank You for this picture of You being like a lamb led to the slaughter. Help me to understand it more. Thank You for what You went through for me, because You love me. Help me to learn to know Your love more and to love You in deeper ways.*

# March 11

## Sheep before its Shearers

*He was oppressed and afflicted, yet he did not open his mouth;*
*he was led like a lamb to the slaughter,*
*and as a **sheep before its shearers** is silent,*
*so he did not open his mouth.*
Isaiah 53:7

**Steps on Your Journey to Know God More Intimately:**

- How was Jesus like a sheep before her shearers?

- Did you know that the difference between a sheep and a goat is that when a sheep is in the shepherd's hands being sheared, it relaxes, whereas a goat resists everything, all the time. Think about this: are you a sheep or a goat?

- Ask the Lord to show you why it compares Jesus' silence to a lamb being shaved?

- Matthew 27:12 and other verses talk about Jesus being silent before His accusers. Why do you think He remained silent?

- Ask the Lord to reveal more of Himself to you today through this name.

**A Prayer for You:**

*Jesus, thank You for another name that is a picture of You. Show me more of what it means, so I can know You more. Thank You, Jesus, that You demonstrated how to go through trials and hard times. Help me to follow Your example.*

## Offering for Sin

*But it was the Lord's good plan to crush him and cause him grief.*
*Yet when his life is made an **offering for sin**,*
*he will have many descendants. He will enjoy a long life,*
*and the Lord's good plan will prosper in his hands.*
Isaiah 53:10 (NLT)

**Steps on Your Journey to Know God More Intimately:**

- *Asham* means offering for sin in Hebrew.

- We've just looked at Jesus being a sheep and a lamb. The animals they used for offerings for sin had no choice as to whether they would die to pay for people's sins. Jesus gave His own life willingly as an offering for sin.

- In John 1:29, John calls Jesus "the Lamb of God, who takes away the sin of the world!"

- Imagine the stress Jesus must have been under—taking all the sins of the world on Himself. I can't even imagine how difficult that must have been for Him.

- I'm so grateful that Jesus was willing to be an offering for my sin. He paid the price once and for all—not like the lambs that had to be continually sacrificed.

- Thank the Lord today for what He's showing you from this name.

**A Prayer for You:**

*Thank You, Jesus, that You willingly became an offering for my sin. You gave Your life to pay for my sin. That is an incredible love that I can't even begin to fully understand. Open my eyes and heart to be able to grasp how much You love me. Forgive me for the times I forget to say thank You.*

## My Righteous Servant

*When he sees all that is accomplished by his anguish, he will be satisfied.
And because of his experience, **my righteous servant**
will make it possible for many to be counted righteous,
for he will bear all their sins.*
Isaiah 53:11 (NLT)

**Steps on Your Journey to Know God More Intimately:**

- *Tsadeek* in Hebrew means just, lawful, clean, to be right in a moral or forensic sense and to cleanse self. *Ebed* means servant or bond servant.

- Earlier this year, we saw Jesus called God's servant. Today Isaiah adds that Jesus is God's *Righteous* Servant. Why do you think it was important to show that Jesus was righteous? If you're not sure, ask the Lord to show you.

- What does this verse say that God's righteous servant would do?

- 2 Corinthians 5:21 says, "For our sake he [God] made him to be sin who knew no sin, so that in him we might become the righteousness of God" (ESV). Think about this.

- Praise the Lord today that Jesus was willing to be God's Righteous Servant *and* that God was willing to send Him to earth—knowing all He would have to go through.

**A Prayer for You:**

*Lord Jesus, I praise You today that You were willing to be God's Righteous Servant to make it possible for me to be counted as righteous, because You bore my sins. Thank You that You took my sin on Yourself to make me righteous. Wow!*

# Him Who Knew No Sin

*God made **Him who knew no sin** to be sin for us,*
*that we might become the righteousness of God in Him.*
2 Corinthians 5:21 (NKJV)

**Steps on Your Journey to Know God More Intimately:**

- Meditate on this verse. God took our sins and traded His righteousness for them. That's an amazing thought! I think this is one of the most incredible verses in the entire Bible. I often return to it, reveling in what God did for me. Ask the Lord to reveal more of Himself through it.

- Isaiah 53:12 says, "He poured out his life unto death, and was numbered with the transgressors. For he bore the sin of many, and made intercession for the transgressors." How did Jesus pour out His life?

- What does it mean to you today that Jesus gave His life so you could have eternal life?

- How does it affect you, knowing that the One who had no sin became sin for you so you might become righteous? Talk to Him about that.

- Thank God for what He did for you.

**A Prayer for You:**

*God, I'm so grateful that You were willing to let Jesus become sin for me so I could become righteous. My mind can't even comprehend why a sinless God would do that for people who hated, rejected and despised You. Open my eyes to understand this name—and You—more.*

## March 15

### *Intercessor*

*He poured out his life unto death,
and was numbered with the transgressors.
For he bore the sin of many, and made* **intercession** *for the transgressors.*
Isaiah 53:12

**Steps on Your Journey to Know God More Intimately:**

- This name is extrapolated from what He does for us.

- Hebrews 7:25 says, "Therefore he is able to save completely those who come to God through him, because he always lives to intercede for them."

- An intercessor is one who prays on behalf of another person. Jesus prayed for us when we were still sinners. And He is still interceding for us. Think about that.

- I am an intercessor. I love praying for people, although it isn't always easy. How encouraging it is to know that Jesus is my intercessor.

- What does it mean to you today that Jesus prayed for you when you were still a sinner?

- How does it affect your life, knowing that Jesus is interceding for you today?

**A Prayer for You:**

*Lord, thank You that You are my Intercessor. It's hard to believe that the Savior of the World is praying for me. But it's comforting to know that You always live to intercede for me. Help me to remember what You've done for me and how You pray for me, especially when I feel alone.*

# Christ the Son of God

*The high priest said to him, "I charge you under oath by the living God:*
*Tell us if you are the **Christ, the Son of God**."*
Matthew 26:63

**Steps on Your Journey to Know God More Intimately:**

- Remember that Christ means Messiah or Anointed One.

- The high priest asked Jesus if He was the Christ, the Son of God. Jesus answered, "Yes, it is as you say." He admitted to them that He is the Messiah, God's Son. In effect, He was saying that He is God.

- Do you ever wonder if Jesus really is God? If you wonder at all, just ask Him to show you. He loves to answer us. But remember to be quiet and just listen for His answer. John 10:27 says, "My sheep hear My voice, and I know them, and they follow Me" (NKJV). Be still and listen.

- Ask the Lord to reveal to you what it means that He is the Christ, the Son of God.

**A Prayer for You:**

*Lord, I praise You that You are the Messiah, the Anointed One. I praise You that You are God's Son. Show me today in new ways what it means that You are the Christ, the Son of God.*

# March 17

## *Lord (in lower case)*

Adon or Adonai (Hebrew); Kurios (Greek)
*The Lord says to my **Lord**: Sit at my right hand,*
*until I make your enemies your footstool.*
Psalm 110:1 (ESV)

**Steps on Your Journey to Know God More Intimately:**

- Psalm 110 is a Messianic psalm. The Jews knew this referred to the Messiah. Jesus quoted it in Luke 20.

- In Luke 20:41-44 Jesus said to them, "How can they say that the Christ is David's son? For David himself says in the Book of Psalms, "The Lord said to my Lord, Sit at my right hand, until I make your enemies your footstool.' David thus calls him Lord, so how is he his son?" (ESV).

- This is the Hebrew word, *adon* (the root of Adonai), that is translated Lord (in lower case in the Old Testament). The Greek word is *kurios*. Both names mean Lord, master, owner or one who is supreme in authority. How do the Greek and Hebrew add to your knowledge of God as Lord?

- Meditate on Jesus being your Lord today. What does that mean to you?

- Are there any areas of your life where Jesus is not Lord? You might want to ask God to reveal them to you. What might you need to change to make Him your Lord and Master?

**A Prayer for You:**

*Lord, I want to praise and worship You more as my Master, recognizing You as the One who is supreme in authority. Show me how to honor You more. Reveal any areas of my life where I don't acknowledge You as my Lord.*

## Son of David

*The crowds that went ahead of him and those that followed shouted,
"Hosanna to the **Son of David**!
Blessed is he who comes in the name of the Lord!
Hosanna in the highest!"*
Matthew 21:9

**Steps on Your Journey to Know God More Intimately:**

- *Huios* is son in Greek. *Dabeed* is David.

- This is a quotation from Psalm 118:26. It is the cry of the multitudes as they thronged in Jesus' triumphal procession into Jerusalem.

- Hosanna means "Oh save!" It is an exclamation of adoration. The people recognized Jesus was their Savior.

- Matthew 1 gives Jesus' genealogy, showing He comes from the line of David. Remember, David was the king over all of Israel. In 2 Samuel 7:16, God promised David that his kingdom and throne would last forever. By Jesus being called the Son of David, it told the Jews that He was the Messiah, especially combining it with the rest of the verse (we'll look at that tomorrow).

- Ask the Lord to show you what difference it makes to you today that Jesus is the Son of David.

**A Prayer for You:**

*Hosanna to Jesus, the Son of David. I worship and adore You, because You, being God, came as a man to earth. You fulfilled promises in Scripture about the Messiah. Show me more about this name today. I want to know You, Lord.*

# He Who Comes in the Name of the Lord

*Then the multitudes who went before and those who followed cried out,*
*saying: "Hosanna to the Son of David!*
*'Blessed is **He who comes in the name of the Lord**!*
*Hosanna in the highest!"*
Matthew 21:9 (NKJV)

**Steps on Your Journey to Know God More Intimately:**

- Blessed means to praise or to celebrate with praises.

- Consider each word in this name. Ask the Lord to reveal to you what it means.

  o He who—Who is He?

  o Comes—It is present tense, not past. Why?

  o In the name—A name represented the entire person, everything about him or her.

  o Of the Lord—The Greek word for Lord is *Kurios*, meaning master or lord.

- By quoting Psalm 118:26 in praise of Jesus, the people were acknowledging that Jesus was their Messiah.

- How can you bless the Lord today?

**A Prayer for You:**

*I bless and praise You today, You who came in the name of the Lord. Thank You that You didn't just come in Your own name. You came in the name of Yahweh, the One True God. Teach me more of what it means to bless You. Show me how You want me to bless You today and in the coming days.*

## Stone that the Builders Rejected

*Then Jesus asked them, "Didn't you ever read this in the Scriptures?*
*'The **stone that the builders rejected***
*has now become the cornerstone.*
*This is the Lord's doing, and it is wonderful to see.'"*
Matthew 21:42 (ESV)

**Steps on Your Journey to Know God More Intimately:**

- This verse is quoted from Psalm 118:22-23.

- Isaiah 53, especially verse 3 talks more about how the Messiah would be rejected by men. Today He is becoming more and more so. How is it for you to follow the One who is rejected?

- Isaiah 28:16 refers to the Messiah as a stone: "Therefore thus says the Lord God, 'Behold, I am laying in Zion a stone, a tested stone, a costly cornerstone for the foundation, firmly placed. He who believes in it will not be disturbed'" (NAS).

- Think about what this name means. Ask the Lord to show you what He wants you to know today. Let's break this name down:

    o The—Not just *any* stone.

    o Stone—What was the stone used for? How is Jesus like a stone?

    o The builders—Who were they? What were they building?

    o Rejected—What does it mean to be rejected? When have you been rejected? What did it feel like? Why was Jesus rejected by the builders?

**A Prayer for You:**

*Jesus, thank You for coming as a foundation stone for my life. Thank You for being willing to be rejected by men. Forgive me for any ways I have rejected You. Help me to trust in You more and build my life on You.*

## Cornerstone

*Then Jesus asked them, "Didn't you ever read this in the Scriptures?*
*'The stone that the builders rejected*
*has now become the **cornerstone**.*
*This is the Lord's doing, and it is wonderful to see.'"*
Matthew 21:42 (ESV)

**Steps on Your Journey to Know God More Intimately:**

- Cornerstone is *Kefalay Goinia* in Greek. *Kefalay* means head. *Gonia* means a corner or an angle.

- The cornerstone is the most important stone in the foundation of a house or wall, because it bears greater weight.

- Growing up in Guatemala, we often had hard earthquakes. I remember my family running outside, night or day, as soon as the ground started to shake. I often wondered if one might cause our house to fall. I'm so glad nothing can cause my life to fall when it is founded on Jesus as my Cornerstone. I can build my life on His solid foundation, without fear of it ever giving way. And so can you.

- This word is also translated as "capstone," which refers to the top stone that finishes off a building or an arch.

- Meditate on how Jesus is the Cornerstone. How has He been a foundation for your life?

- Consider Jesus as the Capstone. How has He finished off or crowned your life?

**A Prayer for You:**

*Jesus, thank You for being the foundation for my life. It's comforting to know that my life is built on a solid foundation that will never be shaken. Teach me more of how You are a Cornerstone, not just of my life, but also of the whole church.*

# Jesus Who Is Called Christ

*So when the crowd had gathered, Pilate asked them,*
*"Which one do you want me to release to you:*
*Barabbas, or **Jesus who is called Christ**?"*
Matthew 27:17

**Steps on Your Journey to Know God More Intimately:**

- Pilate, the Roman governor, used this name. He was using the Jewish terminology, not his own. It seems like he was trying to convince the Jewish leaders not to crucify Jesus.

- Remember Christ means the Anointed One and referred to the Messiah.

- Pilate doesn't say, "Jesus who *is* the Christ." He was not sure that Jesus really was the Messiah. What about you? Is there any part of you that wonders if Jesus really is God come down to earth? If so, talk to Him about that today. Ask God to reveal to you if Jesus really is God.

**A Prayer for You:**

*Jesus, I choose to acknowledge You as the Christ, the Messiah, God who came to earth as a man to die for me. Thank You for what You went through because of Your love for me. Reveal more of who You are today, so I can know You and worship You in greater ways.*

# Jesus of Nazareth (the Nazarene)

Iesous Nazoraios (Hebrew)

*Pilate had a notice prepared and fastened to the cross.
It read: **"Jesus of Nazareth**, King of the Jews."*
John 19:19

**Steps on Your Journey to Know God More Intimately:**

- In Mark 16:6 an angel says, "Don't be alarmed. You are looking for Jesus the Nazarene, who was crucified. He has risen! He is not here. See the place where they laid him."

- We see Jesus' humanity in this name. They knew where He was raised.

- In Israel in Jesus' time, Nazareth was seen in a negative way by other Jews. The word "Nazarene" was a synonym for despised. The Jews were convinced no prophet could come from there (John 1:46). Remember, Jesus only grew up there. He was born in Bethlehem, the town from which the Messiah was to come.

- Why do you think the angel called Jesus "the Nazarene" (in Mark 16:6) instead of another of His many names?

- Consider all Jesus did for you when He died on the cross.

**A Prayer for You:**

*Jesus of Nazareth, thank You for coming to earth as a human, so You could identify with me. I'm so grateful for all You went through for me on the cross. As I prepare to celebrate Easter, remind me of all You endured for me, showing me Your great love.*

# King of the Jews

Basileus Ioudaios (Greek)

*Pilate had a notice prepared and fastened to the cross.*
*It read: "Jesus of Nazareth, **King of the Jews**."*
John 19:19

**Steps on Your Journey to Know God More Intimately:**

- *Basileus* means king. This is the second part to the title Pilate fastened on the cross after Jesus was hung there.

- The first part of this name reveals His humanity. The title *King of the Jews* shows His royalty, power and His authority.

- Pilate, a Gentile who didn't believe in the Messiah, wrote this. Why do you think Pilate called Jesus the King of the Jews?

- Think about how Jesus is your king. What does that look like?

- Take some time today to remember what Jesus went through for you as He hung on the cross. Ask Him to open your eyes to understand more of what He endured and how much He loves you.

**A Prayer for You:**

*Jesus, thank You for using a heathen ruler to remind me that You are both a human like me as well as being royalty—the King not only of the Jews, but also of the Universe. Help me to honor You and worship You as my King. Thank You for being willing to go to the cross to die for my sins so I can have hope, knowing I'll live with You for eternity.*

# March 25

## One They Have Pierced

Hos Ekkenteo (Greek)

*They will look on the **one they have pierced**.*
John 19:37

**Steps on Your Journey to Know God More Intimately:**

- *Hos* is who or whom. *Ekkenteo* means pierce. This is a quotation from Zechariah 12:10. Read John 19:31-37 for the context of this verse.

- Isaiah 53:5 says Jesus was pierced for our transgressions. Transgression means a revolt, rebellion or sin. Jesus was pierced for my sins and yours. Think about what that means.

- Jesus loved us so much He was willing to be pierced, wounded for us, to save us from our sins. What does this name mean to you, personally, today?

- Think about what God the Father endured as He watched His Son go through all the pain and suffering. If you have children, imagine what it would be like to watch one of them go through what Jesus did. Remember, the Father didn't have to allow men to hurt His Son.

- Take some time today to thank both Jesus and Father God for all they went through for you.

**A Prayer for You:**

*Jesus, I'm so grateful for what You endured for me. Thank You for being willing to be pierced for my sins, so I could have a right relationship with You. Thank You, Father, that You allowed Your Son to suffer all the pain, because of Your great love for me. Help me to understand Your love in new and fresh ways.*

## Teacher

*"**Teacher**," they said, "we know you are a man of integrity*
*and that you teach the way of God in accordance with the truth.*
*You aren't swayed by men, because you pay no attention to who they are."*
Matthew 22:16

**Steps on Your Journey to Know God More Intimately:**

- *Didaskalos* in Greek means master, teacher, instructor or doctor. The Pharisees—legalistic, religious leaders—were calling Jesus Teacher in this verse. In Matthew 22:24, the Sadducees—other religious leader—also called Him Teacher. These were both Jewish religious groups. Yet they acknowledged that Jesus was a great Teacher (even if they were trying to trip Him up, by asking Him very difficult questions).

- Jesus always had and has the perfect answer. What is a question you want to ask Him today? Ask, believing He will answer. Then sit quietly and wait for His response.

- Ask yourself, "How has Jesus been my Teacher in the past?"

- How do you need or want Him to be your Teacher today?

**A Prayer for You:**

*Thank You for being my Teacher. Thank You for what You are teaching me about Yourself from Your Word and from this study of Your names. Please make me more open to You to listen to what You want to teach me.*

# Name that Is Above Every Name

*Therefore God exalted him to the highest place and gave him the*
**name that is above every name** *that at the name of Jesus every knee
should bow, in heaven and on earth and under the earth, and every tongue
confess that Jesus Christ is Lord, to the glory of God the Father.*
Philippians 2:9-11

**Steps on Your Journey to Know God More Intimately:**

- The Greek word for name is *onoma*. When the Bible mentions "name" it refers to everything about that person—what he or she is like, personality, looks, character, etc. Think about all that Jesus is when it refers to His Name.

- How is Jesus' Name above every name?

- What do these verses say we should do because of His Name?

- Meditate on these verses.

- Ask the Lord to reveal to you more about this Name that is Above Every Name.

**A Prayer for You:**

*Jesus, I praise You and Your Name that is Above Every Name. Teach me more of what this means. I want to know You and Your Name more intimately.*

## *Name of Jesus*

*Therefore God exalted him to the highest place and gave him the
name that is above every name that at the **name of Jesus** every knee should
bow, in heaven and on earth and under the earth, and every tongue confess
that Jesus Christ is Lord, to the glory of God the Father.*
Philippians 2:9-11

**Steps on Your Journey to Know God More Intimately:**

- Name of Jesus in Greek is *Onoma Iesous.* There is amazing power in Jesus' Name. Think about what these verses say—His Name makes every knee bow and every tongue confess that Jesus Christ is Lord. That's not just people who believe in Him. That's every knee and tongue—Christians, atheists, demons and even Satan himself.

- In John 14:13-14 Jesus says, "I will do whatever you ask in my name, so that the Father may be glorified in the Son. You may ask me for anything in my name, and I will do it." See also John 15:16.

- He has given you the authority to use His name. Do you believe it?

- Do you use Jesus' Name to stand against the enemy? If not, why not? We don't have to do anything on our own. In fact, apart from Him we can do nothing (John 15:5).

- In recent years, I have begun to learn the power in Jesus' Name. I've seen sick people healed and demons flee. Almost every day I ask the Lord to increase my faith. I believe in Jesus' Name and in His power, but not as much as I could. I want to see more miracles, including the dead raised! Just this week, I walked into a tree branch, hurting my eyeball so much that I couldn't even open it, because of the severe pain. A friend touched my eye lid, prayed in Jesus' Name and all pain and redness went away immediately.

- Ask the Lord to show you how you can tap into the power in Jesus' name in new ways.

**A Prayer for You:**

*Lord, I praise You for the Name of Jesus and the power that is in it. Thank You for giving me the ability to use Your Name and its power to accomplish Your will on the earth. Teach me to use the Name of Jesus more, believing in its power.*

## Jesus Christ

*Therefore God exalted him to the highest place and gave him the
name that is above every name that at the name of Jesus every knee should
bow, in heaven and on earth and under the earth, and every tongue confess
that **Jesus Christ** is Lord, to the glory of God the Father.*
Philippians 2:9-11

**Steps on Your Journey to Know God More Intimately:**

- Jesus Christ is *Iesous Christos* in Greek. This compound name reveals His humanity: Jesus, and His deity: Christ. Using the compound name, specifies which Jesus they were talking about, since the name Jesus was common in New Testament times.

- As you read through the New Testament, He is called many different variations of this name: Jesus, Christ, Jesus Christ, Christ Jesus and many other names. Think about each of these names. What significance do you see in the various forms of Jesus' name? If you're not sure, ask Him to show you.

- Confess means to acknowledge. This verse says that every tongue will acknowledge that Jesus Christ is Lord. Every person will eventually have to say that Jesus is Lord. I would rather confess that now, than when Jesus returns and it is too late. If you question whether or not Jesus is Lord, talk to God about that right now.

**A Prayer for You:**

*Jesus Christ, I acknowledge that You are Lord. You are my Master. I choose to follow You. I want to give You glory and bring glory to God the Father by my acknowledgement. Show me how to share this good news with others who don't yet know You.*

## Strength of His People

*The Lord is the **strength of his people**;*
*he is the saving refuge of his anointed.*
Psalm 28:8 (ESV)

**Steps on Your Journey to Know God More Intimately:**

- Strength is *oz* in Hebrew. It also means power, might and boldness. I'm so glad the Lord is the Strength of His people and I'm especially glad that I am one of His people.

- This verse doesn't say God will give you strength, although He does do that. This says He *is* our strength. When you don't have strength in yourself (and even when you think you do have enough of your own) let God be your strength.

- I have often seen God be my strength throughout my life. For example, when I am asked to speak, being an introvert, I am terrified to get up in front of people. I can't do it on my own. I have to rely on the Lord's strength and wisdom.

- How has the Lord been your strength in the past?

- How do you need Him to be your strength right now? Ask Him.

- Lean on Him today and let Him be your strength in whatever you are going through. He's always there and His strength has no limit.

**A Prayer for You:**

*O My Strength, I trust in You. Thank You for being my strength when I am weak. I'm so glad You are the One I can depend on, regardless of what happens in my life. Teach me to lean on You more and allow You to be my strength throughout my life.*

# March 31

## *Fortress of Salvation*

Maoz Mashiah (Hebrew)

*The Lord is the strength of his people,*
*a **fortress of salvation** for his anointed one.*
Psalm 28:8

**Steps on Your Journey to Know God More Intimately:**

- The Hebrew word for fortress, *maoz*, means a place of safety, refuge, protection and a stronghold. *Mashiah* means salvation and deliverance. This word is also used for the Messiah. Refer back to February 18.

- Other translations use the following terms for this name: saving refuge, saving defense, safe fortress and stronghold of salvation. Consider each of these names. What is the Lord saying to you through them?

- 2 Corinthians 1:21-22 says that God anointed us, "Now it is God who makes both us and you stand firm in Christ. He anointed us, set His seal of ownership on us, and put His Spirit in our hearts as a deposit, guaranteeing what is to come." Many Scriptures also talk about Jesus as being the Anointed One, such as Acts 4:26.

- When I was in Israel, my son Timothy and I went to the top of Masada. It was an incredible fortress where the Jews hid from their enemies. Unlike Masada, which was eventually overtaken, our Fortress of Salvation never will be.

- Think about this name. There is so much in it. Ask the Lord to show you what He wants you to see from it today. Then thank and praise Him for what He shows you.

**A Prayer for You:**

*Fortress of Salvation, thank You that You are a place of safety and protection for me. I'm so glad I can run to You for refuge. You are a strong, impenetrable fortress. Teach me not to fear, but instead to hide myself in You.*

## April 1

### *Lord Jesus*

*In everything I did, I showed you that by this kind of hard work
we must help the weak, remembering the words the **Lord Jesus** Himself
said: "It is more blessed to give than to receive."*
Acts 20:35

**Steps on Your Journey to Know God More Intimately:**

- This is a compound name. The Greek word for Lord here is *kurios*, meaning master or sir, showing He is supreme in authority. Jesus is His human name, meaning the Lord saves.

- Meditate on this name. Praise the Lord Jesus.

- Think about what this verse says the Lord Jesus said. How can you apply what He said today?

- What areas of your life clearly show that He is the Lord Jesus?

- How well does your generosity reveal that Jesus is your Lord?

- Are there areas of your life where Jesus isn't Lord?

**A Prayer for You:**

*Lord Jesus, I praise You today for being my Master and the One who saves me. Thank You for all Your teachings. Help me to always honor You as my Lord and to remember that it is more blessed to give than to receive.*

April 2

## *One Who Was Raised from the Dead*

*You died to the power of the law when you died with Christ.*
*And now you are united with the **one who was raised from the dead**.*
*As a result, we can produce a harvest of good deeds for God.*
Romans 7:4 (NLT)

**Steps on Your Journey to Know God More Intimately:**

- Imagine if Jesus had just died and not risen from the dead. Where would you be? What would your future be like?

- Look at the last part of this verse. What is the result of what Jesus did? What does that look like in your life?

- Thank and praise Jesus that He didn't stay dead, but that He was raised and is now alive. Because God raised Jesus from the dead, we have hope! If He wasn't, we would have no hope at all for anything in the future.

**A Prayer for You:**

*Lord, I praise You that You not only died, but that You are the One Who Was Raised from the Dead. Thank You for the hope I have because You are alive. As a result, I want to produce a harvest of good deeds for You—not because it will bring me salvation, but because I'm so grateful for what You did for me.*

93

# God, Who Has Not Rejected My Prayer or Withheld His Love from Me!

*Praise be to **God, who has not rejected my prayer
or withheld His love from me!***
Psalm 66:20

**Steps on Your Journey to Know God More Intimately:**

- Meditate on this name today. God loves you so much that He won't reject your prayer or withhold His love from you. He loves to hear you talk to Him. He loves spending time with you.

- Have you ever been in a relationship where the other person withholds his or her love from you, because you did something wrong? God will never do that to you. Never. Ever.

- There have been times in my life when I felt like God had rejected my prayer. It felt like I might as well be praying to myself. No answers. Have you ever felt that way? Now, when I feel like that, I choose to stand on this name of God.

- I've also felt like God withheld his love from me. He hadn't, but it felt like that. Everything important in my life seemed to be taken away—my marriage, my son, my fiancé, my finances, my best friend and more. For a while, I believed the lie of the enemy that God didn't love me, so I walked away from God. I know now that wasn't true. God has shown me His love in so many ways.

- Think about God's great love for you today. If you don't feel His love, invite Him to reveal it to you in ways you can understand.

- Ask the Lord to show you who needs to hear that He loves them. Then go share what God is showing you about His great love.

**A Prayer for You:**

*Lord, I praise You that You don't reject my prayers and that You will never withhold Your love for me. Thank You for always listening to my prayers. I'm so glad I never have to fear that You'll be too busy to listen or You will think my prayers are a bother to You.*

# LORD, Who Brought You Up Out Of Egypt
## with Mighty Power and Outstretched Arm

*The **Lord**, **who brought you up out of Egypt with mighty power and outstretched arm**, is the one you must worship.*
*To him you shall bow down and to him offer sacrifices.*
2 Kings 17:36

**Steps on Your Journey to Know God More Intimately:**

- Consider this complex name.

- This verse refers back to when God led the Israelites out of Egypt where they were slaves. God did some incredible miracles, revealing His mighty power and outstretched arm. I'd encourage you to read the story in Exodus 13-14.

- God is still the same God as the One who brought them out of Egypt. He can bring you out of difficult situations with His mighty power and outstretched arm. There are many ways He does that, for example, one time years ago when I was rehabbing a mobile home, a greedy contractor took me to court, suing me for more money. The Lord showed me His outstretched arm when the judge laughed at the man and threw the case out of court. Yay God!

- In what areas do you need God to work in your life? Ask Him.

- How have you seen God's power at work in your life in the past? Thank Him.

- Let's celebrate the freedom we have because of our great God.

**A Prayer for You:**

*Lord, thank You that all of Your mighty power is available to me today. You are able to bring me out of any and all difficult circumstances. Show me Yourself through this name and help me learn to trust You more, especially when things seem impossible.*

# April 5

## Spirit of the Lord

*The **Spirit of the Lord**, shall rest upon Him, The Spirit of wisdom and understanding, The Spirit of counsel and might,*
*The Spirit of knowledge and of the fear of the Lord.*
Isaiah 11:2 (NKJV)

**Steps on Your Journey to Know God More Intimately:**

- Spirit of the Lord is *Ruah Yahweh* in Hebrew. Remember *ruah* means spirit, breath or wind in the Hebrew. We'll look at several names from this verse in the next few days.

- The Spirit has many facets and many names. I challenge you to begin a study of the Holy Spirit. You'll be amazed at all you'll learn and how it will change your life.

- In recent years I've begun studying about the Holy Spirit. I'm getting to know Him and letting Him work in my life. As a result, I'm seeing dramatic changes in my life and my family.

- Isaiah 11:2 is talking about the Spirit of the Lord resting on the Messiah, but He also rests on us. There are many verses that talk about us having the Spirit. Here are a few references you can look up: John 20:22; Acts 1:8; Ephesians 1:13, 17; 2 Timothy 1:14; 1 John 3:24; 4:13.

- Ask the Lord to show you what He wants to reveal to you today about the Spirit of the LORD.

**A Prayer for You:**

*Spirit of the Lord, I'm so thankful that You are in me and working through my life. Help me to learn to know You more and tap into all of who You are.*

April 6

*Spirit of Wisdom and Understanding*

*The Spirit of the Lord, will rest on him—*
*the **Spirit of wisdom and of understanding,***
*the Spirit of counsel and of power,*
*the Spirit of knowledge and of the fear of the Lord.*
Isaiah 11:2

**Steps on Your Journey to Know God More Intimately:**

- Proverbs 2:10-12; 3:13-14 says, "For wisdom will enter your heart, and knowledge will be pleasant to your soul. Discretion will protect you, and understanding will guard you. Wisdom will save you from the ways of wicked men. Blessed is the man who finds wisdom, the man who gains understanding." What can you learn from these verses?

- Knowledge is knowing facts. Understanding is knowing the implication of the facts in real life and includes discernment. Wisdom is knowing how to use the knowledge you have.

- We all need wisdom for our lives. Think about where you usually look for wisdom and understanding when you need them.

- In what areas do you need wisdom or understanding today?

- Romans 8:6 says, "letting the Spirit control your mind leads to life and peace" (NLT). Ponder the implications of allowing the Spirit to control your mind.

- I'm learning to rely on God's wisdom and understanding. Every day I choose to give the Spirit control of my mind to direct it in the ways He wants it to go. I couldn't write this book without His wisdom.

- Ask God to give you more of His wisdom and understanding through His Spirit.

**A Prayer for You:**

*Spirit of Wisdom and Understanding, I need You in my life. I constantly need wisdom, discernment and understanding. Teach me to turn to You first when I need direction. I choose to allow You to control my mind and my thoughts, Holy Spirit.*

97

## April 7

*Spirit of Counsel*

*The Spirit of the Lord will rest on Him—*
*the Spirit of wisdom and of understanding,*
*the **Spirit of counsel** and of power,*
*the Spirit of knowledge and of the fear of the Lord.*
Isaiah 11:2 (NKJV)

**Steps on Your Journey to Know God More Intimately:**

- This name is *ruah aytsa* in Hebrew. The Hebrew for counsel is *aytsa*, meaning advice, purpose or counselor.

- The same Spirit who rested on Jesus is also in us and on us! In John 14:16 Jesus promised that the Father would give us a Counselor, the Holy Spirit.

- In what areas do you need counsel? Have you asked your Counselor for His advice? Too often we go to humans for counsel, when the greatest Counselor is always with us—and doesn't cost us anything!

- I've struggled with going first to people for counsel and only later to God. I'm learning to start each day by loosing the Spirit of Counsel into my life and my family to guide every step of the day.

- Thank God throughout this day for His gracious gift of counsel through His Spirit within you.

**A Prayer for You:**

*Spirit of Counsel, thank You that You are always with me, giving me the best counsel I could ever want or need. Teach me to turn to You first when I need advice. Help me to learn to rely on You more.*

# April 8

## Spirit of Power

Ruah Gebura (Hebrew)

*For God did not give us a spirit of timidity,*
*but a **spirit of power**, of love and of self-discipline.*
2 Timothy 1:7

**Steps on Your Journey to Know God More Intimately:**

- Isaiah 11:2 says, "The Spirit of the Lord will rest on Him … the Spirit of counsel and of power" (NKJV).

- The Greek word for power in 2 Timothy 1:7 is *dunamis,* from which we get dynamite. Think about the power of dynamite. The Hebrew word for power is *gebura,* meaning strength, might, valor and bravery. It refers to the mighty deeds of God.

- Consider these two definitions of power. Ask the Lord to reveal more to you about the Spirit of Power.

- In Acts 1:8, Jesus promised us power through the Holy Spirit. In what areas do you need power in your life?

- A few years ago, I changed how I was praying for myself and my sons. I began to bind the enemy and loose the Spirit to work in whatever ways He wanted. Almost immediately, I began to see dramatic results and our lives transformed by the Spirit of Power.

- Read Ephesians 3:14-21 to see some unique ways the Spirit strengthens us with power. We often want external power, yet these verses talk about the Spirit giving us power in our inner beings. Think about that.

- Ask the Lord to show you what you may need to do to experience more of the Spirit's power in your life.

**A Prayer for You:**

*Spirit of Power, I want Your power to be at work in my life, not what humans consider power. Help me to learn to rely on You more and allow You to reveal Your power in my inner being. I long for Your power to show me Christ's love as I see in Ephesians 3.*

# April 9

## Spirit of Knowledge and of the Fear of the Lord

*The Spirit of the Lord will rest on him—*
*the Spirit of wisdom and of understanding,*
*the Spirit of counsel and of power,*
**the Spirit of knowledge and of the fear of the Lord.**
Isaiah 11:2

**Steps on Your Journey to Know God More Intimately:**

- Proverbs 1:7 says, "The fear of the Lord is the beginning of knowledge, but fools despise wisdom and discipline" (NKJV). This is another compound name of the Holy Spirit.

- Knowledge is knowing information, while wisdom is knowing how to apply that information in the best ways. We need both wisdom and knowledge. Meditate on the Spirit of Knowledge.

- In what areas do you need knowledge? Talk to the Spirit about those.

- When the Bible talks about the fear of the Lord, it is referring to a reverence for God because He is holy. That reverence makes us want to live holy and godly lives. The Word often tells us not to fear—be afraid of things or people. The fear (reverence) of the Lord is completely different. You can learn more about the fear of the Lord by reading the book of Proverbs.

- Every day I also loose the Spirit of Knowledge and the Fear of the Lord into my life and my family. When we have the fear of the Lord we want to live holy, righteous lives, not wanting to disrespect our holy God.

- In what areas of your life do you need the Fear of the Lord? Ask the Spirit to show you what that means.

**A Prayer for You:**

*Spirit of the Lord, I praise You for Your knowledge that is greater than any human could provide for me. I want to learn to always seek You and Your knowledge first. Teach me what it means to live in the Fear of the Lord. I want to always please You.*

April 10

## *The Almighty*

*The Spirit of God has made me; the breath of **the Almighty** gives me life.*
Job 33:4 ESV)

**Steps on Your Journey to Know God More Intimately:**

- This name is from the Hebrew word, *Shaddai* meaning all-sufficient, all-powerful and almighty.

- Psalm 91:1 says, "Those who live in the shelter of the Most High will find rest in the shadow of the Almighty" (NLT).

- Meditate on God's name, The Almighty. What does it mean to you?

- How has God been all sufficient for you?

- 2 Corinthians 12:9 talks about God's sufficiency, "He [Jesus] said to me, 'My grace is sufficient for you, for my power is made perfect in weakness.' Therefore I will boast all the more gladly about my weaknesses, so that Christ's power may rest on me." This is a verse where I often return. I have seen over and over how God's grace really is more than enough for my weaknesses. I love my weaknesses now, because I know that I can't accomplish anything on my own. That's a great place to be. I know I have to rely on God and His strength. When I am strong in certain areas, I don't always feel like I need to rely on God.

- Consider how 2 Corinthians 12:9 can help you today.

- In what areas do you need to allow God to be sufficient for you?

**A Prayer for You:**

*Almighty God, thank You that You are all powerful and You are sufficient for everything I need. Teach me to rely on You more and find rest in Your shadow.*

## Christ Jesus Our Hope

*Paul, an apostle of Christ Jesus by the command of God our Savior
and of **Christ Jesus our hope**.*
1 Timothy 1:1

**Steps on Your Journey to Know God More Intimately:**

- Hope in the New Testament means a favorable and confident expectation. It has to do with the unseen and the future. It also means the happy anticipation of God.

- We often use the word "hope" as a desire than as a confident expectation. Many times we don't believe that what we hope for will really happen. One pastor said, "It's not a 'hope so' hope. It's a 'know so' hope. Like the certainty of Christmas morning, you know it's coming. It's a sure thing."

- When people all around are living in fear because of the economy and government decisions, I know I have a choice. I can be fearful, anxious and worried. Or I can focus on Christ Jesus my Hope and find my hope in Him. It's not always easy and I don't always make the right choice, but when I do I find great hope and peace.

- In what areas of your life do you need more hope?

- Meditate on how Christ Jesus is your hope. How is He your hope? How has He been your hope?

**A Prayer for You:**

*Christ Jesus, thank You that You are my hope. I'm so glad that because of You and what You've done, I can have a confidence about the future, regardless of what happens. Teach me to trust You more and allow You to be my hope in every area of my life.*

## Glorious and Blessed God

*... the Good News of the **glorious and blessed God**.*
*This Good News was entrusted to me.*
1 Timothy 1:11 (CJB)

**Steps on Your Journey to Know God More Intimately:**

- Glorious means dignity, honor, worship and praise. Ask the Lord to show you more of what it means that He is a glorious God.

- I'm at a cabin in the mountains as I'm writing this. All around me I can see God's amazing glory. For the past year or two, I've been asking Him to show me His glory, and He has been! He likes to show off His glory, especially in nature.

- Blessed is from the root word meaning large or lengthy. It also means praised, fortunate and well-off. God is the One to be praised, because of His greatness and His largeness.

- Blessed is the same word as is used in the beatitudes in Matthew 5:3-12 and Luke 6: 20-22. "Blessed are the pure in heart…"

- Ask the Lord to show you how to bless Him today.

**A Prayer for You:**

*Lord, You are such a Gorious God and such a great God. You are worthy of praise. Teach me how to praise and bless You. How do You want me to bless You?*

# April 13

## *Mediator*

Meseetase (Greek)

*For there is one God and one **mediator**
between God and mankind, the man Christ Jesus.*
1 Timothy 2:5

**Steps on Your Journey to Know God More Intimately:**

- *Meseetase* is a reconciler, a go-between or a mediator. A mediator is one who goes between two parties, bringing peace and understanding. It is a negotiator who acts as a link between parties. Think about how Jesus is a mediator between us and God—between sinful man and the holy God.

- What did Jesus do to mediate between us?

- I imagine myself in a courtroom. My opponent, Satan, is accusing me of all kinds of sins. The Judge says, "He's right. You have sinned." Then Jesus stands up for me, representing me and says "I already paid for those sins, Dad." With that the Father slams the gavel down and says, "Not guilty."

- Thank Jesus for being willing to go through all that He did to mediate between you and God.

**A Prayer for You:**

*Mediator, thank You for Your role mediating between me and the holy God. Thank You for paying the cost to mediate for me. Teach me more of what it means that You are a mediator.*

# Living God, Who Is the Savior of All Men

*For it is for this we labor and strive,*
*because we have fixed our hope on the **living God**,*
***who is the Savior of all men**, especially of believers.*
1 Timothy 4:10 (NAS)

**Steps on Your Journey to Know God More Intimately:**

- This name has two parts. Contemplate the Living God. What does it mean to you that your God is living?

- What do you think it means that Jesus is the Savior of all people, especially of believers? Is He also the Savior of those who don't believe? How?

- I'm so glad our God is living. He's not like other gods who never were alive or else they died. It reminds me of the pagan gods the people worshiped in the village where I grew up in Guatemala. They were impotent. This living God is my Savior and yours. He paid our price to set us free. Wow!

- Meditate on this name. Think about how the Living God became our Savior. What does that mean to you today? Talk to Him about what He shows you.

**A Prayer for You:**

*Living God, I'm so grateful that You are my Savior. Thank You for saving me from all my sins. Thank You for being the Living God, who will never die. Draw me closer to You as I meditate on Your names. I long to know You more.*

## God, the Blessed and Only Ruler

**God, the blessed and only Ruler**, *the King of kings and Lord of lords.*
1 Timothy 6:15

**Steps on Your Journey to Know God More Intimately:**

- We'll be looking at God's names in this one verse over the next few days.

- Blessed here is *makarios* meaning fortunate, well off and happy. Ruler is *dynastace* meaning great authority, mighty and ruler.

- Meditate on this name. What do you think it means that God is the Blessed and Only Ruler?

- How is God blessed?

- What does He rule? Or, who does He rule?

- Is God your only Ruler? In what ways does your life reveal that God rules it?

- Are there areas that He isn't your Ruler? What might you need to change? Talk to the Lord about this.

**A Prayer for You:**

*God, I praise You that You are the Blessed and Only Ruler. I want to know You more, Lord. Show me what it means to have You as the Ruler of my life. I need Your help, because I like controlling my own life sometimes. Please forgive me.*

# King of Kings

*God, the blessed and only Ruler, the **King of kings** and Lord of lords.*
1 Timothy 6:15

**Steps on Your Journey to Know God More Intimately:**

- Imagine you are in a throne room with thousands of kings, all with gorgeous robes and crowns. They are all assembled in a massive room. Rather than people bowing to the kings, all the kings are bowing down to the King of kings—who is sitting on a gigantic throne. He is your God, your King.

- How do you picture the King of kings?

- How does your life reveal that God is your King?

- In what areas is God not your King? What might you need to change?

- Worship the Lord today as your King.

**A Prayer for You:**

*King of kings, I bow down and worship You. You are worthy of my praise, adoration and worship. Show me how You want me to treat You as my King.*

# Lord of Lords

Kurios Kyrieuo (Greek)

*God, the blessed and only Ruler, the King of kings
and **Lord of lords**, who alone is immortal.*
1 Timothy 6:15

**Steps on Your Journey to Know God More Intimately:**

- *Kurios* is lord, master or owner. *Kyrieuo* means to have dominion over or exercise lordship over.

- Psalm 136:3 says "Give thanks to the Lord of lords. His faithful love endures forever" (NLT).

- Think about God being the Lord of all lords. What does that mean to you today?

- Now consider that this Lord of lords loves you with a love that never quits, according to Psalm 136:3 in The Message. Do you really believe that? If not, ask the Lord to reveal how much He really loves you, personally.

- The more I'm getting to know God's love, the more joy I'm experiencing and the more I can love Him.

**A Prayer for You:**

*Lord of lords, I praise You for Your greatness and power. Thank You that although You are such a great God, You love me so much. Thank You for Your faithful love that endures forever. Help me to understand Your love in new and fresh ways.*

# God … Who Alone Is Immortal

**God**, *the blessed and only Ruler, the King of kings
and Lord of lords,* **who alone is immortal***.*
1 Timothy 6:15-16

**Steps on Your Journey to Know God More Intimately:**

- The Message translates this name as, "The only one death can't touch." Someone who is immortal is exempt from death. He won't die.

- God is not human, not mortal, as we are. Aren't you glad that your God is not human as you are? He can't die. He will never, ever die. That gives me comfort, knowing He'll never die or change.

- Jesus chose to die for our sins, yet death couldn't hold Him in the grave, because He is immortal. He rose again.

- How does this name affect you today?

- Ask the Lord to reveal more of Himself to you through this name.

**A Prayer for You:**

*God, I'm so glad to know that You are immortal. You are not human like I am and You will never die. I praise You for Your greatness and Your immortality.*

## April 19

# *God ... Who Lives in Unapproachable Light*

***God**, the blessed and only Ruler, the King of kings and Lord of lords,
who alone is immortal and **who lives in unapproachable light**.*
1 Timothy 6:15-16

**Steps on Your Journey to Know God More Intimately:**

- The New Living Translation says, "He lives in light so brilliant that no human can approach him."

- Consider this name. Close your eyes and picture the Lord. If you're having a hard time, ask the Lord to open the eyes of your heart, so that you can see Him clearly. In Ephesians 1:17-18 Paul prays, and we can pray too, that God would give them the Spirit of wisdom and revelation, so that they would know Him better. He prayed that the eyes of their hearts would be enlightened.

- If God lives in unapproachable light, does that mean that we can't approach Him? If so, then why does Hebrews 4:16 tell us to approach God's throne of grace with confidence? Ask the Lord to show you what this name means.

**A Prayer for You:**

*God, teach me what it means that You live in unapproachable light. Reveal to me who You are today. I want to know You, Lord, more intimately than I ever have before.*

# God ... Whom No One Has Seen or Can See

*__God__, the blessed and only Ruler, the King of kings and Lord of lords,*
*who alone is immortal and who lives in unapproachable light,*
*__whom no one has seen or can see__.*
*To him be honor and might forever. Amen.*
1 Timothy 6:15-16

**Steps on Your Journey to Know God More Intimately:**

- This verse tells us that no one has seen God or can see Him. What do you think this means? Couple that with Exodus 33:11 that says that Moses spoke with God face to face. How could Moses speak to Him face to face, if no one can see Him? Later we'll look at God as the revealer of mysteries. If this is a mystery to you, ask Him to reveal it to you.

- If no one can see God, does that mean that we won't see Him even when we get to Heaven? Ask the Lord to show you what this name means. Again, we need to ask Him to give us the Spirit of wisdom and revelation so that we will know Him better (Ephesians 1:17).

- The end of 1 Timothy 6:16 says, "To him be honor and might forever. Amen." Take some time today to give God honor and ascribe to Him might. He is worthy.

**A Prayer for You:**

*God, help me to understand and know You more. Show me more of what this name means. I want to bring You honor and glory through my life.*

April 21

## *God, Who Gives Life to All Things*

*I charge you before **God, who gives life to all things**,*
*and before the Messiah Yeshua,*
*who in his witness to Pontius Pilate gave the same good testimony,*
1 Timothy 6:13 (CJB)

**Steps on Your Journey to Know God More Intimately:**

- Meditate on this name today.

- Look around you to see where He has given life. I'm in a cabin in the mountains and can see so much life around me. It brings me so much enjoyment to see the deer, llamas, birds, even the mosquitoes, ants and the blur of white fur I saw scurry behind the barn tonight. I'm so glad God created so many different things with life in them.

- Thank Him for the life He has given you and your family.

- As you go through your day, thank Him for all the life you see around you—in plants, animals, flowers, people, birds, bugs, etc.

**A Prayer for You:**

*God, thank You for giving life to all things, especially to me, my family and friends. I can't imagine what life would be like without all the living things around me. Teach me to enjoy Your creations more, recognizing Your hand in making each one.*

## April 22

### The LORD, the LORD

*The Lord passed before him and proclaimed,
"**The Lord, the Lord**, a God merciful and gracious, slow to anger,
and abounding in steadfast love and faithfulness."*
Exodus 34:6 (ESV)

**Steps on Your Journey to Know God More Intimately:**

- Moses had just gone up Mount Sinai to meet with the Lord for the second time. When he went down the mountain the first time, Moses smashed the tablets on which God had written the commandments. This is the name the Lord first used with him when he returned to the mountain.

- This name is *Yahweh, Yahweh* in Hebrew. Lord is the word *YHWH, Yahweh* or *Jehovah*. It is the holy name of God that the Jews wouldn't even speak out loud. It means self-existent or eternal.

- Why do you think God used this name twice in a row? Do you think it was to remind Moses that He really is holy?

- Ask the Lord to show you more of Himself through this name today.

**A Prayer for You:**

*Lord, I praise You that You are merciful, gracious, slow to anger and abounding in love and faithfulness. I know I don't deserve it, but I sure do appreciate it. Reveal more of Yourself to me through the repetition of Your name. I want to know You more.*

## Compassionate and Gracious God

*He passed in front of Moses, proclaiming,*
*"The Lord, the Lord, the **compassionate and gracious God**,*
*slow to anger, abounding in love and faithfulness."*
Exodus 34:6

**Steps on Your Journey to Know God More Intimately:**

- Think about this name today.

- Compassion is God showing how much He cares about you when you are hurting. Grace is God blessing you, giving you what you don't deserve. How has God been compassionate and gracious to you?

- Throughout my life, I've seen God's compassion reaching out to me when I'm hurting. Sometimes He uses a person with skin on. Sometimes He speaks to me with His still small voice or touches me personally.

- God is so gracious to me—and you. He gives me so much that I don't deserve. I'm learning to thank God for everything in my life and focus on His gifts to me.

- Read the whole verse—each description of who God is. Which ones stand out to you? Which do you need today?

**A Prayer for You:**

*Compassionate and Gracious God, I praise and worship You today for who You are. Thank You for showing Your grace and compassion to me and my family. We need You, Lord.*

April 24

## *My Strength*

*O **my Strength**, I sing praise to You;*
*You, O God, are my fortress, my loving God.*
Psalm 59:17

**Steps on Your Journey to Know God More Intimately:**

- Psalm 18:1 says, "I love You, O Lord, my strength" (ESV).

- The Hebrew word for my strength, *oze*, means help strength, strong, boldness and power.

- Think about this. God *is* our strength. He doesn't just give us strength when we need it. When we are living in Him, we are living in His strength.

- You can stand strong no matter what happens because you don't have just your own human strength, you have God's absolute, complete strength in you.

- God has been my strength so many times in my life. One time was when I had to make extremely tough decisions about one of my sons. I had to use tough love, even though I would rather not have. It was very difficult, but I could feel God holding me up, giving me strength.

- Meditate on what it means that He is your strength. Thank Him for what He shows you.

- In what areas do you need God to be your strength today? Ask Him, then press into Him and allow Him to be your strength.

**A Prayer for You:**

*O My Strength, I praise You today because You not only give me strength, You **are** My Strength. Thank You for being My Strength. I love You, Lord. Teach me to press into You and allow You to be My Strength all the time.*

## April 25

### My Rock

*The Lord is **my rock**, my fortress and my deliverer;*
*my God is **my rock**, in whom I take refuge.*
*He is my shield and the horn of my salvation, my stronghold.*
Psalm 18:2

**Steps on Your Journey to Know God More Intimately:**

- Psalm 62:2 says, "Truly he is my rock and my salvation; he is my fortress, I will never be shaken."

- *Sela* is used in Hebrew in Psalm 18 and means rock, fortress, stone or stronghold. *Tsur* is used in Psalm 62 and is translated rock, strength and Mighty One.

- Each day this coming week we'll be looking at different names of God in Psalm 18:2. I'd encourage you to read this verse several times each day, so you can begin to learn it.

- I grew up in a tiny village in the mountains of Guatemala. On the way up to our village we passed a massive rock by the road. Despite torrential rains, devastating earthquakes and mudslides that often closed the road, the rock never changed. It wasn't affected by wind, rain, earthquakes or anything else. That rock reminds me of God, who is my Rock—only my Rock, and yours, is stronger, bigger and nothing can ever change Him (something could potentially change the rock in Guatemala).

- Meditate on God as your Rock. How is He like a Rock for you?

- As you face various situations today, remind yourself that you are not alone. The One who is your solid Rock is your protection. He never changes and He will be your Rock forever.

**A Prayer for You:**

*My Rock, I praise You and thank You for being unchangeable and dependable. I'm glad I can build my life on You, because You are solid and strong. Help me to learn to rely on You more as I get to know You in new ways.*

## My Fortress

*The Lord is my rock and **my fortress** and my deliverer,*
*my God, my rock, in whom I take refuge,*
*my shield, and the horn of my salvation, my stronghold.*
Psalm 18:2 (ESV)

**Steps on Your Journey to Know God More Intimately:**

- *Mesuda* is the Hebrew word meaning fortress, castle, strong place and defense.

- In the Old Testament a fortress was one of their main sources of protection against attacks by enemy armies. They were thick rock walls that no enemy weapon could penetrate.

- When I was at boarding school as a child, we built fortresses in the play yard to keep other children out. It never worked for long, because they weren't strong enough. With God as my fortress, I know I'm safe and secure. No one can ever break Him down. Thank You, Lord.

- Numerous times in the New Testament it says that we are "in Christ" or "in the Lord." Read Ephesians to see many verses about this. Close your eyes and imagine yourself in the Lord—inside a secure fortress that no enemy weapon can ever penetrate.

- Ask God to show you how He is your Fortress.

- In what ways do you seek God as your Fortress as you face the attacks of the enemy?

- Write Psalm 18:2 on a card or sticky note. Put it where you'll see it every day. Ask the Lord to help you to begin to memorize it.

**A Prayer for You:**

*My Fortress, it is so encouraging to know You are my protection. When I am in You, the enemy can't get to me. Remind me to always stay close to You, hidden away in You, my Fortress.*

## April 27

### *My Deliverer*

*The Lord is my rock, my fortress and **my deliverer**;*
*my God is my rock, in whom I take refuge.*
*He is my shield and the horn of my salvation, my stronghold.*
Psalm 18:2

**Steps on Your Journey to Know God More Intimately:**

- *Palat* is the Hebrew word meaning one who delivers or causes to escape, to carry away safely, to save and to slip away. Meditate on these meanings. What stands out to you?

- From what does God deliver us? It could be Satan and his schemes or possibly bad situations or people. From what has God delivered you?

- Think of a time when you were very aware that God was your deliverer in a difficult situation. How did He deliver you and what was the outcome?

- As you pray today, thank God that He is your Deliverer.

**A Prayer for You:**

*My Deliverer, I'm so glad I can depend on You to protect me and bring me out of bad situations. Thank You for delivering me from Satan and his demons. Lord, please bring me freedom and deliverance from any demonic forces that are anywhere in or around me. In Jesus' Name.*

# April 28

## *My Shield*

*The Lord is my rock and my fortress and my deliverer,
my God, my rock, in whom I take refuge,
**my shield**, and the horn of my salvation, my stronghold.*
Psalm 18:2 (ESV)

**Steps on Your Journey to Know God More Intimately:**

- A shield is something we deliberately take up to protect ourselves. *Magane* is the Hebrew word meaning a protector, a defense and a buckler.

- From what do you need God's protection?

- God is our Shield, but in Ephesians 6:10-18, we are told to put on the full armor of God, including taking up the shield of faith. Why do we need to take up our shield if God is our shield? Ask the Lord to show you.

- Think about this: Each piece of the armor is recognition of who God is and who we are in Jesus Christ. Each piece points back to Him and what He has done for us. When we take up the shield of faith we are recognizing the promises of God. The enemy's fiery darts can't penetrate the promises of God. Letting Him be our shield requires an act of faith.

- Think about how God is your shield. What does that look like?

- Consider what you do to seek God's protection when you need it.

- Thank God that He is your shield against all attacks.

- If you haven't already, write Psalm 18:2 on a card and put it where you'll see it often.

**A Prayer for You:**

*My Shield, thank You for protecting me from anything that may harm me. Help me to trust You to be my shield, rather than feeling like I have to always take care of myself. Increase my faith in Your promises so I can effectively hold the shield of faith for Your glory*

## April 29

### *Horn of My Salvation*

*The Lord is my rock, my fortress and my deliverer;*
*my God is my rock, in whom I take refuge.*
*He is my shield and the **horn of my salvation**, my stronghold.*
Psalm 18:2

**Steps on Your Journey to Know God More Intimately:**

- The New Living Translation says, "the power that saves me." How is God the power that saves you?

- *Qeren* in Hebrew means horn and is a sign of strength and a means of victory. In Micah 4:13 God says to Jerusalem, "Rise and thresh, O Daughter of Zion, for I will give you horns of iron; I will give you hoofs of bronze and you will break to pieces many nations." Our God is powerful. He is our offensive weapon. In Psalm 18:2, God is both our defense (shield) and our offense (our deadly and powerful horn).

- *Yesha* in Hebrew means salvation, deliverance, rescue, safety and welfare. Think about how your salvation today is as strong as the One who provides it—the Creator of the Universe Himself. Could anything or anyone provide more security than Him?

- In Luke 1:69, Jesus is called the Horn of Salvation. Think about how Jesus is a Horn.

- Try to say Psalm 18:2 without looking at it today. It's okay if you need to look at it. I want to encourage you to keep learning it.

**A Prayer for You:**

*Lord, thank You that You are the Horn of My Salvation. Thank You that You are the sign of strength for me and a means of victory. Teach me Lord how to let You be my Horn of Salvation.*

## My Stronghold

*The Lord is my rock and my fortress and my deliverer,
my God, my rock, in whom I take refuge,
my shield, and the horn of my salvation, **my stronghold**.*
Psalm 18:2 (ESV)

**Steps on Your Journey to Know God More Intimately:**

- *Misgab* is the Hebrew word meaning defense, refuge, stronghold, high tower or a cliff.

- A stronghold protects you. It is a place you can go to for protection. I think about NORAD, a United States military stronghold deep under Cheyenne Mountain near Colorado Springs. When people are in there, they are safe from any enemy attack. Close your eyes and imagine the Lord as your Stronghold—like NORAD, only much more secure. Nothing—absolutely nothing and no one—can get to you when the Lord is your Stronghold.

- The New Living Translation calls God, "my place of safety." How is the Lord your place of safety?

- In Psalm 27:1 David wrote, "The Lord is my light and my salvation, whom shall I fear? The Lord is the stronghold of my life—of whom shall I be afraid?" What is one fear you face? Ask God to show you Himself as your Stronghold. Give your Stronghold all your fears today. He's big enough to protect you.

- As you go through today, meditate on God as your Stronghold, the One who protects you from harm.

- As we finish looking at this verse, talk to God about each of His names in it.

**A Prayer for You:**

*Lord, I'm so glad You are my place of safety. You are the place I can go to find protection. Thank You that I don't have to fear anything when You are my stronghold. I give You my fears today. I want to trust You and rest in You more, my Stronghold.*

## May 1

## *Him Who Is Able to Keep You from Falling*

To **Him who is able to keep you from falling** and to present you
before his glorious presence without fault and with great joy—
to the only God our Savior be glory, majesty, power and authority,
through Jesus Christ our Lord, before all ages, now and forevermore! Amen.
Jude 24-25

**Steps on Your Journey to Know God More Intimately:**

- We're going to spend the next few days looking at these verses. I want to encourage you to write them on a card or sticky note and put them where you'll see them often. Meditate on them and ask the Lord to reveal more of Himself to you through them. I'd encourage you to memorize them.

- Why do you think it doesn't say, "to Him who keeps you from falling?" It says He *is able to* keep you from falling. I think you and I have a choice. He is able, but I have a choice whether I want to rely on my own strength and stand on my own two feet or I want to rely on Him and lean on Him. Sometimes I decide to stand on my own—and often fall. When I lean on God, He keeps me standing. Think about that.

- In what areas do you need the Lord to keep you from falling?

- Have you been trying to yourself keep from falling? If so, are you ready to start leaning on the Lord more? He'll help you. You just have to ask.

- Ask the Lord to reveal Himself to you, as well as, more of who you are through this verse. Talk to Him about what He shows you.

**A Prayer for You:**

*Lord, thank You that You are able to keep me from falling and You will also present me before Your glorious presence without fault and with great joy. You are so good to me! Thank You. Forgive me for trying to make it on my own. Please help me to trust You more. Remind me to lean on You.*

# May 2

## *His Glorious Presence*

*To him who is able to keep you from falling and to present you*
*before **His glorious presence** without fault and with great joy—*
*to the only God our Savior be glory, majesty, power and authority,*
*through Jesus Christ our Lord, before all ages, now and forevermore! Amen.*
Jude 24-25

**Steps on Your Journey to Know God More Intimately:**

- Think about His Presence. What does that mean?

- Consider this name today. What do you think God's Glorious Presence looks like? Ask the Lord to show you.

- Deuteronomy 4:37 says, "Because He loved your ancestors and chose their descendants after them, he brought you out of Egypt by his Presence and his great strength."

- What does it mean to you that His Presence is with you?

- I find great comfort knowing the God is always with me, no matter where I go or what happens in my life.

- One day you will be presented before His Glorious Presence. Close your eyes and imagine what that might look like. I'm convinced though that your best picture can't begin to compare with how it will be.

**A Prayer for You:**

*Thank You for Your Glorious Presence and the confidence I have that I will be in Your Presence for eternity. Teach me more about Yourself and Your Presence. I want to see You and know You in greater ways, Lord.*

## May 3

### *Only God Our Savior*

*To him who is able to keep you from falling and to present you
before his glorious presence without fault and with great joy—
to the **only God our Savior** be glory, majesty, power and authority,
through Jesus Christ our Lord, before all ages, now and forevermore! Amen.*
Jude 24-25

**Steps on Your Journey to Know God More Intimately:**

- Today we look at the Only God Our Savior. Think about the parts of this name:

  o He is *the only* God. There is none that even begins to compare with Him.

  o He is our Savior. As we looked at before, Savior comes from the Greek word, *sozo*, meaning to save, heal, deliver and make whole. Jesus did all that for us! Let yourself become amazed at what He did for you on the cross.

- I trust you have been as blessed and filled with joy from these two verses as I have. Isn't our God Incredible! Are you catching the joy of who He is and who you are because of Him? We talk about catching a cold or some other disease. Why not catch joy? If you are struggling with being amazed at who our great God is and finding joy in Him, I'd encourage you to find a friend who is in love with the Lord and full of joy. Hang around with him or her.

**A Prayer for You:**

*Lord, I praise You that You are the Only God. There is no other God. Thank You for being my Savior, who died on the cross to bring me healing, wholeness, deliverance and salvation. Please teach me more about Yourself from this name. I long to know You more intimately.*

## Joy of the LORD

Hedwa Yahweh (Hebrew)

*Don't be dejected and sad, for the **joy of the Lord** is your strength.*
Nehemiah 8:10 (NLT)

**Steps on Your Journey to Know God More Intimately:**

- *Hedwa* means joy, gladness and rejoicing.

- Meditate on this name today. God wants to give you His joy. He wants to be your joy. And when He is your joy, He is also your strength for whatever you are facing.

- This morning I was so filled with joy realizing that little ole me can come right into the presence of the King of kings, the One who created the universe. And not only that, He acknowledges me. He listens to me and He talks to me. Wouldn't you think that Someone who is so important wouldn't have time for the little, seemingly insignificant people like me—and you? But He does. And you know why? Because I'm His precious little girl! And so are you—well, if you're a guy, you are His precious son.

- I trust you are not only getting to know our incredible God, but you are also getting a bigger picture of who you are. And I pray that as you do, you will be filled with overflowing joy.

- Meditate on the Lord being your joy. Ask Him to fill you with joy in His presence (Psalm 16:11).

**A Prayer for You:**

*Lord, I'm so grateful that You are Joy and that Your Joy gives me strength. I want greater Joy in my life. Teach me how to press into You more, to see myself as You see me and see You more clearly.*

# Name of the Lord

Shem Yahweh (Hebrew)

*The **name of the Lord** is a strong tower;
the righteous run to it and are safe.*
Proverbs 18:10 (NKJV)

**Steps on Your Journey to Know God More Intimately:**

- *Shem* is translated as name, renown, fame and famous.

- There is power in the name of the Lord. Remember that God's Name represents all that He is. When you say, "The Name of the Lord" you are referring to all that God is—His power, love, grace, holiness, mercy, compassion, justice, etc.

- In recent years, I've been learning to pray more with the power of Jesus' name. As a result, I've seen so many miracles. I know I have a long way to go to really understand the power in His name.

- Think about this verse. The Lord's name—the Lord Himself—is a place we can go for refuge and protection. Do you run to Him when you are feeling afraid or vulnerable? If not, why not?

- Ask the Lord to reveal more of Himself to you through this name and this verse.

**A Prayer for You:**

*Lord, I praise You for Your name and the power that is in it. Thank You for the protection and safety I can find in You and Your name. Teach me to trust You more and run to You whenever I'm afraid.*

## May 6

### *Holy Spirit*

*But you will receive power when the **Holy Spirit** has come upon you,*
*and you will be my witnesses in Jerusalem*
*and in all Judea and Samaria, and to the end of the earth.*
Acts 1:8 (ESV)

**Steps on Your Journey to Know God More Intimately:**

- *Hagios* in Greek means holy, sacred, pure and blameless. There are other spirits that are not holy. We need to make sure we are connected with the Holy Spirit of God and not to evil spirits.

- *Pneuma* means spirit, breath, breathe or wind.

- John 20:21-22 says, "So Jesus said to them again, 'Peace to you! As the Father has sent Me, I also send you.' And when He had said this, He breathed on them, and said to them, 'Receive the Holy Spirit'" (NKJV). This shows what Jesus said and did to the disciples right after He was raised from the dead. Consider this last symbolic act of Jesus. Why do you think He breathed on them?

- Acts 1:8 contains the last recorded words of Jesus before He was taken up to Heaven. Notice what He says will happen when the Holy Spirit comes on them.

- Meditate on the Holy Spirit. Ask God what He wants you to know about Himself through this name.

**A Prayer for You:**

*Holy Spirit, I praise You and thank You for Your presence in my life. I want to get to know You in deeper ways and experience more of Your power. Please teach me about You. Show me how I can be better connected with You.*

# *Holy Spirit Who Is a Deposit*
## Guaranteeing Our Inheritance

*Having believed, you were marked in him with a seal,
the promised **Holy Spirit, who is a deposit guaranteeing our
inheritance** until the redemption of those who are God's possession.*
Ephesians 1:13-14

**Steps on Your Journey to Know God More Intimately:**

- When you purchase a home, you put a deposit on it that guarantees no one else can take it from you. Jesus left the Holy Spirit as a deposit, guaranteeing our inheritance in Heaven. No one can take the deposit away, although I believe you can choose to remove the deposit, just as you can on a house. You can choose to stop following Jesus. He will never force you to keep following Him or to accept your eternal inheritance. But why would anyone ever want to make that devastating choice?

- Thank the Holy Spirit now for being inside you, guaranteeing your future.

- Meditate on what inheritance is waiting for you. What are you most anticipating?

**A Prayer for You:**

*Holy Spirit, thank You that You are in me as a deposit guaranteeing my inheritance. I'm excited about what You have waiting for me. Show me more of what it means that You are my deposit and what it is that You have waiting for me.*

# May 8

## Helper

Paraklaytos (Greek)

Jesus said, *and I will ask the Father, and he will give you another **Helper**, to be with you forever.*
John 14:16 (ESV)

**Steps on Your Journey to Know God More Intimately:**

- This name is also translated as Counselor, Comforter and Advocate. Meditate on each of these names of the Holy Spirit. What stands out to you today?

- John 14:26 says, "But the Helper, the Holy Spirit, whom the Father will send in my name, He will teach you all things and bring to your remembrance all that I have said to you" (ESV).

- In what ways do you need a helper? Ask Him. He's always ready to help you. Do you need a counselor? The Holy Spirit is the best counselor you can have. Are you sad or grieving? If you need comfort, remember, the Holy Spirit is always right there with you and He'll bring you comfort.

- Do you need an advocate, someone to stand up for you? The Holy Spirit is your advocate before the Father, but He will also be your advocate here on earth.

- I have seen the Holy Spirit be all of these things for me at different times of my life. He helped me raise my sons alone. He counsels me and guides me in the directions I should go in writing this book. He comforts me when I feel lonely. He was my advocate when I was sued by people buying a home from me. What do you need from the *Paraklaytos?*

**A Prayer for You:**

*Holy Spirit, I'm so grateful that You are my Helper, my Counselor, my Comforter and my Advocate. Thank You that I can always depend on You to be there for me. Draw me close to Yourself. Teach me more about who You are. I want to learn to live in a closer connection to You.*

## Spirit of Truth

*When the **Spirit of truth** comes, he will guide you into all the truth,*
*for he will not speak on his own authority,*
*but whatever he hears he will speak,*
*and he will declare to you the things that are to come.*
John 16:13 (ESV)

**Steps on Your Journey to Know God More Intimately:**

- Spirit in Greek is *pneuma*. Truth is *alethia*. Jesus asked the Father to give us the Spirit of Truth. Of all the names of the Spirit He could have used, He chose the Spirit of Truth. Why? If you're not sure, talk to Him about that.

- One of Satan's primary tactics against us is lies. He is a very good liar and the father of lies (John 8:44). He works to get us to believe lies about ourselves, God, others and our situation.

- In Matthew 18:18, Jesus says, "Whatever you shall bind on earth shall be bound in Heaven; and whatever you loose on earth shall be loosed in heaven" (NAS). As I've mentioned before, I use this verse everyday to bind the enemy and to loose the Holy Spirit. I bind using the Name of the Lord Jesus. For example, "In the name of the Lord Jesus Christ, I bind any lying, deceiving, conning and manipulating spirit that is anywhere around me or my family. And I loose the Spirit of Truth in and around my family so we will know the truth in every situation." I encourage you to try this. It is very powerful.

**A Prayer for You:**

*Spirit of Truth, thank You that You are with me and in me, guiding me and revealing the Father's heart and mind. I want to be more connected with You. Reveal the truth about myself, Yourself, the enemy, other people and my life. Help me to be so connected to You that I can instantly recognize lies from the enemy.*

## Forgiving God

*They refused to listen and failed to remember the miracles
you performed among them. They became stiff-necked and in their
rebellion appointed a leader. But you are a **forgiving God**, gracious and
compassionate, slow to anger and abounding in love.*
Nehemiah 9:17

**Steps on Your Journey to Know God More Intimately:**

- *Eloah* in Hebrew means God or a deity. *Selikha* means forgiveness or pardon.

- Wow! Even when they failed to remember God's miracles in their lives and they became stubborn and rebellious, God *still* was a forgiving God. He was still gracious and compassionate. He was still slow to anger and abounding in love. Would you be as forgiving and loving to others if they didn't even notice what you had done for them? Most of us wouldn't.

- Meditate on this name: a Forgiving God. Think about how much God has forgiven you.

- Thank the Lord for His forgiveness, but also for the miracles He has performed. If you don't think you've seen any, ask God to show you some of the miracles He has done in your life and in those around you. I can almost guarantee there have been miracles, although often we don't recognize them.

- Matthew 6:12 tells us to forgive others as we have been forgiven. How did God forgive us?

- How can you imitate God's forgiveness?

**A Prayer for You:**

*Forgiving God, thank You for not treating me as I deserve. Thank You for forgiving me completely, even when I rebel against You. I don't deserve Your forgiveness, but I'm so thankful for it. Teach me how to forgive others as You forgave me.*

# Him Who Rides on the Clouds

*Sing to God, sing in praise of his name,*
*extol **Him who rides on the clouds**;*
*rejoice before him—his name is the Lord.*
Psalm 68:4

**Steps on Your Journey to Know God More Intimately:**

- The Message puts it this way: "Sing hymns to God; all heaven, sing out; clear the way for the coming of Cloud-Rider. Enjoy GOD, cheer when you see him!"

- Meditate on this name.

- Close your eyes and ask the Lord to show you Himself as the Cloud-Rider. What does He look like? What's He doing?

- This week I've been watching the cloud formations. They have been so interesting. They are always different. This morning as the sun rose, there were brilliant pinks turning to golden and then to yellows.

- When you notice the clouds, remember the One who rides on them.

- What does this verse say to do? (It tells us to do three things!) Will you do them today?

- Thank and praise Him for what He shows you through this name.

**A Prayer for You:**

*Cloud-Rider, I want to see You more clearly. I want to see You riding on the clouds. Remind me when I see cloud formations that You are the One who rides on them. Help me to see You more in the clouds. I praise You and sing to You. I choose to rejoice before You today.*

# May 12

## Father to the Fatherless

Ab Yatom (Hebrew)

*A **father to the fatherless**, a defender of widows,*
*is God in His holy habitation.*
Psalm 68:5 (NKJV)

**Steps on Your Journey to Know God More Intimately:**

- The Message translates this verse, "Father of orphans, champion of widows, is God in His holy house."

- *Ab* means father. *Yatom* means fatherless, coming from the root meaning to be lonely, an orphan or a bereaved person.

- Think about this name. If you haven't had a father who was there for you, or your dad died, the Lord wants to be your Father. He is your Father. He is everything that a good father should be and so much more.

- Ask the Lord to show you how He is your Father, whether or not you have an earthly father who is there for you.

- Thank Him for being a Father to the fatherless.

**A Prayer for You:**

*Father, thank You that You are a Father to the Fatherless. Thank You that You care for me and love me so much more than any earthly father ever could. Please heal my heart from any and all wounds I've received from my earthly father (or lack of one). Remind me that You are the best Dad I could ever want.*

## May 13

### *Defender of Widows*

Dayyan Almana (Hebrew)

*A father to the fatherless, a **defender of widows**,*
*is God in his holy dwelling.*
Psalm 68:5

**Steps on Your Journey to Know God More Intimately:**

- The word defender in Hebrew is *dayyan*, meaning judge or advocate. The Greek word for widow means one lacking a husband. The Hebrew for widow, *almana*, means her husband is departed, a desolate place, forsaken and discarded (as a divorced woman). We often think of widows as just someone whose husband has died. It can also mean someone who doesn't have a husband—from death, divorce or singleness.

- Whether or not you fall into the category of being a widow, we all know people who are widows, by the above definition. Isn't it just like our God to defend widows—those who don't have anyone else to defend them? I personally have seen God be my defender as I raised my sons alone.

- Ask the Lord to reveal what He wants to show you through this name today.

- Is there someone you know who might be encouraged by you sharing this name?

**A Prayer for You:**

*Lord, thank You that You are a defender of widows. Thank You that You care about me when I'm feeling all alone, forsaken or discarded. Teach me more of what this means. I want to know You in deeper ways.*

## May 14

### *God-for-Us*

*Blessed be the Lord—day after day he carries us along.*
*He's our Savior, our God, oh yes!*
*He's **God-for-us**, he's God-who-saves-us.*
Psalm 68:19-20 (MSG)

**Steps on Your Journey to Know God More Intimately:**

- I love the way the Message talks about God here. Read the verse again, meditating on what it says.

- Romans 8:31 says, "If God is for us, who can be against us?" Think about that. What does it mean to you today that God is for you?

- How have you seen God-for-you in your life? If you haven't experienced Him in this way, ask the Lord why you haven't. It might just be that you weren't looking. I know there have been times in my life when I have felt like God abandoned me, yet when I looked back His fingerprints were all over my life in many ways.

- In what ways do you need to know that God is for you? Talk to Him about that.

**A Prayer for You:**

*God, thank You that You are for me. I bless You today and praise You that You are my protector and my advocate. Open my eyes to see You more as God-for-me.*

## May 15

# *God Who Can Save You*

*You have turned from the **God who can save you**.*
*You have forgotten the Rock who can hide you.*
Isaiah 17:10 (NLT)

**Steps on Your Journey to Know God More Intimately:**

- The English Standard Version says, "You have forgotten the God of your salvation." Could this be said of you, that you have forgotten the God Who Can Save You? If so, spend time today to reconnect with Him. You might need to tell Him you're sorry and ask for His forgiveness.

- Take time to remember what God has done for you, how He came to earth to be your Savior. I don't know about you, but I don't want anyone to ever say that I have forgotten the God who saved me. Just about every day I thank the Lord for what He did for me on the cross. Don't let it ever be said of you that you have turned from God your Savior.

- God saves us in different ways. Just yesterday when I was out walking in the forest alone, He saved me from a potentially harmful situation. He did it in a very unusual way—with a severe pain in my knee, so I couldn't keep walking. As soon as I turned around, the pain went away. I found out, if I had continued that path, I would have walked right by some men committing a crime. Who knows what they might have done? Thank You, Lord!

- Ask the Lord to reveal more of Himself through this name.

**A Prayer for You:**

*God Who Can Save Me, thank You for all the ways You have saved me—from my sins, as well as from people, situations and even from myself. Help me to learn to see how You are working in my life every day. I want to always acknowledge when You save me.*

# Rock Who Can Hide You

### Tsur Maoz (Hebrew)

*You have turned from the God who can save you.*
*You have forgotten the **Rock who can hide you**.*
Isaiah 17:10 (NLT)

**Steps on Your Journey to Know God More Intimately:**

- *Tsur* means rock or strength. *Maoz* means fortress, strength or strong. In what ways is God like a rock?

- How has the Lord been the Rock Who Can Hide You? Think about when you've seen Him in that way. If you can't remember, ask Him to remind you.

- The New International Version translates this name, "The Rock, your fortress." Think about what a fortress is like. When I think of a fortress, I think about when my son Timothy and I were on top of Masada in Israel. It was a tall rock mountain where the Jews hid from their enemies, virtually impenetrable. They were safe there for a long time. I say virtually, because their enemies did end up overpowering them.

- Our God is not like any manmade fortress. We are completely safe when we run to Him. He is the One Who Can Hide You. What are you waiting for? You can run to Him and you will be safe and secure.

**A Prayer for You:**

*Lord, I praise You that You are the Rock Who Can Hide Me. You are unchangeable, solid and secure. You are a place I can run to for refuge, knowing You'll always hide me and protect me. Help me to learn to live in You, in Your hiding place.*

# Him Who Rides Across the Highest Heavens

*Sing to God, you kingdoms of the earth, sing praise to the Lord,*
*to **him who rides across the highest heavens**,*
*the ancient heavens, who thunders with mighty voice.*
Psalm 68:32-33

**Steps on Your Journey to Know God More Intimately:**

- The Message translates this name Sky-Rider. How is this name similar and different from the Cloud-Rider we saw earlier?

- How do you think God rides across the highest heavens? What does that look like? If you're not sure, ask Him to show you.

- I love watching sunrises and sunsets, because I can see God's glory in some beautiful ways. Do you think they might be different every day, because God is riding across the heavens, stirring up the clouds?

- Sing praise to Him Who Rides Across the Highest Heavens as these verses say to do.

**A Prayer for You:**

*Lord I sing praise to You today, to the One Who Rides Across the Highest Heavens. Show me more of what that means. I want to know You. You are such an incredible God. I am constantly amazed at all of Your different names. Each one shows Your unique character.*

# May 18

## *Him Who Thunders with Mighty Voice*

*Sing to God, you kingdoms of the earth, sing praise to the Lord,*
*to **Him** who rides across the highest heavens,*
*the ancient heavens, **who thunders with mighty voice**.*
Psalm 68:32-33

**Steps on Your Journey to Know God More Intimately:**

- Do you think this is talking about the thunder we hear in a storm? Or could it be some other sound? Ask God to show you.

- When we hear thunder, is that just a natural occurrence with a storm and as a result of lightning? Or could it be God's voice we're hearing?

- As I'm sitting here writing, the clouds are rolling in and I hear thunder in the distance. Lord, is that Your voice? What are You saying?

**A Prayer for You:**

*Lord, thank You for showing me another of Your names. Show me what it means. I choose to sing praise to You today, to the One Who Thunders with Mighty Voice.*

May 19

## God Whose Majesty Is Over Israel

*Proclaim the power of **God**, **whose majesty is over Israel**,*
*whose power is in the heavens.*
Psalm 68:34

**Steps on Your Journey to Know God More Intimately:**

- Meditate on this name today. It's unique, as many of His names are.

- The word for majesty here also means excellency, a rising up, highness and pride. Think about these meanings.

- Ask the Lord to show you what it means that His Majesty is over Israel.

- If I were writing this name today, I would call Him *The God Whose Majesty Is Over Colorado.* I can see God's majesty all around me. I see it in the mountains, trees, flowers, sky, animals and so much more.

- What do you want to say to God, Whose Majesty Is Over Israel?

- What do you want Him to say to you?

**A Prayer for You:**

*God, thank You for majesty that I can see all around me. Please open my eyes to see more of Your majesty and excellency. I want to learn to recognize You in new ways.*

## May 20

# God Whose Power Is in the Heavens

*Proclaim the power of **God**, whose majesty is over Israel,*
***whose power is in the heavens**.*
Psalm 68:34

**Steps on Your Journey to Know God More Intimately:**

- Have you ever watched a lightning storm? I'm sure you have. You can see God's power in it. When I was in college in Dallas, I remember watching the most phenomenal lightning storm I've ever seen. The entire sky lit up every few seconds. I could see the light bouncing around the heavens from the flashes.

- How else is God's power in the heavens?

- When you look at the universe with the sun, moon and all the stars held in place, you can see God's power. If you can, go outside tonight to see the stars and consider God, Whose Power Is in the Heavens.

- Ask Him to reveal more of Himself to you through this name.

**A Prayer for You:**

*God, Your power in the heavens is so amazing. I can't imagine how big You are to hold all the stars and planets in their orbits. Show me more of Your greatness and power in the heavens.*

## God of Israel

*Awesome is God from his sanctuary; the **God of Israel**—*
*he is the one who gives power and strength to his people.*
*Blessed be God!*
Psalm 68:35 (ESV)

**Steps on Your Journey to Know God More Intimately:**

- If you are a Gentile, like me, (that's anyone who is not a Jew) it's easy to overlook the names of God that have to do with Israel. However, the book of Romans talks about Gentiles being grafted into Israel because of Jesus. So whether you are from Israel or not, this name is applicable to all of us. You might want to call Him the God of _____ (the country where you live).

- First Chronicles 4:10 says, "Jabez cried out to the God of Israel, 'Oh, that you would bless me and enlarge my territory! Let your hand be with me, and keep me from harm so that I will be free from pain.' And God granted his request."

- About a year ago, I started praying Jabez's prayer (see above) everyday, for myself and for my family and others. Note: he prayed it to the God of Israel. I have seen some incredible miracles happen since I started praying—better jobs for my sons, open doors for my ministry, my mind able to concentrate better and so much more. I want to encourage you to take at least the next month and pray the prayer for yourself and your family. See if God doesn't answer you in some remarkable ways.

- Think about what Psalm 68:35 says the God of Israel does. How has He done that for you?

- Spend some time praising your great God.

**A Prayer for You:**

*God of Israel, thank You that You give power and strength to Your people, and I am one of them. Lord, I ask that You would bless me and enlarge my territory! Let Your hand be with me and keep me from harm so that I will be free from pain. Thank You so much for all of Your amazing blessings.*

## May 22

# *The Name*

Onoma (Greek); Shem (Hebrew)

*The apostles left the Sanhedrin, rejoicing because
they had been counted worthy of suffering disgrace for **the Name**.*
Acts 5:41

**Steps on Your Journey to Know God More Intimately:**

- *Onoma* shows authority and character. In *With Christ in the School of Prayer,* Andrew Murray said, "What is a person's name? It is a word or expression in which a person is represented to us. When I mention or hear a name, it brings to mind the whole man, what I know of him and also the impression he has made on me. His name is the symbol of His power. And so each name of God embodies and represents some part of the glory of the Unseen One. The name of Christ is the expression of everything He has done and everything He is and lives to do as our mediator."

- Psalm 20:7 says "Some trust in chariots and some in horses, but we trust in the name of the Lord our God."

- Over and over in the Word we hear about the *Name* of the Lord. When you see that, it should remind you of everything He is.

- I started studying references to God's Name about five years ago. I'm amazed at all the times the Bible just mentions "name," rather than a specific name of the Lord. Why do you think God does that?

- Think about this name of God today. There is no one that even begins to compare with our God. The people in the New Testament just referred to Jesus as "The Name." Think about that.

**A Prayer for You:**

*Lord, thank You for Your Name and all that it represents—Your power, Your presence, Your character, Your qualities and so much more. Teach me to know Your Name in new ways.*

# LORD Who Brought You out of Egypt,
## out of the Land of Slavery

*Be careful that you do not forget*
*the Lord, **who brought you out of Egypt, out of the land of slavery.***
Deuteronomy 6:12

**Steps on Your Journey to Know God More Intimately:**

- This verse is referring back to when the Israelites were enslaved in Egypt (Exodus 1-14). We also can be enslaved—not necessarily physically. We are more likely to be in slavery to our past, our emotions, Satan and his demons, bad relationships, etc.

- What is your "Egypt?" Out of what has the Lord brought you?

- To what were you a slave? How has the Lord brought you freedom?

- This verse and many others in the Bible remind us: "do not forget." Don't forget what God has done for us. In the past, I often got so caught up with my life and problems that I forgot about the things God had done for me. Now, I choose to daily thank God for everything I can remember. I'm keeping a list of what He's done. I challenge you to do the same.

- Ask the Lord to reveal to you if you are still in slavery. If so, ask Him to bring you out of it, just as He brought the Israelites out of their situation.

- Thank and praise Him that He is the LORD Who Brought You out of _____ (fill in the blank).

**A Prayer for You:**

*Thank You, Lord, for freeing me from my sins, because of Your death on the cross. Thank You for freeing me from my past and from Satan's grip in my life. Reveal to me any areas where I need freedom. I want complete freedom in You. If I need someone to help me find it, show me where to turn.*

# May 24

## *LORD Who Is Great and Awesome*

*Remember the **Lord**, **who is great and awesome**,
and fight for your brothers, your sons, your daughters,
your wives and your homes.*
Nehemiah 4:14 (ESV)

**Steps on Your Journey to Know God More Intimately:**

- Over and over in the Word we are reminded to remember the Lord or to not forget the Lord. Why do you think that might be? When everything is going great, do you tend to forget the Lord? Or what about when times get hard and you are so focused on surviving? Whether times are good or bad, we need to remember the Lord.

- I love this name of the Lord. Our God is great and awesome in so many ways. Think about this name. In what ways is the Lord great and awesome? How have you seen His greatness and awesomeness?

- I'm up in the mountains for the whole week by myself in a very secluded cabin (the nearest neighbors are a half mile away!) I'm able to see God's greatness and awesomeness here in ways I don't always see when I'm in the city: the huge trees and the massive rock formations, the deer and llamas that stop by to visit, the most brilliant blue birds I've ever seen, as well as the ground hogs, squirrels and rabbits playing. All of this with the mountain peaks in the background and the calmness of the pond outside my front door. I feel overwhelmed by God's greatness, awesomeness and goodness to me.

- Sometimes you can't miss God's greatness—like here in this cabin on 200 acres, surrounded on four sides by the national forest. But other times, we have to choose to see His greatness and awesomeness. It's in the normal, mundane times that we need to make that choice.

**A Prayer for You:**

*Lord, I praise You for Your greatness and awesomeness. Help me to learn to see You clearly wherever I am. I choose to focus on seeing You more. I want to see Your greatness and awesomeness more.*

## May 25

## *Your Creator*

Bawraw (Hebrew)

*Remember now **your Creator** in the days of your youth.*
Ecclesiastes 12:1 (NKJV)

**Steps on Your Journey to Know God More Intimately:**

- Remember your Creator. He created your entire being. Because He created you He knows you intimately. He made you just the way you are, although sometimes we mess up His creation by what we do to our bodies or minds.

- I used to complain about my body, because I didn't like things about it. But I realized when I do that, I'm saying God didn't do a good job when He made me. *Forgive me Lord and remind me never to do that again.*

- Do you recognize your Creator? Or do you tend to take credit for who you are?

- Thank the Lord today that He is your Creator. Spend some time focusing on how He created you—your mind, your body, your heart and your spirit.

**A Prayer for You:**

*Creator, thank You for making me just the way You did. Forgive me for complaining about things I don't like about myself. Help me to remember that You made me and You don't make mistakes or inferior quality in Your creations.*

# May 26

## Righteous Father

Dikaios Pater (Greek)

**Righteous Father**, *though the world does not know you,*
*I know you, and they know that you have sent me.*
John 17:25

**Steps on Your Journey to Know God More Intimately:**

- *Dikaios* means holy, innocent, righteous and just. *Pater* is father.

- Meditate on this name today. God is righteous and He cannot tolerate sin. He forgave our sins on the cross, but He wants us to live holy, righteous lives now. We can only do that in His power. When we confess our sins, He will forgive us, but we don't want to take His forgiveness for granted. I've heard people say that they will go ahead and do something they know is wrong, because they know God will forgive them.

- What does it mean to you that God is your Righteous Father? You are His precious child. Since He is your Father, remember that He loves you so much.

- Take some time to talk to your Righteous Father today and let Him talk to you.

**A Prayer for You:**

*Righteous Father, I bless You and praise You today that You are both righteous and You are my loving Father. Thank You that because Jesus knows You, I also can know You. Teach me to know You more intimately each day.*

# *LORD Your God*

*Remember that you were a slave in Egypt
and that the **Lord your God** brought you out from there
with a mighty hand and by an outstretched arm.*
Deuteronomy 5:15 (NKJV)

**Steps on Your Journey to Know God More Intimately:**

- Today is Memorial Day (in the United States in 2012). As we are grateful for those who gave their lives to give us our freedom, let's remember the One who gave us freedom from sin, fear, death and more. He died to give us eternal freedom.

- This name is a combination of the Hebrew words *Yahweh* (the eternal, self-existent God) and *Elohim* (the plural form of God). This name makes God more personal—He is *your* God.

- Ask the Lord to reveal to you what He wants you to see today from this name.

- What does it mean to you that the Lord is your God? How does your life reveal that?

- Stop right now and remember what the Lord your God has done for you. In what ways have you seen His mighty hand and outstretched arm working in your life?

**A Prayer for You:**

*Lord, thank You that You are a personal God, that You are my God. Thank You that although You are the God who created the universe, You care about my life. Thank You that You are big enough to deal with my problems, just like You did with the Israelites in Egypt. Help me to remember what You've done and trust You for my future.*

# His Great Name

## Gadole Shem (Hebrew)

*For the sake of **his great name** the Lord will not reject his people,*
*because the Lord was pleased to make you his own.*
1Samuel 12:22

**Steps on Your Journey to Know God More Intimately:**

- *Gadol* means great, high and greater. Remember when the Bible mentions God's name, it is referring to all that He is.

- Meditate on His Great Name today and praise Him for it and for how multifaceted it is. Ask the Lord what He wants to show you today.

- Look at what this verse says God won't do because of His great name—He won't reject His people. That's very encouraging, because we blow it all the time. God won't give up on us, no matter what.

- Look at the last part of this verse, "The Lord was pleased to make you His own." Think about that. God made *you* His own. You are His precious child. But He didn't just do it because He had to; He was pleased to make you His child. Think about that. If you struggle with a low self-esteem, write this verse on a card and read it often. God chose you. He picked you, because He wanted to.

**A Prayer for You:**

*Thank You, Lord, for Your Great Name. I want to learn to know You more and see You more clearly. Thank You that You were pleased to make me Your very own. I want that fact to sink deep within my being, so that it changes how I see myself as well as how I see You.*

# His Majesty

*Remember today that your children were not the ones who saw and experienced the discipline of the Lord your God:* **his majesty**, *his mighty hand, his outstretched arm.*
Deuteronomy 11:2

**Steps on Your Journey to Know God More Intimately:**

- Webster defines majesty as sovereign power, authority, or dignity; it's used in addressing or referring to reigning sovereigns and their consorts; royal bearing or aspect; and greatness or splendor of quality or character.

- The Hebrew of majesty, *godel*, means magnitude, to magnify and greatness.

- Think about this name, especially in relation to these definitions.

- Imagine you are appearing before a great King—the King of the Universe, the King of kings. When you speak to Him, you call Him Your Majesty. What does it mean to you to call God His Majesty or Your Majesty?

- How will you react to His Majesty today?

- What do you want to say to His Majesty?

**A Prayer for You:**

*Lord, I'm so honored to appear before You without fear and with great boldness, because while You are a great King, You are also my Daddy. I worship You and praise Your holy, majestic name today. Teach me to know You, love You and honor You more.*

# His Mighty Hand

*Remember today that your children were not the ones who saw and experienced the discipline of the Lord your God: his majesty, **his mighty hand**, his outstretched arm.*
Deuteronomy 11:2

**Steps on Your Journey to Know God More Intimately:**

- *Khazak* in Hebrew means strong or mighty. This word for hand in ancient Hebrew, *yawd,* is an open hand indicating power, means and direction.

- God's hand is strong and powerful. Because of that He is able to save you and care for you, just as He did with the children of Israel.

- How have you seen His Mighty Hand at work in your life? If you don't think you have, stop and ask the Lord to show you. I'd be surprised if He hasn't been at work in your life and your family.

- In what ways would you like to see His Mighty Hand at work in your life today?

**A Prayer for You:**

*Lord God, I'm so glad that You are my God. I wouldn't want Your mighty hand at work against me and my family. Thank You for Your power that is available for me today. Teach me to reach out for Your hand when I feel weak. Help me to remember that Your power is always available to me.*

## His Outstretched Arm

*Remember today that your children were not the ones who saw and
experienced the discipline of the Lord your God:
his majesty, his mighty hand, **his outstretched arm**.*
Deuteronomy 11:2

**Steps on Your Journey to Know God More Intimately:**

- *Nawtaw* in Hebrew means outstretched. In Hebrew when it talks about God's arm, *zeroa*, it is also referring to His might, power and strength. Think about this. God's strong arms are reaching out to you today.

- We've been looking at Deuteronomy 11:2 for the last few days. What is God saying to you through it?

- Sometimes when I want to see the Lord, I close my eyes and see His arms reaching out for me, waiting for me to run into them for comfort, protection or whatever I need at the time.

- Close your eyes and ask the Lord to show you His Outstretched Arm. What do you see? Can you see Him? If not, you might ask Him to remove anything that is keeping you from being able to see Him clearly.

- Ask God to reveal more to you about this name today.

**A Prayer for You:**

*All Powerful God, I worship You today and praise Your name. Thank You
for Your powerful arm that is always outstretched, reaching for me. You long
to reveal Your power in my life and in those around me. Help me to see Your
arms reaching out to me and remind me to reach back, letting You pick me
up and work in my life.*

June 1

## *Bread of God*

Artos Theos (Greek)

*For the **bread of God** is he who comes down from heaven*
*and gives life to the world.*
John 6:33 (ESV)

**Steps on Your Journey to Know God More Intimately:**

- *Artos* is bread. *Theos* is God or the supreme divinity.

- Bread was very important throughout the Old Testament, both in ceremonial and common use. Bread gives sustenance, strength, life and enjoyment. What else does bread do for us?

- When my mom and dad were translating the New Testament into the Chuj language in Guatemala when I was a child, the Chuj people didn't understand this concept. To them bread was an extra. Tortillas were what sustained them, so they had to translate this name the Tortilla of God, so they understood the meaning.

- Micah 5:2 says, "But you, O Bethlehem Ephrathah, are only a small village among all the people of Judah. Yet a ruler of Israel will come from you, one whose origins are from the distant past" (NLT). Is it coincidence that the prophet Micah said that the Messiah would be born in Bethlehem, which means "House of Bread"?

- Meditate on what it means that Jesus is the Bread of God. How is Jesus like Bread?

- How do you need Jesus to be your Bread?

**A Prayer for You:**

*Bread of God, I'm so grateful that You came down from Heaven to give us life. Thank You that in You I can find strength, sustenance, life and so much more. Help me to rely on You more as my Bread.*

# He Who Comes Down From Heaven

## and Gives Life to the World

*For the bread of God is*
***He who comes down from heaven and gives life to the world.***
John 6:33

**Steps on Your Journey to Know God More Intimately:**

- Jesus was willing to come down out of a perfect place—where He was loved and respected—Heaven to Earth—where people hated Him, rejected Him and betrayed Him.

- What does this name mean to you?

- What kind of life does He bring you?

- In John 10:10 Jesus says, "I have come that they may have life, and have it to the full." Many people try to fill their lives with things, success and people, thinking those will give them full lives. I've done those things, but they are empty. It's only in the Lord, that I have a full and fulfilled life.

- Take some time to thank Him for coming to Earth to give you eternal life.

- Here is one of the many times that Jesus affirms His deity. He has the power and authority to give us eternal life. In fact, the life He gives is available to all who believe in Him. Praise Him that He is God's Son.

**A Prayer for You:**

*Jesus, thank You for being willing to leave the beauty and peace of Heaven to come down to Earth to bring us life—eternal life and abundant life now.*

## Shepherd

*For the Lamb in the midst of the throne will be their **shepherd**,
and he will guide them to springs of living water,
and God will wipe away every tear from their eyes.*
*Revelation 7:17*

**Steps on Your Journey to Know God More Intimately:**

- *Poimane* in Greek means shepherd or pastor. A shepherd cares for the sheep. He provides for them, protects them, guides them and much more. Read Psalm 23 to learn more about God being the Shepherd.

- In John 10:14 Jesus says, "I am the good shepherd. I know my own and my own know me" (ESV).

- Read John 10:1-18. What do you learn about the Shepherd? What do you learn about being a sheep?

- When I was in a head-on collision in college, my car was totaled. People who saw it said no one should have lived through it. However, I walked away from the accident with only bruises to my body and cuts on my face. I believe my Shepherd put His arms in front of me, during the impact, protecting me from serious damage or death. I wonder how often my Shepherd has protected me, but I've only focused on what He didn't do, rather than on what He did.

- Think about how Jesus is your Shepherd. What does that mean to you today? When has He been a Shepherd to you?

**A Prayer for You:**

*Shepherd, thank You for guiding me, providing for me and protecting me. I'm so glad I can depend on You. I want to be like a sheep that knows the Shepherd's voice and follows the Shepherd without question. Help me to know You more as my Shepherd.*

## *Lamb*

*For the **Lamb** in the midst of the throne will be their shepherd,*
*and he will guide them to springs of living water,*
*and God will wipe away every tear from their eyes.*
Revelation 7:17

**Steps on Your Journey to Know God More Intimately:**

- Yesterday, we looked at Jesus as the Shepherd. Today we see Him as the Lamb, *arnion* in Greek. Think about this: How can Jesus be both the Shepherd and the Lamb?

- Revelation 5:13 says, "And I heard every creature in heaven and on earth and under the earth and in the sea, and all that is in them, saying, 'To him who sits on the throne and to the Lamb be blessing and honor and glory and might forever and ever!'"(ESV).

- In John 1:29, John the Baptist saw Jesus coming and said, "Behold, the Lamb of God, who takes away the sin of the world" (ESV).

- Revelation 17:14 says, "They will make war on the Lamb, and the Lamb will conquer them, for he is Lord of lords and King of kings, and those with him are called and chosen and faithful" (ESV).

- Lambs were used as sacrifices for sins in the Old Testament.

- Think about each of the verses above. In what ways is Jesus like a lamb?

**A Prayer for You:**

*Lamb of God, thank You for coming to earth to be the perfect sacrifice for our sins, once for all. Just as a lamb is helpless, so You came as a helpless baby. Thank You for being the Lamb, but also my Shepherd. I'm so glad You will guide me to springs of living water and will wipe every tear from my eyes.*

# My Servant, Whom I Uphold

*Here is **my servant**, **whom I uphold**, my chosen one in whom I delight;
I will put my Spirit on him and he will bring justice to the nations.*
Isaiah 42:1

**Steps on Your Journey to Know God More Intimately:**

- This is God talking about the Messiah. Jesus is God's servant. How can He be both God and God's servant? Think about that.

- When might God have upheld Jesus?

- How do you think God upheld Jesus?

- How have you seen God uphold you?

- Meditate on this name. Ask God to show you what it means to you today.

**A Prayer for You:**

*Jesus, thank You for being willing to be God's Servant even though You are His Son. You chose to be obedient to the Father, giving me an example of how to obey You. Thank You that as the Father upheld You, You also hold me up when I'm weary and tired. Teach me more of what this name means.*

# My Chosen One in Whom I Delight

*Here is my servant, whom I uphold, **my chosen one in whom I delight**;
I will put my Spirit on him and he will bring justice to the nations.*
Isaiah 42:1

**Steps on Your Journey to Know God More Intimately:**

- Jesus is God's Chosen One. God chose Him to bring us salvation and peace with Him.

- Delight means great pleasure, joy and something that gives great pleasure or enjoyment.

- Who do you delight in? Your children, grandchildren, spouse? Think about how you delight in that person. What does that look like?

- How do you think the Father delights in Jesus? How do you think He might show it?

- Psalm 16:3 says, "As for the saints who are on the earth, they are the excellent ones, in whom is all my delight." You are a saint, If you believe in the Lord God. That means that God delights in you. Think about that. How does that make you feel?

**A Prayer for You:**

*Father, thank You that You chose Jesus to come to earth to bring me into a right relationship with You. Help me to understand more of what this name means and how You delight in Jesus. I'm overwhelmed by the fact that You also delight in me. Show me how to bring You more joy and delight.*

# My God and King

El Melek (Hebrew)

*Your procession has come into view, O God—*
*the procession of **my God and King** as he goes into the sanctuary.*
Psalm 68:24 (NLT)

**Steps on Your Journey to Know God More Intimately:**

- Think about these two names—*El*, God and *Melek*, King.

- How are they similar?

- How are they different?

- Your God and King is to be worshipped, honored, obeyed, etc. Are there any ways you treat Him that you need to change?

- Ask the Lord to show you how you are to respond to Him today as your God and King.

**A Prayer for You:**

*My God and King, I worship and honor You for who You are. I choose to obey You in whatever You ask me to do. Teach me how to honor You more as my God and King.*

June 8

## He Who Comforts You

*I am **be who comforts you**;*
*who are you that you are afraid of man who dies,*
*of the son of man who is made like grass?*
Isaiah 51:12 (ESV)

**Steps on Your Journey to Know God More Intimately:**

- *Nahkham* in Hebrew means to comfort, sigh, repent and console.

- Isn't it amazing that the mighty God of the universe cares for us and comforts us in our troubles? Thank Him today for His comfort for you.

- 2 Corinthians 1:3-4 says, "Blessed be the God and Father of our Lord Jesus Christ, the Father of mercies and God of all comfort, who comforts us in all our affliction, so that we may be able to comfort those who are in any affliction, with the comfort with which we ourselves are comforted by God."

- God has comforted me so many times throughout my life, but especially when I found out my son was dying and then after my fiancé was killed. I experienced His comfort mostly during the long nights when no one was around. I could talk to Him or let Him talk to me. Just knowing He was there brought great comfort.

- When has God comforted you? How?

- In what ways do you need Him to comfort you right now? Ask Him. He really loves you and cares about you. He's always there for you, regardless of what circumstances look like.

**A Prayer for You:**

*Lord, thank You for being the One who comforts me. Because You know all about me, You can comfort me better than anyone else. Teach me how to find comfort in You when I am hurting and sad. And help me to be able to share Your comfort with others when they are hurting.*

## June 9

## He Who Filled Their Houses with Good Things

*Yet it was **He who filled their houses with good things**,*
*so I stand aloof from the counsel of the wicked.*
Job 22:18

**Steps on Your Journey to Know God More Intimately:**

- How has God filled your house with good things? No matter how old or worn your things are, God has still given you everything. And if you compare what you have with many of the very, very poor people around the world, you are wealthy. It's easy to compare ourselves with those who have more than us, but that only makes us discontent.

- I've been looking at the things I have in my house recently, thanking God for each one. For example, I'm so grateful for my nice, soft couch. I have no idea how old it is, I got it from a garage sale seventeen years ago. When I choose to be thankful for the things I have, God fills me with joy. If I focus on how old my stuff is, how do you think I would feel?

- Look around your house and thank God for everything you see. It's amazing how being thankful can change your perspective and fill you with joy.

**A Prayer for You:**

*Thank You, Lord, that You are the One who has filled my house with good things. You have given me so much. Forgive me for taking for granted what You have given me. I want to have a heart full of gratitude for You and what You have done for me.*

# He Who Formed Me in the Womb
## To Be His Servant

*And now the Lord says—**he who formed me in the womb to be His servant** for I am honored in the eyes of the Lord
and my God has been my strength.*
Isaiah 49:5

**Steps on Your Journey to Know God More Intimately:**

- God personally formed you when you were in your mother's womb. Think about that.

- Ephesians 2:10 says, "For we are God's masterpiece. He has created us anew in Christ Jesus, so we can do the good things He planned for us long ago."

- When you are tempted to complain about your appearance or something else about yourself, remember that you are complaining about God's creation—His masterpiece.

- Consider God's unimaginable attention to the smallest detail. Your complete set of DNA contains about 3 billion base pairs of chromosomes and the total length of your DNA equals nearly 70 trips from the earth to the sun and back! Isn't that amazing?!

- God created you to be His servant. Ask the Lord to show you what that means for your life.

- Thank God for creating your unique DNA.

**A Prayer for You:**

*Thank You, Lord, that You created me when I was in my mother's womb. You created me to be Your masterpiece. I'm perfect just the way You created me. Forgive me for complaining about what I'm like. Show me why You created me to be Your servant.*

# *Glorious Name*

*Stand up and bless the Lord your God from everlasting to everlasting.
Blessed be your **glorious name**,
and may it be exalted above all blessing and praise.*
Nehemiah 9:5 (ESV)

**Steps on Your Journey to Know God More Intimately:**

- This name is *Kabod Shem* in Hebrew. *Kabod* means glory, glorious, weight, splendor and honor. Merriam-Webster defines glorious as, "possessing or deserving glory; marked by great beauty or splendor; delightful, wonderful." *Shem* means name.

- How is the Lord's name glorious? What do you think that means?

- How can you bless God's Glorious Name today?

- How can you exalt it above all blessing and praise? You may need to ask the Lord to show you what this might look like. Then do it!

- I find that the more I praise and exalt the Lord's name, the more I am filled with joy and peace. I never get tired of getting to know the Lord and His names. He is continually showing me new names that I never saw in the Word before. It's amazing to think how many names the Lord has.

**A Prayer for You:**

*I bless Your Glorious Name. Show me how to bless Your name and exalt it. Teach me what it means that Your Name is Glorious.*

## Eternal Spirit

*Just think how much more the blood of Christ will purify our consciences
from sinful deeds so that we can worship the living God.
For by the power of the **eternal Spirit**,
Christ offered himself to God as a perfect sacrifice for our sins.*
Hebrews 9:14 (NLT)

**Steps on Your Journey to Know God More Intimately:**

- I encourage you to read all of Hebrews 9 to get the context for this verse.

- The Greek word for eternal is *aionios*, meaning perpetual, eternal, everlasting and forever. *Pneuma* means spirit, breath or breeze.

- Meditate on this name. What does it mean to you that the Spirit is eternal?

- Notice what this verse says—that the blood of Christ was offered for us through the eternal Spirit. Meditate on what this verse says God did for us and why. What is the Lord saying to you through it?

- Ask the Lord to reveal to you what He wants to show you about this name today.

**A Prayer for You:**

*Eternal Spirit, I thank and praise You today that it was through You that the blood of Christ was offered to cleanse me. Show me more of what You want me to see about this verse and about Yourself today.*

# Father of the Heavenly Lights

*Every good and perfect gift is from above,
coming down from the **Father of the heavenly lights**,
who does not change like shifting shadows.*
James 1:17

**Steps on Your Journey to Know God More Intimately:**

- *Pater* is Father in Greek. *Phos* mean light, shine, luminous or fire.

- How is God the Father of the Heavenly Lights? What does that mean? If you're not sure, ask Him.

- Read this verse again. Why might it use this particular name to describe the Lord?

- I'm glad God created the heavenly lights—the sun, moon, stars. Imagine what life would be like without them.

- I'm learning more and more to see the gifts the Father gives me—the sunshine, singing birds, friends, my messy desk and challenges I face. The more I thank Him, the quicker my perspective changes.

- Thank the Lord for this name. Then thank Him for the beginning of the verse—that He gives you every good and perfect gift. Think about what some of those have been for you.

**A Prayer for You:**

*Father, I praise You that You are the Father of the Heavenly Lights. Thank You for creating them for our enjoyment as well as to provide light for us to see. And thank You for giving me every good and perfect gift. You know just what I need.*

# Father ... Who Does Not Change
## Like Shifting Shadows

*Every good and perfect gift is from above,*
*coming down from the **Father** of the heavenly lights,*
***who does not change like shifting shadows.***
James 1:17

**Steps on Your Journey to Know God More Intimately:**

- Think about how shadows change and shift so quickly.

- What does it mean to you today that your Father in Heaven doesn't change like shifting shadows?

- It is fun to sit and watch shadows changing as the sun moves or lights shift, however I'm so glad I can depend on my Father, knowing He will never change.

- Numbers 23:19 says, "God is not human, that He should lie, not a human being, that He should change His mind. Does He speak and then not act? Does He promise and not fulfill?" What does that say to you?

- What do you want to say to the Lord right now, based on what He is showing you?

**A Prayer for You:**

*Thank You, Father, that You don't change, so I can depend on You. So much in this world changes and people change, but You never will. Teach me to trust You and depend on You more and more.*

## Father Who is Unseen

*But when you pray, go into your room,*
*close the door and pray to your **Father**, **who is unseen**.*
*Then your Father, who sees what is done in secret, will reward you.*
Matthew 6:6

**Steps on Your Journey to Know God More Intimately:**

- Our Heavenly Father is always with us, even though we can't see Him. He is always there to listen to us and help us. There is nowhere we can go where He can't hear or see us.

- Even though I can't see my Father with my physical eyes, I love slowing down long enough to let Him reveal Himself to me. I often ask Him to open the eyes of my heart so I can see Him clearly (Ephesians 1:18). When I take the time to see Him, He always shows up. Sometimes I ask Him to reveal Himself to me, but then I don't stop and look for Him. Then I wonder why I can't see Him. I encourage you to ask your Father who is Unseen to open the eyes of your heart to see Him.

- Meditate on this name. Ask your Father to reveal more of Himself to you today through it.

- Thank Him that even though you can't see Him, He is always with you and He hears your prayers.

**A Prayer for You:**

*Father, thank You that though You are unseen, You always hear my prayers. I can be in a closed room and You still see me and hear me. I'm so grateful to have a Father like You.*

June 16

## *Father Who Sees What is Done in Secret*

*But when you pray, go into your room, close the door*
*and pray to your Father, who is unseen.*
*Then your **Father**, **who sees what is done in secret**, will reward you.*
Matthew 6:6

**Steps on Your Journey to Know God More Intimately:**

- Think about this name. Ask the Father to reveal more of Himself through this name today.

- Knowing that our Heavenly Father sees what we do in secret can be either comforting or distressing. If we are living our lives to please Him, we won't mind Him seeing everything we do. However, if we are doing things we know we shouldn't do, remember God still sees everything. Is there anything you might need to change or confess?

- My favorite times with the Father are when I am home alone spending time with Him. I love praising Him, thanking Him and learning about Him. He does reward me for my time spent in secret. He multiplies the rest of my time and He fills me with such contentment.

- Ask the Lord to remind you that He sees everything you do, even when you think no one sees or will ever know.

- I want to encourage you to take time daily alone with your Father.

- Look what this verse says your Father Who Sees What is Done in Secret will do when we pray to Him. He rewards us. Think about how He rewards us. How has He rewarded you?

**A Prayer for You:**

*Father, I'm glad to know You see what is done in secret, when I'm alone with You. Thank You for rewarding me for my time with You. Thank You for being such a good Father to me. I love You.*

# God our Father

*Grace and peace to you from **God our Father** and the Lord Jesus Christ.*
Ephesians 1:2 (NKJV)

**Steps on Your Journey to Know God More Intimately:**

- The God who created the universe is our Father. He is your Father, your Heavenly Father. Consider what that means that the God of gods is your Daddy.

- In what ways is God a Father to you? How does He show it?

- If you don't feel like God loves you, ask Him to show you. He does love you, even if you can't feel it.

- As you relate to God today, thank Him that He is truly your Heavenly Father and loves you as His precious child.

**A Prayer for You:**

*God, thank You for being my Father. Thank You for being the best Father I could ever ask for. Thank You for loving me and caring for me. Show me more of Your love for me. Teach me how to be Your child that brings You joy.*

June 18

*Lord Jesus Christ*

Kurios Iesous Christos (Greek)

*Grace and peace to you from God our Father and the **Lord Jesus Christ**.*
Ephesians 1:2 (ESV)

**Steps on Your Journey to Know God More Intimately:**

- In the coming days we'll be looking at names of God from the book of Ephesians. I want to encourage you to read this short book. There is so much incredible truth in it.

- Lord comes from the Greek, *kurios*, meaning master, authority, supremacy, sir and owner. What does it mean to you that Jesus is your Lord, your master?

- *Christos* means Messiah or Anointed One. What does it mean that Jesus was anointed?

- Meditate on this name, the Lord Jesus Christ.

- Philippians 2:11 says that every tongue will "confess that Jesus Christ is Lord, to the glory of God the Father." Throughout this day confess (or acknowledge) Jesus as Lord every time you think of Him.

**A Prayer for You:**

*Jesus, I acknowledge that You are my Lord and Savior. You are my master. I want to learn to praise You, worship You and honor You more, because You are worthy of praise. Thank You for the grace and peace You give me.*

# God and Father of our Lord Jesus Christ

*Praise be to the* **God and Father of our Lord Jesus Christ,**
*who has blessed us with every spiritual blessing
in the heavenly places in Christ.*
Ephesians 1:3 (NLT)

**Steps on Your Journey to Know God More Intimately:**

- Think about this and talk to the Lord about it—how can God be Jesus' God since Jesus is God?

- Why do you think this verse calls Him both the God *and* Father of Jesus?

- Jesus' relationship with God the Father is an example of the Father's relationship with us. Think about that. How is that true?

- Look at what this God has done for us! I'd encourage you to read all of Ephesians 1. It goes into detail about some of the spiritual blessings we have in Christ.

**A Prayer for You:**

*I praise You, Lord, because You are both the God and the Father of my Lord Jesus Christ. Teach me what this means and how You can be both. I honor You because You are also my God and Father. Thank You for all the spiritual blessings You have given me.*

## One He Loves

*He predestined us to be adopted as his sons through Jesus Christ,*
*in accordance with his pleasure and will—*
*to the praise of his glorious grace,*
*which he has freely given us in the **One He loves**.*
Ephesians 1:5-6

**Steps on Your Journey to Know God More Intimately:**

- The original Greek meaning of this name, *agapao,* is the Loved One. It comes from the word Greek word, *agape,* meaning unconditional love. Jesus is the Loved One. He is loved by God, but He is also loved by us.

- Thank Jesus that He is the Loved One today. He is loved by the Father. Thank Him that you have the privilege of loving Him, because He first loved you.

- God has freely given us His grace in Jesus. Think about that. How has He shown you His glorious grace?

- Look at the beginning of the verse. He predestined us and adopted us as His sons (and daughters). Think about what that means for your life. How does that affect you today?

**A Prayer for You:**

*Father, thank You that You love Jesus and that You have freely given me Your grace because of Jesus. Reveal Yourself to me today through this name. Father, as You love Jesus, I too want to love Him more.*

## June 21

## *Father of Glory*

Pater Doxa (Greek)

*I pray that the God of our Lord Jesus Christ, the **Father of glory**,*
*may give you a spirit of wisdom and of revelation in the knowledge of him.*
Ephesians 1:17 (ESV)

**Steps on Your Journey to Know God More Intimately:**

- Glory in Greek is *doxa*, meaning dignity, glorious, honor, praise and worship. *Pater* means father.

- Consider this name today. Ask the Lord to show you more of who He is through this name.

- God is the one who is worthy of all glory, praise and worship. Ask the Lord to show you how you can bring Him glory.

- He loves to reveal His glory to us, especially in nature. Psalm 19:1 says, "The heavens declare the glory of God and the earth shows His handiwork." Since I started asking God to show me His glory, I've seen His glory in nature in ways that I had never seen before. I started taking pictures of God showing off His glory. I now have over 1400 pictures. I'm having so much fun! You should try it.

- Ask the Lord to show you Himself in a clearer way as the Father of Glory.

**A Prayer for You:**

*Father of Glory, show me Your glory in new ways. I want to see You and know You more. I praise and worship You for Your glory.*

## Spirit of Wisdom and Revelation

*I keep asking that the God of our Lord Jesus Christ,*
*the glorious Father, may give you the **Spirit of wisdom and revelation**,*
*so that you may know him better.*
Ephesians 1:17

**Steps on Your Journey to Know God More Intimately:**

- This is part of Paul's prayer for the Ephesians. I'd encourage you to read the whole prayer in Ephesians 1. It is a wonderful prayer to use for youself, your family and friends. Build the habit of praying it regularly for those close to you: "Lord, give _____ the Spirit of wisdom and revelation, so that he or she may know You better." I pray this for me and my family almost every day.

- The purpose for this name, Spirit of Wisdom and Revelation, is to reveal more of who the Lord is, so you will know Him better.

- The Greek for revelation means disclosure, appearing, manifestation, lighten and revealed. Think about these meanings. Revelation is when God reveals something to you personally. In this case the purpose is to know God better.

- In what ways do you need wisdom or revelation? Ask God to give you His Spirit of Wisdom and Revelation.

**A Prayer for You:**

*Spirit of Wisdom and Revelation, I invite You to come and reveal Yourself to me in new and fresh ways. Show me who You are and more about the Father and Jesus. The more I get to know You, the more I want to know You in deeper ways.*

# Head over All Things for the Benefit of the Church

*God has put all things under the authority of Christ and has made him*
**head over all things for the benefit of the church.**
Ephesians 1:22 (NLT)

**Steps on Your Journey to Know God More Intimately:**

- Meditate on the fact that Jesus is the Head over All Things for the Benefit of the Church. He is supreme over everything in all creation. But He does it for the church. Ask Him to show you what this means.

- How does Jesus being the head of all things benefit you, who are part of the church? Ask Him to show you.

- What do you need, that Christ can give you, because He is the head over everything?

**A Prayer for You:**

*God, thank You that You put everything under the authority of Christ and made Him the Head over All Things for the Benefit of the Church. Your ways and plans are so much higher and greater than mine. Help me to know You more through this name today.*

# Him Who Fills Everything in Every Way

*And God placed all things under his feet and appointed him to be
head over everything for the church, which is his body,
the fullness of **Him who fills everything in every way**.*
Ephesians 1:22-23

**Steps on Your Journey to Know God More Intimately:**

- Our God is so amazing. He fills everything in every way.

- Ask the Lord to show you what it means that He is the One who fills everything in every way.

- Psalm 139 says that there is nowhere we can go to get away from God's Spirit. That is encouraging and comforting to me. No matter where I go, I know He is already there. There is nowhere I can go that He isn't there.

- Thank Him that He fulfills every need you have. He fills you and He fills everything around you!

**A Prayer for You:**

*Jesus, thank You that You fill everything in every way. I praise You that I can go wherever You lead me with complete confidence because I know You are already there. Help me learn to recognize Your presence wherever I go.*

## June 25

## *God, Who is Rich in Mercy*

*But **God, who is rich in mercy**, because of His great love
with which He loved us, even when we were dead in trespasses,
made us alive together with Christ (by grace you have been saved).*
Ephesians 2:4-5 (NKJV)

**Steps on Your Journey to Know God More Intimately:**

- An easy way to understand the difference between God's grace and His mercy is: Grace is God giving us what we don't deserve. Mercy is Him *not* giving us what we *do* deserve.

- I'm so grateful that God doesn't give me what I deserve. I deserve to go to hell, because I'm a sinner. But I don't have to—that's mercy. Instead I get to go to Heaven—that's grace. I am so blessed. And so are you. Consider that.

- Here is an example where human language struggles to express infinite truth. God's rich mercy is so great, so wonderful and so tremendous that it will take eternity for us to experience it fully. Ask the Lord to show you the depths of His mercy toward you. Don't forget to listen for His answer.

- In what ways have you seen God's mercy in your life?

- In what areas do you need God's mercy?

**A Prayer for You:**

*Lord, I praise You that You are infinitely rich in mercy. Your mercy never ends. I deserve to be punished for my sins; instead You paid for my sins so I can have a relationship with You. Thank You for Your great love for me. Help me to learn to understand how much You really do love me.*

June 26

## Our Peace

Eiraynay (Greek)

*For he himself is **our peace**, who has made us both one and
has broken down in his flesh the dividing wall of hostility.*
Ephesians 2:14 (ESV)

**Steps on Your Journey to Know God More Intimately:**

- This word for peace, *eiraynay*, comes from the Greek word, *eiro*,
  which means to join. It also means prosperity, quietness, rest and set
  at one again.

- Peace in this context referred to the end of conflict between believing
  Jews and believing Gentiles. Thank God that Jesus included Gentiles
  in His salvation and brought us peace with His chosen people.

- Jesus came to bring us peace with God (Romans 5:1), peace within
  ourselves (John 14:27) and peace with others. He is everything
  we need.

- The Complete Jewish Bible translates this, "For He himself is our
  shalom." *Shalom* means safe, well, happy, friendly, welfare, good
  health, rest and wholeness.

- Meditate on Jesus being our peace. What does it mean to you today?

- How do you need Jesus to be your peace? Talk to Him about that.

**A Prayer for You:**

*Jesus, I thank You and praise You that You are my Peace, my Shalom. You
bring me peace in every area of my life. Help me to learn to rest in You and
find peace and security, regardless of what is going on in my life.*

# Manifold Wisdom of God

*His intent was that now, through the church,*
*the **manifold wisdom of God** should be made known to the rulers and*
*authorities in the heavenly realms, according to his eternal purpose*
*that he accomplished in Christ Jesus our Lord.*
Ephesians 3:10-11

**Steps on Your Journey to Know God More Intimately:**

- This is the only time the word manifold, *polopoikilos*, is used in the New Testament. It means, many and varied; of many kinds; having many features or forms. *Sophia* means wisdom.

- This name is also translated multi-faceted, how many-sided God's wisdom is and His wisdom in its rich variety.

- 1 Corinthians 1:24 calls Jesus the "Wisdom of God." Meditate on what it means that Jesus is the Wisdom of God.

- Why is it important that Jesus is made known to the rulers and authorities in the heavenly realms as the Manifold Wisdom of God?

- In what areas do you need God's varied wisdom today?

- I trust you are enjoying our study getting to know the Lord better. I know I am. I am constantly amazed at how much I continue to learn about the Lord, even though I've been studying about Him and getting to know Him for over 45 years!

**A Prayer for You:**

*Lord, thank You for this unique name. Thank You that in Jesus we see Your multi-faceted wisdom. I need wisdom in so many ways. I'm glad I can depend on Your wisdom that has such rich variety. Teach me to lean on Your wisdom more and my own less.*

# Him Who Is Able to Do Immeasurably More
## Than All We Ask or Imagine

*Now to **Him who is able to do immeasurably more
than all we ask or imagine**, according to his power that is at work within
us, to him be glory in the church and in Christ Jesus.*

Ephesians 3:20

**Steps on Your Journey to Know God More Intimately:**

- It would have been enough just to say that He is able to do all we ask. But the Holy Spirit wanted us to know that there is absolutely no limit to what He is able to do. His power goes infinitely beyond anything we can imagine. I don't know about you, but I have a very good imagination. Yet God is able to do *immeasurably* more than you or I can imagine. Wow! I'm amazed at this thought. I hope you are too.

- This verse says God *is able to do* … Think about why God didn't just say that He *does* more than we can ask or imagine. Do you think it could be because we have a choice whether or not we will let Him work in our lives? Meditate on that.

- Are you keeping God from doing any incredible things in your life? I'm sure there are times that I hold God back from doing what He wants, because I don't have enough faith. How about you?

- Let your imagination run wild for a few minutes. What would you like God to do for you? Ask Him in faith.

**A Prayer for You:**

*Thank You, Lord, that You are able to do immeasurably more than all I can ask or imagine. I want to see You do miracles in my life and through me. Increase my faith to trust You more and to believe that You really are able to accomplish infinitely more than I might ask or think.*

June 29

*One Spirit*

Heis Pneuma (Greek)

*There is one body and **one Spirit**—just as you were called to one hope
when you were called—one Lord, one faith, one baptism.*
Ephesians 4:4-5

**Steps on Your Journey to Know God More Intimately:**

- Ephesians 2:18 says, "For through Him we both have access by one Spirit to the Father"(NKJV). We are looking at many different facets of the Holy Spirit in this study, but there is still only One Spirit.

- Believers today often focus on our differences–in doctrine, form of worship, etc. There is only one Spirit—not a different Spirit for each church or denomination. So long as others are not going contrary to what the Word says about Him, we should not judge them.

- I enjoy teaching mission groups, because they are often have people from all different denominations and spiritual backgrounds. Yet we are all united in Christ and in our desire to reach the lost for Him.

- The Word has so much to say about the Spirit, however if you are like me, you may have missed a lot of it in the past. I want to challenge you to make a study, with an open mind, about who the Holy Spirit really is and all that He wants to do in and through you. You may just be amazed, like I have been.

- Today, think about how all who have a relationship with Jesus are followers of Christ because of His One Spirit.

- Are there believers you don't fellowship with because they have different beliefs than you do about the Holy Spirit? What might you need to do to change that?

**A Prayer for You:**

*Spirit, I want to know You more. Thank You that You are One Spirit, with many facets. Forgive me for keeping You from working in and through me, because of my lack of knowledge about You and faith in You. Teach me more about Yourself, who You are and what You want to do in my life.*

## One Lord

*For there is one body and one Spirit,*
*just as you have been called to one glorious hope for the future.*
*There is **one Lord**, one faith, one baptism.*
Ephesians 4:4-5 (NLT)

**Steps on Your Journey to Know God More Intimately:**

- *Heis* in Greek means one. *Kurios* is the Greek word meaning master, lord, sir or supreme authority.

- Think about what it means that there is only one master, only one supreme authority. Ask the Lord to show you what that means.

- Like we looked at yesterday, we need to be careful not to judge other believers that have different beliefs that are not critical to our faith. If they worship the same God as we do and believe in the same Bible, then let's be careful not to judge them or slander them. Now, I'm not saying that all roads lead to God. I do believe there is only One God, One Lord.

- Meditate on this name. What insights do you get from it?

**A Prayer for You:**

*Lord, thank You that there is only one of You. Thank You that each denomination does not have their own Lord. You are big enough for all of us. You are also multi-faceted. Help me to learn to accept others who believe in You, but have slightly different beliefs (so long as they don't go contrary to Your Word).*

# One God and Father of All

*There is one body and one Spirit—just as you were called to one hope when you were called—one Lord, one faith, one baptism;*
**one God and Father of all**, *who is over all and through all and in all.*
Ephesians 4:4-6

**Steps on Your Journey to Know God More Intimately:**

- There is only *One* God. There is only *One* Father of all. What does that mean to you today? Ask the Lord to show you what difference that makes to you.

- What can you do to promote unity in the body of Christ? Our enemy wants to separate us and cause division among us.

- I love my church, because we fellowship together with many other churches. We all help each other, rather than seeing other churches as our competition. We even have a combined service with four separate churches once a quarter. In addition, we promote events at other churches.

- Thank the Lord for the unity this name brings.

**A Prayer for You:**

*Thank You that there is only One God and there is only One Father of All. Thank You that I can go anywhere in the world and fellowship with other believers in You, because we have the same God and Father (even if they worship differently than I do).*

# God ... Who Is Over All and Through All
## and In All

*There is one body and one Spirit—just as you were called to one hope when you were called—one Lord, one faith, one baptism;*
*one **God** and Father of all, **who is over all and through all and in all**.*
Ephesians 4:4-6

**Steps on Your Journey to Know God More Intimately:**

- Think about this name. Consider each part of it:

    o He is *over* all.

    o He is *through* all.

    o He is *in* all.

- What do you think it means that He is through all and in all? Is He in atheists? Or is this just talking about believers? Is He in inanimate things?

- Ask the Lord to show you how this name affects you.

- Praise the Lord for His amazing greatness and His presence everywhere.

**A Prayer for You:**

*God, You are so awesome. You are everywhere. There is nowhere I can go to get away from You. That is so comforting. Open my eyes and heart to understand this name better.*

# July 3

## Savior of His Body

Soter Soma (Greek)

*For the husband is the head of the wife as Christ is the head of the church.*
*he is the **Savior of his body**, the church.*
Ephesians 5:23 (NLT)

**Steps on Your Journey to Know God More Intimately:**

- *Soma* means body. Jesus is your personal Savior, *soter*, but He is also the Savior of His Body, the Church. Consider how Jesus is the Savior of His Body.

- Earlier we looked at the meaning of the Greek word *sozo*, which is the root of *soter*. It means the One who saves, heals, delivers and makes us whole.

- I do a one-on-one ministry with people called *Sozo*. It's exciting to watch God work in people's lives bringing wholeness, deliverance and healing.

- Ask the Lord to reveal to you more of this name today.

- What does it mean to you that God *sozos* you?

- Thank Him that He came as your Savior——the One who *sozos* you. Jesus did so much for us when He came.

- What did it cost Christ to be the Savior of His body, the Church?

- In what ways does He *sozo* the body?

**A Prayer for You:**

*Jesus, thank You for being my Savior, but also the Savior of Your whole body, the Church. When I have conflict with others in Your body, remind me that You came to save them too, not just me.*

## July 4

### Spirit of the Lord God

*The **Spirit of the Lord God** is upon me,*
*because the Lord has anointed me to bring good news to the poor;*
*he has sent me to bind up the brokenhearted, to proclaim liberty to the*
*captives, and the opening of the prison to those who are bound.*
Isaiah 61:1 (ESV)

**Steps on Your Journey to Know God More Intimately:**

- Jesus quoted this verse about Himself in Luke 4:17-19.

- Spirit of the LORD God is a compound name in Hebrew. *ruah* means spirit, breath or wind. *Adonai* means lord, master and controller. *Yehwih* is a variation of *Yahweh*. It is only used after *Adonai*, but the Jews pronounce it *Elohim* so they don't say the same word twice in a row.

- Meditate on this name. Ask the Lord to reveal more of Himself to you through it.

- Today, as we celebrate the freedom we have in the United States as a nation, we want to look at the freedom that God brings us. As this verse says, Jesus came to bring us freedom.

- In what ways do you need the Lord to bring you freedom?

- Ask Him to show you any ways you are held captive—it could be in your thoughts, your feelings, relationships, people you need to forgive, etc. The Lord wants you to have complete freedom. Thank Him that He came to bring you freedom.

- The Spirit is also on us, sending us to bind the brokenhearted and proclaim freedom for captives. How can you do that in your sphere of influence? One way I do it is through the *Sozo* ministry that I mentioned yesterday.

**A Prayer for You:**

*Spirit of the Lord God, I worship You today. Thank You that You came upon Jesus and anointed Him to do all the things in this verse. And thank You Holy Spirit that I can claim this verse for myself, because I know You have anointed me to do Your work. Teach me more about Yourself and this name.*

# He Who Descended

Katabaino (Greek)

**He who descended** *is the one who also ascended*
*far above all the heavens, that he might fill all things.*
Ephesians 4:10 (ESV)

**Steps on Your Journey to Know God More Intimately:**

- *Katabaino* means descend, come down or fall down.

- In case you haven't noticed, we are still going through names of God from the book of Ephesians.

- There are various interpretations of this name. Rather than me telling you what they are, you can ask the Lord to reveal to you what it means.

- Jesus came down to earth to show us how to live as well as to pay the price for our sins.

- 2 Corinthians 5:21 says, "God made Christ, who never sinned, to be the offering for our sin, so that we could be made right with God through Christ" (NLT). Try to imagine how much it cost the One who knew no sin to become sin for you.

- Spend some time thanking Him for being willing to descend to earth.

**A Prayer for You:**

*Jesus, thank You that You came down to earth to pay for my sins, but also to show me how to live my life in connection with the Holy Spirit. Teach me more about You today through this name.*

# One Who Ascended Far Above All the Heavens

*He who descended is*
**the one who also ascended far above all the heavens,**
*that he might fill all things.*
Ephesians 4:10 (ESV)

**Steps on Your Journey to Know God More Intimately:**

- Aren't you grateful that Jesus didn't just die? He rose and is in Heaven waiting for us, preparing a place for us (John 14:2-3) and interceding for us (Romans 8:34).

- Think about what this means. It doesn't say He just went back to Heaven. He ascended far above all the heavens. I like to close my eyes and ask God to show me Himself and His greatness. Sometimes He'll show me the universe. He is sitting on a throne, out in space. He looks down at all the stars and planets. From that vantage point, they all look very small. He points to a tiny speck and says, "that's earth!" Our God is incredibly great and awesome.

- Consider how He fills the whole universe. That is one *huge* God. Try to imagine what that means. Praise Him today for what He shows you.

**A Prayer for You:**

*Jesus, I praise You that You didn't stay dead, but that You rose and are in Heaven waiting for me. Show me what it means that You ascended far above all the heavens. Thank You for revealing so many of Your different names, so I can see various facets of Who You are.*

# El-Shaddai—God Almighty

*When Abram was ninety-nine years old, the Lord appeared to him and
said, "I am **El-Shaddai—'God Almighty.'**
Serve me faithfully and live a blameless life."*
Genesis 17:1 (NLT)

**Steps on Your Journey to Know God More Intimately:**

- *El Shaddai* in Hebrew means the all-sufficient God, God Almighty or the One Who is all-powerful.

- In 2 Corinthians 12:9, Jesus said, "My grace is sufficient for you, for my power is made perfect in weakness." God's grace is all you need. *El Shaddai* is sufficient for you and for me.

- Meditate on the name, God Almighty. He is all powerful. He is sufficient for all that you need.

- What does it mean to you today, knowing He is all you need and His grace is enough?

- Thank and praise the Lord that He is God Almighty.

**A Prayer for You:**

*El Shaddai, I'm so grateful that You are the all-sufficient God. You are all I need in every area of my life. Thank You that I can depend on You. Teach me to rely less on myself and more on You, God Almighty.*

# Son of God, Who Loved Me

## and Gave Himself for Me

*I have been crucified with Christ. It is no longer I who live,*
*but Christ who lives in me. And the life I now live in the flesh I live by*
*faith in the **Son of God**, **who loved me and gave himself for me**.*
Galatians 2:20 (ESV)

**Steps on Your Journey to Know God More Intimately:**

- Look at the first part of the name. What does it mean that Jesus is the Son of God?

- Think about this name. Although Jesus is the Son of God—the God of the Universe—He loved you and gave Himself for you. He took your place, paying for your sins so you could live with Him forever. Now that's love! Can you imagine a love greater than that?

- I'm sitting in the Jericho Center, an incredible house of prayer (one of my favorite places to be!). The worship team just sang a song with these words: "You laid Your glory aside. You signed up for our death row. You paid the penalty that I owe,"

- Think about the words to that song. Jesus was in Heaven, surrounded by astounding glory and adoration. He laid all that aside for you and me. We were on "death row," condemned to die for our sins, because we couldn't stand before a holy God. Jesus, the perfect Son of God, signed up to take our place on death row. He paid our penalty. That is incredible love!

**A Prayer for You:**

*Thank You, Lord, for Your marvelous love for me. Thank You that though You are the Son of God, yet You loved me so much that You gave Yourself for me. I can't even begin to understand the depths of Your love. Open my eyes to be able to see how much You really love me.*

July 9

## *Son of Man*

*In my vision at night I looked, and there before me was*
*one like a **son of man**, coming with the clouds of heaven.*
*He approached the Ancient of Days and was led into his presence.*
Daniel 7:13

**Steps on Your Journey to Know God More Intimately:**

- Matthew 20:28 says, "The Son of Man came not to be served but to serve, and to give his life as a ransom for many."

- *Bar* in Hebrew and *huios* in Greek both mean son. *Enosh* in Hebrew and *anthropos* in Greek mean man. The title, the Son of Man, is used in the Old Testament as a title of the Messiah. It shows the true humanity of our Lord. Jesus was a perfect man. Consider why Daniel referred to Jesus as a Son of Man rather than the Son of God.

- Jesus often referred to Himself as the Son of Man, reminding us of His humanity. Because He was human, we can relate to Him.

- Notice what happens in Luke 22:69-70 when Jesus refers to Himself as the Son of Man. "'From now on the Son of Man shall be seated at the right hand of the power of God.' So they all said, 'Are you the Son of God, then?' And he said to them, 'You say that I am.'" The religious leaders recognized that He was calling Himself God.

- What does it mean to you today that Jesus is the Son of Man—fully human as well as fully God?

- Thank Jesus that He's human so He can relate to you and you can relate to Him. Then thank Him that He is coming back for you.

**A Prayer for You:**

*Son of Man, thank You for coming to earth as a human as well as the Son of God. And thank You that You are coming back one day to take me home to be with You forever.*

# He Who Was Seated on the Throne

*He who was seated on the throne* said, *"I am making everything new!"*
*Then he said, "Write this down, for these words are trustworthy and true."*
Revelation 21:5

**Steps on Your Journey to Know God More Intimately:**

- Look at Revelation 19:16: "On his [Jesus'] robe and on his thigh he has a name written, King of kings and Lord of lords."

- Jesus is the King of kings and Lord of lords. He is in Heaven seated on His throne making everything new for us.

- Close your eyes and picture Jesus on His heavenly throne. If you have a hard time seeing Him, ask Him to remove anything that may keep you from seeing Him clearly.

- Read Revelation, chapters 1 and 4, for a picture of Heaven.

**A Prayer for You:**

*Lord, thank You that You are the King of kings and the Lord of lords. I praise You, that though You are right here with me, You are also seated on Your throne. Thank You that I am seated with You in the heavenly realms (Ephesians 2:6). Show me more of Who You are and who I am when I'm with You.*

# He Who Will Sustain You

*Even to your old age and gray hairs I am he,*
*I am **he who will sustain you**. I have made you and I will carry you;*
*I will sustain you and I will rescue you.*
Isaiah 46:4

**Steps on Your Journey to Know God More Intimately:**

- Some of the definitions of sustain are support, provide for, maintain and encourage.

- God is the One who holds us up and keeps us going. Look at the verses below to see how God sustains us.

    o Psalm 3:5: "I lie down and sleep; I wake again, because the LORD SUSTAINS ME."

    o Psalm 41:3: "The Lord will sustain him on his sickbed and restore him from his bed of illness."

    o See also Nehemiah 9:21; Psalm 54:4; 55:22.

- In what ways have you seen God sustain you?

- In what ways do you need the Lord to sustain you?

- When I was doing a single-parent family ministry, it was exhausting. I taught weekly classes, made meals for single parents, had a food bank, did one-on-one ministry, plus raised my own sons on my own. I became weary. During that time, the Lord sustained me. He held me up, encouraged me and provided for me.

- Thank God that He will sustain you throughout your life—to your old age and gray hairs!

**A Prayer for You:**

*Thank You, Lord, that You are the One who sustains me. You encourage me, support me and provide for me. Thank You that You made me, will carry me, sustain me and rescue me even to my old age. That is so comforting. Help me to remember this throughout all my days.*

# *He Who Forms the Hearts of All,*
## Who Considers Everything They Do

**He who forms the hearts of all, who considers everything they do.**
Psalm 33:15

**Steps on Your Journey to Know God More Intimately:**

- Not only does God form our bodies, He also forms our hearts. Do you ever wish you were different? Remember God made you just the way you are. Thank God for forming your heart the way He did.

- He not only made your heart, but He also made the hearts of the people you may struggle to like or understand. Ask God to help you accept others, because He created them the way they are too.

- The Lord pays attention to *everything* you do. How does that statement affect you? That thought could be either very frightening (if you're not obeying Him) or very comforting (if you're living your life to please Him). Either way, He is aware of how you live.

- Make a decision today that you will always choose to bring Him joy when He looks at you. But remember, He doesn't expect perfection. Isaiah 43:25 says, "He remembers our sins no more." I'm so glad!

**A Prayer for You:**

*Thank You, Lord, that You formed my heart and You see and understand everything I do (as well as what others do). You know me better than I even know myself. Thank You for making me just the way I am. I want to always please You in all that I do.*

# God Our Savior

Elohim Yesha (Hebrew)

*Cry out, "Save us, **God our Savior**…*
*that we may give thanks to your holy name, and glory in your praise."*
1 Chronicles 16:35

**Steps on Your Journey to Know God More Intimately:**

- *Elohim* is the plural name of God. *Yesha* means salvation, liberty, deliverance and prosperity. It's amazing all our Savior has done and continues to do for us. Think about what *Yesha* means and how that relates to you.

- 1 Timothy 2:3 says, "This is good, and pleases God our Savior" (NLT).

- Meditate on all God your Savior did for you.

- What is God showing you through this name?

- From what has God saved you?

- How has He healed you and made you whole?

- From what did He deliver you?

- *Yesha* also means prosperity. Think about that.

- Take some time to express your gratitude for all He has done for you.

**A Prayer for You:**

*God Our Savior, I'm so grateful for all You did for me. Thank You that You not only saved me from my sins, but You also healed my body and soul (and continue to heal me). Thank You that You delivered me from Satan and his demons and that You made me whole. Forgive me for forgetting all that You did and do for me.*

July 14

## *Hope of All the Ends of the Earth*
### and of the Farthest Seas

*You answer us with awesome and righteous deeds, God our Savior,*
*the **hope of all the ends of the earth and of the farthest seas.***
Psalm 65:5

**Steps on Your Journey to Know God More Intimately:**

- The Hebrew word for hope, *mibtakh*, means confidence, security, a refuge, hope, trust and sure.

- How is God the Hope of All the Ends of the Earth and of the Farthest Seas? Think about that.

- Why doesn't this verse just say that God is *our* hope?

- How has God given you hope in the past?

- In what areas do you need hope today?

- Thank Him for being your hope and for giving you hope.

- If you don't yet have a personal relationship God, then you may not have much hope. If you'd like to learn more about how you can find more hope, go to page 369.

- Notice the beginning of this verse. God answers us with awesome and righteous deeds. How have you seen Him do that?

**A Prayer for You:**

*Thank You, Lord, that You are the Hope of All the Ends of the Earth and You are also my Hope. Thank You for the hope You bring me in every area of my life. I want to always find my Hope in You, rather than in people or things, because You are the only One I can completely depend on.*

## Father of Compassion

Pater Oiktirmos (Greek)

*Praise be to the God and Father of our Lord Jesus Christ,
the **Father of compassion** and the God of all comfort.*
2 Corinthians 1:3-4

**Steps on Your Journey to Know God More Intimately**:

- The Greek word for compassion, *oiktirmos*, means compassion, pity or mercy. One definition of compassion is a feeling of distress and pity for the suffering or misfortune of another, often including the desire to alleviate it.

- Our Heavenly Father has compassion on us. He cares about the things that hurt us and frustrate us. He knows all about what is going on in our lives.

- In what areas do you need your Father to show you compassion? Ask Him. He loves you so much.

- Meditate on your Father, who is the Father of Compassion. Talk to Him about what's bothering you. He cares about you.

- One of the first verses I remember from my childhood is 1 Peter 5:7: "Cast all your cares on him, because the Lord cares for you." He really does care for you. Don't ever forget that. No matter how hard things seem, He does care about you.

**A Prayer for You:**

*Father of Compassion, I praise You for Who You are and what You do. You don't just show compassion, You are the Father of Compassion. Thank You for being so caring and kind to me. I'm so glad I can run to You when I am hurting and know You will always love me.*

## God of All Comfort

*Praise be to the God and Father of our Lord Jesus Christ,*
*the Father of compassion and the **God of all comfort**,*
*who comforts us in all our troubles, so that we can comfort those in any*
*trouble with the comfort we ourselves receive from God.*
2 Corinthians 1:3-4

**Steps on Your Journey to Know God More Intimately:**

- This name in Greek is *Theos Pas Paraklesis*. *Theos* means God. *Pas* means all, any, every and always. *Paraklesis* means comfort, consolation, exhortation and encouragement.

- Isn't it comforting to know the God of *all* comfort? When we are sad, hurting, depressed, stressed or grieving, He is the One we can turn to for comfort. He comforts us in *all* our troubles.

- I've experienced the Lord as my Comfort so many times. Let me share two times He was my Comforter.

  o He held me close when I was all alone in boarding school in Guatemala from age six to thirteen. He comforted me when no one seemed to care.

  o He brought comfort as I lay curled up in bed, wanting to die, after my fiancé was killed on his motorcycle.

- How has God comforted you in the past?

- How do you need the Lord to comfort you today? Let Him be your comforter in whatever your situation.

- These verses say He comforts us so we can comfort others with the comfort He gave us. Who in your life needs comfort? Call or visit that person and share God's comfort with him or her.

**A Prayer for You:**

*Lord, I praise You that You are the God of All Comfort. I'm so glad to know that You are always with me, holding me and comforting me, even when I can't see You. Show me more of how You are my Comforter and how You want me to bring comfort to others.*

July 17

## *Head of the Body*

*And he [Jesus] is the **head of the body**, the church;*
*he is the beginning and the firstborn from among the dead,*
*so that in everything he might have the supremacy.*
Colossians 1:18

**Steps on Your Journey to Know God More Intimately:**

- *Kephalay* in Greek means head. *Soma* means body. Jesus is the Head of His body. Meditate on how Jesus is the Head of the church. What do you think that looks like?

- How have you seen Jesus be the Head of the Church?

- How is He your Head?

- Is there anything you need to do to give Him His rightful place?

- The end of this verse gives the reason that Jesus in the Head of the Body—"so that in everything he might have the supremacy."

- Supremacy in Greek means to be first. It is also translated preeminence. This is the only time this Greek word is used.

- Is Jesus first in your life, family and your world? If not, why not? What may you need to do to make Him supreme in your life?

**A Prayer for You:**

*Jesus, I praise You that You are the Head of Your Body, whether or not we treat You as the Head. Thank You that You are the One who leads me and guides me as my Head. Help me learn to always put You first in my life and in my family. Forgive me for the times I make someone or something else first.*

## Firstborn from Among the Dead

*And he is the head of the body, the church;
he is the beginning and the **firstborn from among the dead**,
so that in everything he might have the supremacy.*
Colossians 1:18

**Steps on Your Journey to Know God More Intimately:**

- The Greek word for firstborn is *prototokos*. The word prototype comes from this word. How is Jesus the prototype?

- Jesus is Firstborn From Among the Dead, so He is sovereign over all those who will rise from the dead.

- Because Jesus conquered death, and rose by God's power (John 10:18), we too will resurrect to eternal life by the power of God if we trust Jesus. 1 Corinthians 6:14 says, "By his power God raised the Lord from the dead, and he will raise us also."

- Ask the Lord to show you more of what it means that Jesus is the Firstborn From Among the Dead.

**A Prayer for You:**

*Jesus, thank You that You are the Firstborn From Among the Dead. It brings me hope knowing that because You were raised from the dead, I know that I will also be raised up with You one day. Thank You. Show me more of what this name means.*

## Christ the Power of God

*We preach Christ crucified: a stumbling block to Jews and foolishness to Gentiles, but to those whom God has called, both Jews and Greeks,* **Christ the power of God** *and the wisdom of God.*
1 Corinthians 1:23-24

**Steps on Your Journey to Know God More Intimately:**

- *Christos* in Greek means Christ. *Theos* is God. *Dunamis* means force, miraculous power, ability, abundance, power, strength and mighty work.

- Think about God's power displayed throughout the Word.

- Consider how God's power was revealed through Jesus—healing the sick, casting out demons, opening blind eyes and raising the dead.

- I want to see more of God's power in my life. I've seen a little, but I know there's so much more that I haven't tapped into. One example was a friend who had a massive headache. Nothing would take it away. I laid hands on her, prayed briefly and the headache went away completely.

- Look what Jesus said in John 14:12-14: "Very truly I tell you, whoever believes in me will do the works I have been doing, and they will do even greater things than these, because I am going to the Father. And I will do whatever you ask in my name, so that the Father may be glorified in the Son. You may ask me for anything in my name, and I will do it." Do you really believe that? See also John 15:4 and 16:24. If we truly believed these verses we would be doing so much more.

**A Prayer for You:**

*Christ, thank You that You are the power of God. In You is all of God's power. I want to know and experience more of Your power in my life. Increase my faith so You can reveal more of Your power in and through me.*

## July 20

## *Christ ... the Wisdom of God*

***Christ** the power of God and **the wisdom of God**.*
*For the foolishness of God is wiser than human wisdom,*
*and the weakness of God is stronger than human strength.*
1 Corinthians 1:24-25

**Steps on Your Journey to Know God More Intimately:**

- *Sofia* in Greek means wisdom.

- James 1:5-6 says, "If any of you lacks wisdom, you should ask God, who gives generously to all without finding fault, and it will be given to you. But when you ask, you must believe and not doubt, because the one who doubts is like a wave of the sea, blown and tossed by the wind." What does that say to you today?

- 1 Corinthians 2:6 says, "We have the mind of Christ." I believe we have His mind in us, but we can choose whether or not we'll let Him control our thoughts. It's so easy to rely on our own wisdom rather than on His. What do you think about that?

- Every day I have to choose to rely on God's wisdom rather than my own. I do that by beginning my day in the Word and prayer, seeking God. I admit there have been many times I haven't done that. When I rely on my own wisdom, I struggle with whatever I'm doing. When I'm letting Christ be my wisdom, it's amazing what I can accomplish. So why would I ever choose to use my own wisdom? Thankfully, I'm learning.

- In what areas do you need God's wisdom today? Ask Him in faith, without any doubting that He will answer you.

**A Prayer for You:**

*Christ, I praise You that You are the Wisdom of God. All of God's wisdom is in You. Thank You that You gave me the mind of Christ. Teach me how to tap into Your wisdom more of the time.*

# One Who Called You to Live in the Grace of Christ

*I am astonished that you are so quickly deserting*
**the one who called you to live in the grace of Christ**
*and are turning to a different gospel.*
Galatians 1:6

**Steps on Your Journey to Know God More Intimately:**

- Remember, grace means unmerited favor or blessings.

- We have a choice. We can live under the law, with all its dos and don'ts. Or, we can live in the grace of Christ. I don't see much of a choice there. Why would I want to live under the law when I can live in God's favor and blessing? That's an amazing place to be. Yet, we often forget and end up choosing to live under the law.

- What does it mean to you that God called you to live in the grace of Christ?

- Are you ever like the Galatians turning from God's grace to a different gospel? If you're not sure, ask the Lord to show you.

- Meditate on this name today. Ask the Lord to show you more of what it means.

**A Prayer for You:**

*Lord, thank You that You called me to live in the grace of Christ. What a wonderful place to live! Help me to always live there and not desert You, like the Galatians did. Forgive me, Lord, for the times I have deserted You. I want to learn to live more in Your grace.*

# My Song

## Zimrath (Hebrew)

*The Lord is my strength and **my song**; he has become my salvation.*
*He is my God, and I will praise him, my father's God, and I will exalt him.*
Exodus 15:2

**Steps on Your Journey to Know God More Intimately:**

- How is God your song? If you're not sure, ask Him.

- God gives me songs, but is that the same as Him being my song? Think about that.

- I've seen God as my song as He often puts a song in my heart. I find that throughout the day I'm singing or humming a song. Sometimes it's one I've known before. Sometimes it is a new song. Ask God to be your song and put a song in your heart.

- Ask the Lord to show you what His song is for you right now.

- Zephaniah 3:17 says that God rejoices over you with singing. What song is He singing over you today? Stop and listen. Ask Him to let you hear—and see—Him singing over you. You won't hear Him unless you slow down long enough to listen.

- We'll be looking at names of God from this one verse over the next few days. I'd encourage you to write it out and begin to memorize it.

**A Prayer for You:**

*Lord, thank You that You are my Song. Reveal Yourself to me more as my Song. I want to continually have Your Song in my heart. And I want to hear You singing over me.*

# My Salvation

## Yeshua (Hebrew)

*The Lord is my strength and my song; he has become **my salvation**.
He is my God, and I will praise him, my father's God, and I will exalt him.*
Exodus 15:2

**Steps on Your Journey to Know God More Intimately:**

- Remember, salvation in Hebrew is *Yeshua* meaning salvation, deliverance, victory, prosperity and welfare.

- *Yeshua* is Jesus' Hebrew and Aramaic name. Messianic Jews call Jesus *Yeshua* today.

- Consider the meanings of salvation. What does it mean to you that God is your Salvation?

- How does it affect you knowing that the word for salvation is Jesus' name? Is Jesus your Salvation?

**A Prayer for You:**

*Yeshua, thank You for being my salvation and for bringing me deliverance, victory, prosperity and welfare. You have done so much for me. Thank You. Open my eyes to see more clearly who You are and what You've done for me.*

## My God

*The Lord is my strength and my song; he has become my salvation.*
*He is **my God**, and I will praise him,*
*my father's God, and I will exalt him.*
Exodus 15:2

**Steps on Your Journey to Know God More Intimately:**

- This verse has so many names of God in it. I'm amazed how many can be fit into one little verse.

- This name, *El* in Hebrew, reveals the all-powerful God who is personal. He is not just the God of the Universe. He is also my personal God. He cares about me personally. And He cares about you personally.

- What does it mean to you that He is your God?

- How do those around you recognize that the Lord is your God?

- Spend some time talking to your God today, the God who loves you and cares about you.

**A Prayer for You:**

*My God, I'm so blessed to know that You care about me personally. I know I don't deserve to have You interested in me, but I'm grateful. Teach me more of what it means that You are my God. I want to learn to know You and worship You in greater ways.*

## My Father's God

*The Lord is my strength and my song; he has become my salvation.*
*He is my God, and I will praise him,*
**my father's God**, *and I will exalt him.*
Exodus 15:2

**Steps on Your Journey to Know God More Intimately:**

- The Hebrew for this name is *Ab Elohim*. *Ab* means father or ancestor. *Elohim* is the plural form of God.

- If your parents or other ancestors were believers, what does it mean to you that God is your Father's God? How does that affect you?

- Growing up as a missionary kid I watched God provide for my family. Whenever my sisters or I asked my parents for anything expensive, their response was, "Let's ask God." It was incredible how God provided for us, including giving us a very nice house to live in rent-free when we came back from Guatemala with no money. I have a great view of God because of my parents.

- What if you don't know anyone in your family who are or were believers? How can you relate to this name? Ask the Lord to show you. Is it possible you have ancestors in the past who you didn't know who knew God?

- Meditate on this name today. Ask the Lord what He wants you to see from it.

**A Prayer for You:**

*God, I want to praise You and exalt You because You are such a great God. You deserve praise and adoration, whether or not my parents are or were believers. I want future generations to be able to look back to me and praise You, because of my relationship with You.*

# Only True God

## Monos Alethinos Theos (Greek)

*Now this is eternal life: that they know you,
the **only true God**, and Jesus Christ, whom you have sent.*
John 17:3

**Steps on Your Journey to Know God More Intimately:**

- *Monos* means only or alone. *Alethinos* means true or truthful. *Theos* is God. Meditate on this name. What does it mean that God is the only true God?

- The word "true" in Greek means the real nature corresponding to the name. It includes everything about that person. It means real, genuine and sincere. It is the opposite of counterfeit, imaginary, simulated or pretend.

- Look at the above definitions. How do they add to your understanding of the Only True God?

- Aren't you grateful to know the Only True God? If you're not convinced that He really is Who He says He is, talk to Him. Ask Him to show you Himself. You are welcome to email me and we can dialog about Him with no pressure. Go to page 369.

**A Prayer for You:**

*God, I praise You for being the only true, genuine, sincere God. Thank You that I can depend on You and trust You. Show me more of Yourself so I can trust You more.*

## July 27

## *Jesus Christ, Whom You Have Sent*

*Now this is eternal life: that they know you, the only true God,
and **Jesus Christ, whom you have sent**.*
John 17:3

**Steps on Your Journey to Know God More Intimately:**

- Once again, this name "Jesus Christ," shows both His humanity (Jesus) and His deity (Christ).

- Meditate on this whole verse.

- Knowing the only true God and Jesus Christ is what gives us eternal life. Do you have eternal life? If not, what do you need to do? If so, thank the Lord for what He has done for you. If you're not sure, ask the Lord to show you. You can also contact me and we can dialog about the topic.

- Jesus was sent by the Father to earth. How does it affect your life knowing God sent Jesus to earth?

- Consider what your life would be like today if God had not sent Him.

**A Prayer for You:**

*Jesus Christ, I'm so grateful that God sent You to earth to bring me eternal life. Thank You for being willing to come. You didn't have to. You could have stayed in the peace and glory of Heaven. Instead You came because You loved me. Thank You.*

July 28

## Holy Father

*[Jesus said,] "I am coming to you. **Holy Father**,*
*protect them by the power of your name, the name you gave me,*
*so that they may be one as we are one."*
John 17:11

**Steps on Your Journey to Know God More Intimately:**

- In John 17:1, Jesus referred to God as Father. Here He adds that God is a Holy Father. God is not only a loving and kind Father to us, but He is also holy.

- The Greek word for holy, *hagios*, means sacred, pure, moral or blameless. Merriam-Webster defines holy as "exalted or worthy of complete devotion as one perfect in goodness and righteousness." *Pater* means Father.

- Meditate on this name. What does it mean to you that God is a Holy Father? He is Jesus' Holy Father, but He is also your Holy Father.

- Notice what Jesus was asking His Father to do — protect us by the power of His name. Think about that. What does it mean to you that God protects you by the power of His name?

- Jesus was also asking His Holy Father to make us one, as He is one with the Father. How are they one?

- How do you think God wants us to be one with other believers? What might that look like? Ask the Lord to show you.

**A Prayer for You:**

*Holy Father, I worship You because You are worthy of my complete devotion. You are pure, blameless and perfect, yet You are also my loving Father. Thank You. Teach me to know You and honor You more.*

210

# July 29

## *Trainer of Nations*

Yasar Goy (Hebrew)

*Do you think the **trainer of nations** doesn't correct,
the teacher of Adam doesn't know?*
Psalm 94:10 (MSG)

**Steps on Your Journey to Know God More Intimately:**

- *Yasar* means correct, chastise, instruct, train and punish. *Goy* means heathen, nation or Gentile.

- The New International Version translates this name, "he who disciplines nations."

- Contemplate this name. How does God train or discipline nations?

- How do you believe He is training or disciplining your nation now?

- How does this affect how you should pray for your nation?

- 2 Chronicles 7:14 says, "If my people, who are called by my name, will humble themselves and pray and seek my face and turn from their wicked ways, then I will hear from heaven and I will forgive their sin and will heal their land." What is God saying to you through this verse?

- Ask the Lord what He wants to say to you today through this name.

**A Prayer for You:**

*Trainer of Nations, I praise You that You are a big enough God to correct entire nations. Show me more of Your greatness. I pray for my nation that we will follow You and obey Your laws so You don't have to discipline us.*

# He Who Teaches Mankind

## Lamad Adam (Hebrew)

*Does he who disciplines nations not punish?*
*Does **he who teaches mankind** lack knowledge?*
Psalm 94:10

**Steps on Your Journey to Know God More Intimately:**

- *Lamad* means to teach, instruct or learn. *Adam* means man or human.

- How does God teach mankind? What does that look like?

- What has the Lord taught you?

- How would you answer the question, "Does he who teaches mankind lack knowledge?"

- I'm so glad that the Lord has unlimited knowledge and wisdom. I can go to Him anytime for anything. No question will ever be too hard for Him. I can never stump Him with anything I may ask.

- What do you want or need God to teach you? Ask Him. He loves to give wisdom and knowledge to those who ask Him sincerely (James 1:5-6).

**A Prayer for You:**

*Lord, thank You that You have the wisdom to teach me what I need to know. You have unlimited knowledge, so there isn't anything that You don't understand. Teach me what You know I need to learn. I want to be more teachable.*

# You Who Have Done Great Things

## Awsaw Gadol (Hebrew)

*Your righteousness, God, reaches the high heavens.*
**You who have done great things**, *O God, who is like you?*
Psalm 71:19 (ESV)

**Steps on Your Journey to Know God More Intimately:**

- *Awsaw* mean do or make. It is translated with numerous different words. *Gadol* means great, high or mighty.

- Just read the Bible and you will see so many of the amazingly great things God has done in the past. I want to encourage you to take time every day to read the Bible. That is the best way to get to know God better. He wants you to know Him and to have a relationship with Him, but you have to take the time to seek Him and get to know Him.

- What are some of the great things God did in the Bible?

- What great things has God done in your life?

- I encourage you to keep a record of what God has done and is doing in your life and in those around you. It's so easy for us to forget God's work in our lives. I wish I had been better at keeping a journal of all God has done. It is so encouraging for me to go back and see what God did in the past.

**A Prayer for You:**

*God, You have done great things in my life and in those around me. Thank You for all You have done and are doing. Help me to remember all the things You did in the past. I don't want to miss any of them.*

# August 1

## *Jehovah-Raah (or Rohi)*
### Lord Is My Shepherd

*The **Lord is my shepherd**, I shall not want. He makes me lie down in green pastures, he leads me beside still waters, he restores my soul. He guides me in paths of righteousness for his name's sake.*
Psalm 23:1-3 (ESV)

**Steps on Your Journey to Know God More Intimately:**

- Before we look at the Shepherd, let's look at sheep. Here are just a few of the traits of sheep: timid, fearful, easily panicked, dumb, stupid, gullible, and vulnerable to fear, frustration, pests and hunger. They have very little discernment in choosing food or water. They are totally dependent on the shepherd for every need. How are you like a sheep?

- The Lord is our Shepherd. In Psalm 23, He reveals how He shepherds us. Here are just a few: He meets all our needs (verse 1); He gives rest and refreshment (verse 2); He restores our souls when life brings us grief, worries and sorrows (verse 3). Read Psalm 23 looking for each way God shepherds us (I found at least six others!).

- In John 10, Jesus calls Himself our Shepherd, our Good Shepherd. Read John 10:1-18 to see our Shepherd in the New Testament.

- How is Jesus your Shepherd? What does that mean to you?

- When has He been a Shepherd to you?

- In what ways do you need the Lord to be your Shepherd today?

**A Prayer for You:**

*My Shepherd, Jehovah-Raah, I'm so grateful for all the ways You shepherd me. Thank You for meeting all my needs, guiding me, protecting me, giving me rest and refreshment and restoring my soul. I want to learn to listen to Your voice and follow You all the days of my life.*

# Brilliant Lord

Adon Adeer (Hebrew)

*God, **brilliant Lord**, yours is a household name.*
Psalm 8:1 (MSG)

**Steps on Your Journey to Know God More Intimately:**

- *Adon* means lord, sovereign or controller. It is a shortened form of *Adonai*. *Adeer* means excellent, glorious or famous.

- The New Living Translation says: "O Lord, our Lord, your majestic name fills the earth! Your glory is higher than the heavens."

- Ponder this name today. What is God saying to you through it?

- How is our God a Brilliant Lord? Ask Him to show you.

- How is His name majestic?

**A Prayer for You:**

*Brilliant Lord, Your name is so majestic. You are great and awesome. Your glory fills the earth and is higher than the heavens. Show me Your glory, Lord. I want to know You and Your greatness more.*

## August 3

### *Your Dwelling Place*

*Because you have made the Lord **your dwelling place**—*
*the Most High, who is my refuge no evil shall be allowed to befall you,*
*no plague come near your tent.*
Psalm 91:9-10 (ESV)

**Steps on Your Journey to Know God More Intimately:**

- *T*his name in Hebrew is *mawon,* meaning habitation, dwelling place or a retreat.

- The Message translates this name as, "Your Very Own Home."

- Meditate on this name today.

- In my earthly dwelling, I have safety, peace, happiness and security. What do you have in your earthly dwelling? If you don't have peace and security in your home, ask God to be your home and bring you safety and happiness.

- How have you experienced God as your home, your dwelling?

- What do these verses say you need to do?

- What is the promise, in these verses, *if* you make the Lord Your Dwelling Place?

- In what ways are you making the Lord Your Dwelling Place in your day-to-day life?

**A Prayer for You:**

*Lord, thank You for being my very own home. You are the place I can turn to for rest, peace, comfort and all that I need. Remind me to let You be the place I live. Thank You that when You are my Dwelling Place, that no evil will be able to affect me.*

## August 4

# God of My Life

El Hay (Hebrew)

*By day the Lord directs his love, at night his song is with me—*
*a prayer to the **God of my life**.*
Psalm 42:8

**Steps on Your Journey to Know God More Intimately:**

- *El* means God. *Hay* is translated live or life.

- Think about this name. In what ways is the Lord the God of your life?

- How do you show that He is? How do your family and friends know He is the God of your life?

- You can pray to the God of your life anytime. He is always there, always listening, always loving you and always interested in anything you have to say. How does this affect you?

- If you don't know what prayer is, it's just talking to God like a friend. Just imagine that He is sitting in a chair next to you, listening. Talk to Him just as you would any good friend (although if you're in the habit of swearing, you might not want to do that!) If you want to learn more about prayer, feel free to email me directly. Go to page 369.

- Ponder this name. What does it mean to you that God is the God of your life?

- This verse says God's song is a prayer to Him. I find myself singing throughout the day and night. The songs keep me constantly connected to God.

**A Prayer for You:**

*God of My Life, I praise You that, as this verse says, You direct Your love toward me and give me Your song at night. I want to learn to let You be the God of My Life. Teach me, Lord.*

# Fountain of Life

## Makor Hay (Hebrew)

*For you are the **fountain of life**, the light by which we see.*
Psalm 36:9 (NLT)

**Steps on Your Journey to Know God More Intimately:**

- *Makor* is a fountain or a spring. *Hay* is life.

- Think about this name. Close your eyes and imagine God as a fountain of life and "cascading light" (MSG). What do you see? Talk to the Lord about what you see.

- Think about a fountain. What is it like?

- What is the difference between a pool and fountain? What difference might that make in this name?

- How is God like a fountain to you?

- In John 10:10, Jesus says, "The thief comes only to steal and kill and destroy; I have come that they may have life, and have it to the full." Think about that. Jesus came to bring us a full, abundant life.

- What does it mean to you that He is your fountain of life?

**A Prayer for You:**

*Fountain of Life, thank You that You are an ever-fresh source of life for me. Show me how You are my Fountain of Life and how I can discover more abundant life in You today.*

# August 6

## Light by Which We See

Or Rawa (Hebrew)

*For you are the fountain of life, the **light by which we see**.*
Psalm 36:9 (NLT)

**Steps on Your Journey to Know God More Intimately:**

- *Or* is light. *Rawa* means see, look or behold.

- Jesus referred to Himself as the Light three times in John 12:35-36.

- In John 8:12, Jesus said, "I am the light of the world. Whoever follows me will never walk in darkness, but will have the light of life."

- Meditate on God being the Light.

- How has He been your Light?

- In what ways do you need Jesus to be your Light right now?

- We live in a very dark world and need Jesus to be our Light. I go to a cabin in the mountains miles from any town. One night when I was there recently, it was pitch black outside. I couldn't see anything. Then the next night, the almost full moon came up and I could see the lake, trees and mountain clearly. Jesus is like the light of the moon in my life.

- Psalm 36:9 adds "by which we see." This makes His Light more personal. He's not just a light that is out there in the world, but also one that affects you and me. How does the Light affect your life?

**A Prayer for You:**

*Lord, thank You that You are the Light by which I can see. You make everything clear because of Your Light. I'm so glad I don't have to walk in darkness anymore. Lord, please be my Light, lighting each step of my way.*

# God My Stronghold

## Elohim Maoz (Hebrew)

*You are **God my stronghold**. Why have you rejected me?*
*Why must I go about mourning, oppressed by the enemy?*
Psalm 43:2

**Steps on Your Journey to Know God More Intimately:**

- The Hebrew word for stronghold, *maoz*, means place or means of safety, protection and refuge. Merriam-Webster defines stronghold as a fortified place; a place of security or survival. In the Old Testament, a stronghold was a fortified dwelling used as a means of protection from an enemy.

- Some Bible versions translate this "the God in whom I take refuge," or "the God of my strength."

- As you look at these definitions and translations, what does it mean to you that God is your stronghold? How has He provided security and protection for you?

- In this verse, David asked why God had rejected him. Do you ever feel like God has rejected you?

- Even though God does not reject us, sometimes it feels like it. You can tell God how you're feeling. He knows anyway and it just helps you to be able to express it.

**A Prayer for You:**

*God, thank You for being my Stronghold, my place of safety, my protection and my refuge. It is so encouraging to know I am safe when I am with You. When I feel like You have rejected me, show me once again how much You love me and how You protect me.*

# Earth-Tamer

*All your salvation wonders are on display in your trophy room.*
***Earth-Tamer**, Ocean-Pourer, Mountain-Maker, Hill-Dresser.*
Psalm 65:5-6 (MSG)

**Steps on Your Journey to Know God More Intimately:**

- For the next few days, we'll be looking at the names in this verse from the Message.

- Meditate on this name: Earth-Tamer.

- How does God tame the earth?

- What difference does it make to you that God is the Earth-Tamer?

- How can you praise God today with this name?

**A Prayer for You:**

*Earth-Tamer, I praise You because You are the God who is over all the earth. Since You have the power to tame the earth, I know You have the power to handle anything and everything that comes into my life. Thank You.*

## August 9

### *Ocean-Pourer*

*All your salvation wonders are on display in your trophy room.*
*Earth-Tamer, **Ocean-Pourer**, Mountain-Maker, Hill-Dresser.*
Psalm 65:5-6 (MSG)

**Steps on Your Journey to Know God More Intimately:**

- I was recently in California and had an opportunity to spend time by the ocean. It is so vast, majestic and powerful. It reminds me of the Ocean-Pourer. Wouldn't it have been fun to watch Him pour it?

- Think about this name. How did He pour the oceans? I can just see the Lord holding a pitcher of water, pouring it into the oceans. The pitcher doesn't look that big in the Lord's hands, because He is so huge. Talk to the Lord about what this might have looked like.

- What does it mean that God is the Ocean-Pourer?

- How does this name affect your life today?

**A Prayer for You:**

*Ocean-Pourer, You are so majestic, vast and awesome. Thank You for pouring the oceans so we can enjoy them. Reveal to me more of Yourself through this name today.*

## August 10

### Mountain-Maker

*All your salvation wonders are on display in your trophy room.*
*Earth-Tamer, Ocean-Pourer, **Mountain-Maker**, Hill-Dresser.*
Psalm 65:5-6 (MSG)

**Steps on Your Journey to Know God More Intimately:**

- I can see the 14,115-foot Pikes Peak mountain out my window every day. I'm reminded what an amazingly great God we have. Even though I can see the whole mountain range (and I live at almost 7000 feet), one of my favorite things to do is to go up into the mountains. There is so much peace surrounded by the majestic mountains.

- Think about what mountains are like. Each one is different, unique. Some are rocky (like the Rocky Mountains, where I live). Others have lush, grassy slopes. The lower parts of the mountains have trees and other vegetation, while above 11,000 feet (at least in Colorado) there are no trees. Our God didn't just make one mold for a mountain so they were all the same. He is so creative.

- I'm thankful for God's creativity in making the mountains. How about you?

**A Prayer for You:**

*Mountain-Maker, I praise You for Your creativity as You made the mountains. You could have made them all the same—or just made things flat—but You didn't. I want to know You more. Open my eyes to see You all around me (even if I don't live where there are mountains).*

## August 11

### Hill-Dresser

*All your salvation wonders are on display in your trophy room.*
*Earth-Tamer, Ocean-Pourer, Mountain-Maker, **Hill-Dresser**.*
Psalm 65:5-6 (MSG)

**Steps on Your Journey to Know God More Intimately:**

- How does the Lord dress the hills? I recently went for hikes with my sister in the mountains of California. It was remarkable all the beautiful variations of flowers, trees and plants. Our God is the One who creates all of those.

- Close your eyes and imagine God dressing the hills. He didn't have to make hills, or He could have made them all the same. Instead, He clothed them with all kinds of trees, rocks, shrubs, etc.

- Each season of the year, God dresses the hills differently. In the spring, they are clothed with new green growth on the trees and plants. In the summer, the colorful wild flowers decorate the hills. In the fall, the brilliant colors of the trees show off God's glory. In the winter, the dazzling white snow blankets everything. In each season, we can see God's creativity.

- Thank the Lord that He is the Hill-Dresser—even if you can't see any hills where you live. He is the One who creates beauty. Thank Him for whatever beauty you see around you.

**A Prayer for You:**

*Hill-Dresser, thank You for creating beauty all around me, whether or not I can see any hills. Help me to learn to recognize You and Your beauty wherever I am.*

# Lord Most High

Yahweh Elyon (Hebrew)

*For the **Lord Most High** is awesome,
the great King over all the earth.*
Psalm 47.2

**Steps on Your Journey to Know God More Intimately:**

- Remember *Yahweh* is the sacred name of God. *Yahweh* means the Covenant-keeping God, the Unchangeable and Intimate God.

- *Elyon* means high, Most High, supreme and uppermost.

- Think about the meanings for the two parts to this name. Ask the Lord to reveal more of Himself to you through them. He loves it when we genuinely seek Him.

- What does it mean to you that God is the Lord Most High?

- How does this name affect your life?

- Notice what this verse says about the Lord. He is awesome. In what ways have you seen that He is awesome?

**A Prayer for You:**

*Lord Most High, I praise and worship You, because You are so awesome. Thank You for being the Covenant-keeping God. Thank You for being an intimate, personal God even though You are the supreme, Most High God.*

# Great King of All the Earth

### Gadol Melek Erets (Hebrew)

*For the Lord Most High is awesome.*
*He is the **great King of all the earth**.*
Psalm 47:2 (NLT)

**Steps on Your Journey to Know God More Intimately:**

- *Gadol* is great or high. *Melek* is king and *erets* means land, earth or country.

- Yesterday we looked at the first part of this verse. Meditate on the Great King of All the Earth.

- Imagine one King over the entire earth. What might that look like?

- How does God act as a King?

- How should we respond to the Great King?

- Do you need to change anything in your life to treat God as the Great King?

- Worship your King today.

**A Prayer for You:**

*Great King of all the Earth, I bow down and worship You today. You are worthy of my worship and honor, because You are in the highest position there is on earth. Forgive me for all the times I fail to recognize You and treat You as my King.*

# He Who Weighs the Heart

*If you say, "But we knew nothing about this,"*
*does not **he who weighs the heart** perceive it?*
*Does not he who guards your life know it?*
*Will he not repay each person according to what he has done?*
Proverbs 24:12

**Steps on Your Journey to Know God More Intimately:**

- *Takan* in Hebrew means weigh, ponder and equal. *Liba* means heart.

- The New Living Translation says it a little differently, "For God understands all hearts, and he sees you."

- What if you were always conscious of the reality that God knows every thought, every feeling, every attitude and every motivation of your heart? And He sees everything you do. How would this knowledge affect how you live?

- This name can either be encouraging, because God cares enough about you to know you. Or it could be frightening, if there are things you don't want anyone to know. Meditate on this name. What does it mean to you today knowing that God weighs your heart?

- Talk to the Lord about how you're feeling about this name.

- Remind yourself of this awesome truth.

**A Prayer for You:**

*Lord, thank You for weighing my heart. I'm glad that You know me and You see me. Help me to always live my life in such a way that I won't be ashamed, knowing You see me.*

# He Who Guards Your Life

*If you say, "But we knew nothing about this,"*
*does not he who weighs the heart perceive it?*
*Does not **he who guards your life** know it?*
*Will he not repay each person according to what he has done?*
Proverbs 24:12

**Steps on Your Journey to Know God More Intimately:**

- In Hebrew this name is *Natsar,* meaning keep, preserve and guard. *Nephesh* means soul, life or person.

- Imagine God being like your personal bodyguard. What does a bodyguard do? What would it be like to have someone who is always with you, guarding your life?

- Think about how God guards your life.

- I find immense comfort in knowing that God not only guards my physical life on earth, but He is guarding my eternal life until Jesus returns.

- Ask the Lord to show you more of what He wants you to know about Himself through this name today.

**A Prayer for You:**

*Thank You, Lord, that You guard my body, soul and spirit, both now and throughout all eternity. I am so glad I can trust You and depend on You, because You will never change. Remind me that You are always with me, guarding and protecting me.*

## August 16

# God of Glory

Theos Doxa (Greek)

*The **God of glory** appeared to our father Abraham*
*while he was still in Mesopotamia, before he lived in Harran.*
Acts 7:2

**Steps on Your Journey to Know God More Intimately:**

- *Theos* means God. *Doxa* means glory or glorious.

- Psalm 29:3 says, "The voice of the Lord is over the waters; the God of glory thunders, the Lord thunders over the mighty waters."

- As I've been asking God to show me His glory, He keeps showing me His glory through nature. His glory is all around us.

- Last night I took my grand-dog (my son Jonathan's dog) for a walk. As I left, it started to rain. I almost went back inside, but figured I probably wouldn't melt in the rain. As I turned the corner at the end of my street, I could see a tiny piece of a very faint rainbow. As I kept walking, it got brighter and brighter and then became a double rainbow—absolutely brilliant. Its beauty was overwhelming. I started laughing because God was reminding me of His glory. He was also reminding me of some of His promises to me. I felt like the God of Glory reached down and kissed me, showing me His great love once again.

- Contemplate the God of Glory. Ask God to reveal more of Himself to you today through this name.

- I pray that you also will see God's glory in new ways. Ask the Lord to reveal it to you. And don't forget to watch for it. It's all around you! I guarantee you'll be blessed.

**A Prayer for You:**

*God of Glory, You are so beautiful, so glorious. I love watching You show off Your glory in nature. Open my eyes to see more of Your glory around me. I don't want to stay focused on just my own life.*

229

# The Lord Will Provide

*Abraham looked up and there in a thicket he saw a ram caught by its horns.*
*He sacrificed it as a burnt offering instead of his son.*
*So Abraham called that place **The Lord Will Provide**.*
*To this day it is said, "On the mountain of the Lord it will be provided."*
*Genesis 22:13-14*

**Steps on Your Journey to Know God More Intimately:**

- *Jehovah-Jireh* means *Yahweh* sees or God provides. God revealed Himself as *Jehovah-Jireh* to Abraham when He was in a very tough spot. God had asked Him to sacrifice his only son, Issac. At the very last minute God provided a ram to be sacrificed instead. Read Genesis 22 to learn more.

- I love this name. God is our provider, providing for our all our needs. But sometimes we get our "needs" and "wants" confused. He always provides for our needs and He often provides for our wants—but not always.

- As a missionary, I live on what people donate to the ministry. It's been fun to watch God provide for all my needs, sometimes in very unexpected ways. I choose to trust *Jehovah-Jireh*, regardless of how He chooses to provide.

- What unmet needs do you have today? Ask *Jehovah-Jireh* to provide them, in His time and way.

- Thank God for all the ways He has provided for you. Sometimes it's easy to focus on what we don't have, rather than on what we do have.

**A Prayer for You:**

*Jehovah-Jireh, thank You for being my provider throughout my life. Just as You have provided in the past, I choose to trust you to provide for all my and my family's needs in the future.*

## God of Love

*Finally, brothers, rejoice. Aim for restoration, comfort one another,
agree with one another, live in peace;
and the **God of love** and peace will be with you.*
2 Corinthians 13:11 (ESV)

**Steps on Your Journey to Know God More Intimately:**

- Psalm 111:4 says, "This God of Grace, this God of Love" (MSG).

- God's love for us is unconditional—not based on who we are or what we've done. It's unfailing, never ending.

- I've been so blessed recently as I'm been focusing on God's love, asking Him to reveal more of His love to me. I'm learning so much and I'm excited about all God is showing me. I've been meditating on Ephesians 3:14-21 almost every day for the past few months. I'm amazed at all the new insights the Lord keeps giving me into His love. I'd encourage you to commit to read and meditate on that passage every day for a minimum of a month. You'll be so blessed.

- Ask the Lord to reveal to you how much He loves you. The more I'm learning, the more I'm convinced that we only understand a tiny bit of how much our God loves us.

- How have you experienced God's love for you? If you are having trouble seeing His love, look around you at the things and people in your life. And don't forget what He did for you on the cross!

**A Prayer for You:**

*God of Love, I praise You for Your perfect, unconditional love for me. Thank You that Your love for me will never end. I'm so glad I can depend on it. Help me to learn to see Your love around me, recognizing it comes from You.*

## God Our Strength

Elohim Oze (Hebrew)

*Sing for joy to **God our strength**; shout aloud to the God of Jacob!*
Psalm 81:1

**Steps on Your Journey to Know God More Intimately:**

- *Elohim* means God. *Oze* means strength or strong.

- When I am weak, it's so comforting to know that God is my strength. He has superhuman strength—much better than the strongest person in the world. I often lean on Him for His strength. I'm learning to *always* lean on Him. And I trust you are too.

- Isaiah 40:29-31 talks about God giving us strength. Meditate on what the Lord does for us: "He gives strength to the weary and increases the power of the weak. Even youths grow tired and weary, and young men stumble and fall; but those who hope in the Lord will renew their strength. They will soar on wings like eagles; they will run and not grow weary, they will walk and not be faint."

- In what areas do you need strength? Ask God to be your strength.

- Isaiah 40 tells us that "those who hope in the Lord will renew their strength." The word hope means to wait, expect and look for. What does this say to you today?

- Thank God that He is your strength. Lean on Him. He's strong enough and big enough for whatever you are facing. As you lean on Him, He will increase your strength.

**A Prayer for You:**

*God My Strength, thank You that You both give me strength and You are my strength. Thank You that You are always there to lean on, regardless of what I face. Remind me to lean on You rather than on my own limited strength.*

August 20

*God of Jacob*

*Blessed is he whose help is the **God of Jacob**,*
*whose hope is in the Lord his God.*
Psalm 146:5 (ESV)

**Steps on Your Journey to Know God More Intimately:**

- Jacob was Isaac's son and Abraham's grandson. You can read about Jacob's life starting in Genesis 25. Abraham, Isaac and Jacob were Israel's patriarchs. It's like saying that God is the God of *your* ancestors, assuming they acknowledged Him.

- The God of Jacob is the God of the Universe. He is the holy God who loves you.

- This verse says that we are blessed if our help is the God of Jacob, if our hope is in the Lord our God. This word for hope means expectation. It is not dreaming, as we often use the word hope. Consider what it means to put your hope in the Lord.

- How has God been your helper? Think about that. If you're not sure, ask Him.

- How would you like Him to be your help? Ask Him. He loves to answer our prayers.

**A Prayer for You:**

*God of Jacob, I praise You for being my helper and for giving me hope. Teach me how to put my hope in You. Show me how this name applies to me today. I want to know You more in new ways.*

# High and Exalted One

*For this is what the **high and exalted One** says—he who lives forever,*
*whose name is holy: "I live in a high and holy place,*
*but also with him who is contrite and lowly in spirit,*
*to revive the spirit of the lowly and to revive the heart of the contrite."*
Isaiah 57:15

**Steps on Your Journey to Know God More Intimately:**

- Other translations of this name say the High and Lofty One, the One who is high and lifted up, and the high and towering God. The Hebrew word for exalted is *nasa*, meaning to lift, exalt and carry along.

- Meditate on this name today. Ask the Lord to show you what it means and how you can use it to worship Him.

- In our culture, it's tempting to think of God as our buddy, "the man upstairs" or other such trite ideas. Worship Him as not only your Daddy, but also as the High and Exalted One—infinitely worthy of your humble praise and adoration.

- Ask the Lord to show you if you have lowered Him to someone less than He is—the High and Exalted One. If you have, tell God, then ask Him to help you see Him as He really is and treat Him with utmost respect.

- Notice what the rest of this verse says. Look where God lives and what He does there. Meditate on this and talk to Him about it.

**A Prayer for You:**

*High and Exalted One, I worship and honor You. You are worthy of my complete respect, because You are so great. You are lifted up above everything. Thank You that You not only live in a high and holy place, but You also live with me, when I have a contrite, humble heart.*

# He Who Lives Forever

*For this is what the high and Exalted One says—*
**he who lives forever**, *whose name is holy: "I live in a high and holy place,*
*but also with him who is contrite and lowly in spirit, to revive the spirit of*
*the lowly and to revive the heart of the contrite."*
Isaiah 57:15

**Steps on Your Journey to Know God More Intimately:**

- Another translation of this name is He Who Inhabits Eternity.

- Consider both versions of this name. Ask the Lord to reveal to you what He wants you to see from this name for your life.

- I'm so often amazed at how God shows me different things about Himself, based on what I'm going through at the time. He is a personal God, who wants to meet us right where we are! How does that affect you today?

- What does it mean to you that God lives forever or that God inhabits eternity? Think about it.

- How does this name change your perspective of your life?

**A Prayer for You:**

*Lord, I'm so grateful that You live forever. You have always been and You will constantly be alive. Thank You that I can trust You to be there for me forever. You're never going away. Thank You.*

## Holy

*For thus says the One who is high and lifted up, who inhabits eternity,*
*whose name is **Holy**: "I dwell in the high and holy place,*
*and also with him who is of a contrite and lowly spirit,*
*to revive the spirit of the lowly, and to revive the heart of the contrite."*
Isaiah 57:15 (ESV)

**Steps on Your Journey to Know God More Intimately:**

- This verse says God's name is Holy, *kadosh* in Hebrew. In the Bible, a person's name represents everything the person is.

- *Kadosh* means pure, devoted, sacred, exalted or worthy of complete devotion. Think about God as Holy.

- 1 Peter 1:15 says, "As he who called you is holy, you also be holy in all your conduct." If you really realized He is completely holy, how might that impact your daily life? Is there anything you need to change?

- Spend some talking to the One whose name is Holy.

- Ask the Lord what He has to say to you today (see the rest of Isaiah 57:15).

**A Prayer for You:**

*Holy One, I worship and adore You. You are worthy of my complete devotion. Thank You that although You are Holy and You live in a high and holy place, You also live with me, when I have a humble, contrite heart. Open my ears to hear what You want to say to me.*

# August 24

## *Rock Eternal*

Olam Tsur (Hebrew)

*Trust in the Lord forever, for the Lord,*
*the Lord, is the **Rock eternal**.*
Isaiah 26:4

**Steps on Your Journey to Know God More Intimately:**

- *Olam* means ever, everlasting, perpetual and evermore. *Tsur* means rock, boulder, strength and strong.

- This name is translated in the following ways: Everlasting Rock, Eternal Rock, Everlasting Strength and Rock of Ages.

- Think about the properties of a rock. It's hard, durable, and not changed by wind, rain or anything else. How else would you describe a rock?

- Now think about the most massive rock you have ever seen or heard about. Then imagine it much bigger. Our Lord is a solid rock, unchangeable. How is God like a rock?

- *Vines Complete Expository Dictionary* says "the 'rock' serves as a figure of security." It also says, "'Rock' is frequently used to picture God's support and defense of His people (Deuteronomy 32:15)." What does this mean to you?

- He is the Rock *Eternal*. He will always be the same. He'll never, ever change. I'm so grateful for that. Forever He will be a solid rock on which you can depend.

- Thank the Lord for being your Rock Eternal.

**A Prayer for You:**

*Rock Eternal, I bless You and praise You for being such a strong rock that will never be destroyed or change. Thank You that You are the One I can depend on in every area of my life.*

## Sovereign Lord

*So this is what the **Sovereign Lord** says: "See, I lay a stone in Zion,
a tested stone, a precious cornerstone for a sure foundation;
the one who trusts will never be dismayed."*
Isaiah 28:16

**Steps on Your Journey to Know God More Intimately:**

- For the next few days, we'll be looking at God's names in this one verse. I want to encourage you to write it out and begin to memorize it. Isaiah 28:16 is quoted in 1 Peter 2:6, referring to Jesus.

- Acts 4:24 says, "And when they heard it, they lifted their voices together to God and said, 'Sovereign Lord, who made the heaven and the earth and the sea and everything in them'" (ESV).

- Merriam-Webster defines sovereign as one possessing supreme, political power; one who exercises supreme authority; an acknowledged leader.

- Meditate on God's name, the Sovereign Lord. Ask Him to reveal to you what that means. Praise Him and thank Him for what He shows you.

- In what areas of your life have you not allowed God to exercise His authority?

- Look at what these verses say the Sovereign Lord did. How do you respond to what He did?

**A Prayer for You:**

*Sovereign Lord, You are my leader. You have supreme authority over the entire universe. I want to give You supreme authority in my life. You deserve it, because of Who You are and what You've done.*

## Tested Stone

*Therefore thus says the Lord God, "Behold, I am laying in Zion a stone,
**a tested stone**, a costly cornerstone for the foundation, firmly placed.
He who believes in it will not be disturbed."*
Isaiah 28:16 (NAS)

**Steps on Your Journey to Know God More Intimately:**

- *Bokhan* in Hebrew means tried or tested. *Eben* means stone or a weight.

- This verse is quoted in 1 Peter 2:6 referring to the Messiah, Jesus: "Behold, I am laying in Zion a stone, a cornerstone chosen and precious, and whoever believes in him will not be put to shame" (ESV).

- Why would the Messiah be called a stone?

- What does it mean that the Lord is a *tested* stone? Think about how Jesus was tested when He was here on earth. Thank the Lord for all He went through for you.

- Meditate on this verse and ask the Lord to reveal to you what it means. Then use these names to worship Him.

**A Prayer for You:**

*Father God, thank You that You were willing to send Jesus to earth to be a Stone, a Tested Stone. You knew all He would go through. Jesus, thank You that You were willing to come to earth, knowing You would endure severe testing.*

## August 27

### *Precious Cornerstone*

*So this is what the Sovereign Lord says: "See, I lay a stone in Zion,
a tested stone, a **precious cornerstone** for a sure foundation;
the one who trusts will never be dismayed."*
Isaiah 28:16

**Steps on Your Journey to Know God More Intimately:**

- This name in Hebrew is *Yaqar Pinna Yasad*. *Yaqar* means precious or costly. *Pinna* means corner or chief. *Yasad* means foundation.

- This verse refers to Jesus (See 1 Peter 2:6). Think about how He is precious to you. You might want to write out what the Lord is showing you or share it with someone else.

- A cornerstone is the most important stone in the foundation of a building. The entire house rests on this stone. Consider how Jesus is a precious cornerstone.

- When I was thirteen, I was so excited about getting to know God. I would spend two to three hours a day in the Word. I went to church almost every night. I would have gone every night, but my parents said I could only go five nights a week, until I was old enough to drive. During those years, I was building a firm foundation on the cornerstone of my life.

- How is Jesus the Cornerstone in your life?

- Have you built your life on Jesus as the Cornerstone? If not, what might you need to change?

**A Prayer for You:**

*Precious Cornerstone, thank You for making my foundation so secure. I know it will never shake or crumble no matter what storms or earthquakes may hit it. Help me to remember to never seek another human on whom to build my life. No one will ever be as secure as You are.*

## Sure Foundation

*So this is what the Sovereign Lord says: "See, I lay a stone in Zion,
a tested stone, a precious cornerstone for a **sure foundation;**
the one who trusts will never be dismayed."*
Isaiah 28:16

**Steps on Your Journey to Know God More Intimately:**

- *Yasad* in Hebrew means to set, to found and settle. *Musad* means foundation.

- 1 Corinthians 3:11 says, "For no one can lay any foundation other than the one already laid, which is Jesus Christ."

- Jesus is the foundation of our lives. Think about the foundation of your house. What if it was not solid? How safe would you feel?

- I bought a house recently that had major foundation problems. It cost a lot of money to get them fixed. If you have not founded your life on the Lord Jesus Christ, your foundation may have some major cracks. When the winds of hardship hit your life, you need that foundation to be able to stand firm. Unlike my having to fix the foundation on the house I bought, when you trust in the Lord, He will give you a whole new foundation on which you can build your life.

- Jesus is the best foundation you could ever want for your life. How has He been your Sure Foundation?

- I'm grateful that no matter what problems I face, the Lord is always there holding my life together, giving me a firm foundation.

- Jesus is a Sure Foundation, solid and unchanging. You can depend on Him never to change. Praise Him that He is your Foundation.

**A Prayer for You:**

*Lord, I'm so grateful that You are my Sure Foundation. You are the One on whom I can build my life. You are the One who will never change. You'll never shift. Thank You that when I believe in You, I am unshakable as Isaiah 28 says. Why would I ever want to move away from You?*

## August 29

### *Your Maker*

*For **your Maker** is your husband—*
*the Lord Almighty is his name—*
*the Holy One of Israel is your Redeemer;*
*he is called the God of all the earth.*
Isaiah 54:5

**Steps on Your Journey to Know God More Intimately:**

- *Asa* in Hebrew means to create, to do, to make and to accomplish.

- We'll be looking at this verse again tomorrow I'd encourage you to write it out, meditate on it and memorize it.

- Meditate on this name. Since God created you, then He knows you—better than you even know yourself. If He knows you, then He knows what you need and want. How encouraging that is!

- What does it mean to you that God is your Maker? Talk to Him about this name.

- If there is any way God made you that you don't like, consider confessing your feelings to God. Then begin thanking Him for that very thing.

**A Prayer for You:**

*Thank You, Lord, that You made me just the way I am. Thank You that because You created me, You know all about my needs, wants, hopes and dreams, and You care enough to take care of me.*

242

## August 30

## *Your Husband*

*For your Maker is **your husband**—*
*the Lord Almighty is his name—*
*the Holy One of Israel is your Redeemer;*
*he is called the God of all the earth.*
Isaiah 54:5

**Steps on Your Journey to Know God More Intimately:**

- *Baal* in Hebrew means marry or husband.

- Think about this: the One who created you, made you, is your husband. If He created you, then He knows you—better than you even know yourself. Imagine a Husband who knows you better than you know yourself. He knows what you need or want before you even mention it. God is a perfect Husband, the best one you could ever find. It might be easier for those of us who are single to see God as a husband. However, regardless of whether you are married or not, God still wants to be your Husband.

- Meditate on this name. How has God been your Husband?

- How would you like Him to be a Husband to you?

- What does it mean to you today that God is your Husband? Ask Him to reveal more about what that means.

**A Prayer for You:**

*Lord, thank You that You are my Husband. You love me as Your lover and Your bride. Thank You for being my protector, provider, best friend and so much more. When I desire a human to fill my needs, remind me that You are the best Husband I could ever want.*

# He Who Created the Heavens

*For this is what the Lord says—**he who created the heavens**, he is God;*
*he who fashioned and made the earth, he founded it;*
*he did not create it to be empty, but formed it to be inhabited—*
*he says: "I am the Lord, and there is no other."*
Isaiah 45:18

**Steps on Your Journey to Know God More Intimately:**

- This name is *Yahweh Bara Shamayim* in Hebrew. *Yahweh* means Lord, God or Jehovah. *Bara* means create or creator. *Shamayim* means Heaven or air.

- Our God is the One Who Created the Heavens. When we look up into the sky, we can only see a tiny portion of the heavens. Even powerful telescopes can only see a minuscule part of what God created.

- Louis Giglio has an incredible way of showing how great our God is, by looking at stars. If you haven't already seen it, I encourage you to watch his "How Great is Our God" DVD. It is totally amazing. After watching this video, my view of God changed dramatically.

- Think about this name. What is God showing you through it?

**A Prayer for You:**

*Lord, I praise You for Your greatness, power and creativity in creating the heavens. Teach me to know You more and enjoy what You created.*

# He Who Fashioned and Made the Earth

*For this is what the Lord says—he who created the heavens, he is God;*
***he who fashioned and made the earth**, he founded it;*
*he did not create it to be empty, but formed it to be inhabited—*
*he says: "I am the Lord, and there is no other."*
Isaiah 45:18

**Steps on Your Journey to Know God More Intimately:**

- Today, pay special attention to different aspects of God's earth, whether it is majestic mountains, tall trees, a placid lake, a churning ocean or a delicate flower.

- Think about this: God could have made everything in black and white. But He didn't. He could have made only one type of tree, one type of plant and everything flat. But He didn't! He could have made everything with no smell and no texture. But He didn't! He could have made only one taste. I'm so grateful everything doesn't taste like Ranch dressing, though its creators have tried to introduce it into everything. He created the earth for our enjoyment and I believe, for His as well.

- What parts of the earth do you most enjoy? Thank Him.

**A Prayer for You:**

*Thank You, Father, that You fashioned and made the earth. You created so much beauty for us to enjoy. Help me to notice Your creation more and always let it remind me of You.*

## Apostle

### Apostolos (Greek)

*Therefore, holy brothers, who share in the heavenly calling,*
*fix your thoughts on Jesus, the **apostle** and high priest whom we confess.*
Hebrews 3:1

**Steps on Your Journey to Know God More Intimately:**

- An apostle is a messenger, an ambassador or one sent on a mission. How does this name describe Jesus? How was He an apostle?

- This verse tells us to fix our thoughts on Jesus. I believe this little phrase is one of the main keys to our entire lives. No matter what is going on, if we choose to focus on Jesus, we will find joy and peace. And, an amazing thing happens: no matter how big our problems may seem, when we focus on Jesus (really focus on Him, not just talking about doing it), our problems begin to shrink in comparison. I did this when my second son, Daniel, was dying. I experienced so much joy and peace when I focused on the Lord, but so much discouragement and depression when I focused on my problems.[1]

- Take some time right now to focus on Jesus, your ambassador, the one who represents you before the Father. Ask the Lord what He wants to show you today.

**A Prayer for You:**

*Jesus, I praise You that You are the Apostle, the One who came to earth on a mission from the Father. I want to keep my eyes focused on You, but I need Your help, because it is rarely easy.*

## September 3

# *High Priest*

### Archiereus (Greek)

*Therefore, holy brothers, who share in the heavenly calling,*
*fix your thoughts on Jesus, the apostle and **high priest** whom we confess.*
Hebrews 3:1

**Steps on Your Journey to Know God More Intimately:**

- *Archiereus* means chief priest or high priest.

- High priests were over the other priests. They were the only ones who could go directly into the Holy of Holies, where God was. They represented the people before God. Once a year on the Day of Atonement, the high priest entered the Holy of Holies and offered sacrifices for his own sins and the sins of the people. Jesus offered His own life as a sacrifice, once and for all, to save everyone from their sins.

- Hebrews 2:17 says, "For this reason he had to be made like his brothers in every way, in order that he might become a merciful and faithful high priest in service to God, and that he might make atonement for the sins of the people." What does this verse add about our high priest?

- Think about how Jesus is your high priest. Thank Him for what He does for you.

**A Prayer for You:**

*Jesus, I'm so grateful that You were willing to come to earth as my High Priest. You not only offered the sacrifice for my sins, You offered Yourself as the sacrifice. Thank You so much. I choose to keep my thoughts fixed on You.*

# Your High God

*Step out of the traffic! Take a long,*
*loving look at me, **your High God**,*
*above politics, above everything.*
Psalm 46:10 (MSG)

**Steps on Your Journey to Know God More Intimately:**

- The New Living Translation translates this verse: "Be still, and know that I am God! I will be honored by every nation. I will be honored throughout the world."

- Think about this name. What does it mean to you that God is your High God?

- God is above everything and will be honored by every nation. Do you honor Him as your High God? If not, what may you need to change?

- How does—or can—this name affect your life?

- The beginning of this verse tells us to take a long, loving look at the Lord, or to be still and know He is God. Think about this. Take some time today to look lovingly at Your High God.

**A Prayer for You:**

*Lord, You are the High God above everything and everyone. You are worthy of honor and praise. I choose to take a long loving look at You, remembering who You are. I love You, Lord, and want to continue to grow in my love for You.*

# Our God Forever and Ever

## Elohim Olam Ad (Hebrew)

*For this is God, **our God forever and ever**;*
*he will be our guide even to death.*
Psalm 48:14 (NKJV)

**Steps on Your Journey to Know God More Intimately:**

- Consider this name today.

- The Hebrew word for God here is *Elohim*, meaning the Almighty God, the Creator. This word for God is plural, hinting at the Godhead: the Father, Son and Holy Spirit. *Olam* is everlasting. *Ad* is ever or everlasting.

- How long does it say God will be your God? Think about how long that is. He could have just said forever, but He added "and ever" to emphasize that He will never, ever stop being your God.

- What does it mean to you that God is your personal God forever and ever? How does that affect your life?

- He can also be the God of your marriage and family. My parents had Psalm 48:14 engraved in their wedding rings. It has guided their marriage.

- Talk to God about this name. Ask Him to show you more of what it means to you.

**A Prayer for You:**

*God, I'm so grateful that You are my God, You are my family's God, and not just for today. You are our God forever and ever. I don't have to worry or wonder if You are going to leave me because I sin. Thank You that You'll never stop being my God.*

September 6

## *Our Guide*

Nahag (Hebrew)

*For this God is our God for ever and ever;*
*he will be **our guide** even to the end.*
Psalm 48:14

**Steps on Your Journey to Know God More Intimately:**

- *Nahag* means to lead, guide, drive forth and proceed.

- Meditate on this name.

- How has God been your Guide?

- In what areas do you need Him to be your Guide today?

- This verse says He will be your Guide even to the end. Think about that. You will never, ever be alone. He will always be there with you, guiding you in the way you are to go.

- He is your Guide, but you have a choice whether or not to follow His leading. Have you been following Him? If not, what might you need to change?

- Are there any areas of your life in which you are not letting God be your Guide?

- Talk to Him about this name. Thank Him for all the ways and times He has guided your life.

**A Prayer for You:**

*Lord, thank You that You have always guided my life and that You will be my Guide even to the very end. Thank You that I don't need to fear the future or death, because You will be there with me, guiding me. Forgive me for failing to follow You. I want to see You more clearly and follow You wherever You lead me.*

September 7

*Maker of Heaven and Earth, the Sea,*
and Everything in Them

*He is the **Maker of heaven and earth, the sea,**
**and everything in them**—the Lord, who remains faithful forever.*
Psalm 146:6

**Steps on Your Journey to Know God More Intimately:**

- Think about this name. Our God made everything. Your Father made Heaven, the Earth, the Sea and *Everything* in them. What an amazing God! Take a few minutes to meditate on how incredible He really is.

- Sometime today, go out and look up at the sky and around you at the earth and the ocean, if you're close to it. Think about how God made all of it. In addition, we can only see a tiny portion of what He has made—a miniscule speck. Actually, what we can see would not even amount to a tiny speck compared to all He made.

- Ask the Lord to help you begin to comprehend what a great God He is.

- Worship Him as the Maker of Heaven and Earth, the Sea, and Everything in Them.

- Thank Him that He remains faithful forever. We can trust this incredible God, because He is, and always will be, faithful.

**A Prayer for You:**

*You are such an incredible God. My mind can't even comprehend how great You are. Wherever I go, I see Your handiwork—in the sun, moon, stars, clouds, mountains, oceans, lakes, animals and so much more. Thank You for Your creativity in making so much beauty for us to enjoy. And thank You that I can trust You because You remain faithful forever.*

# Lord Who Remains Faithful Forever

*He is the Maker of heaven and earth, the sea, and everything in them—*
*the **Lord**, **who remains faithful forever**.*
**Psalm 146:6**

## Steps on Your Journey to Know God More Intimately:

- The New Living Translation says, "He keeps every promise forever."

- The Hebrew word for faithful, *emet*, here means firmness, faithfulness, truth, sureness, reliability and stability.

- Think about this—God will be faithful to you forever. He'll never, ever change. He'll never stop being faithful.

- I've seen God's faithfulness in so many ways. He has always been there for me through the hard circumstances and the easy times. He's carried me through many tough times, like when my son was dying, or as I raised my sons alone. He has always provided for me and protected me.

- How have you seen God's faithfulness in your life? You might want to start a list of all the ways God has been faithful to you. Then when times get difficult you can look back at the list, knowing that since He was faithful in the past, He will be faithful in your present and future.

- In what areas are you struggling with seeing God's faithfulness? Talk to God about them. You might want to find another believer to share those struggles.

## A Prayer for You:

*Lord, thank You that You remain faithful forever. You have always been faithful, even when I couldn't see it. I know even when storms come, You will always remain firm, secure and stable for my family and me.*

September 9

## *My Refuge in Times of Trouble*

*But I will sing of your strength, in the morning I will sing of your love;
for you are my fortress, **my refuge in times of trouble**.*
Psalms 59:16

**Steps on Your Journey to Know God More Intimately:**

- The New Living Translation says: "For you have been my refuge, a place of safety when I am in distress."

- Think about how God has been your Refuge in Times of Trouble. What has that looked like? How has God shown you that He has been your place of safety?

- If you are troubled in any way, remember you can run to the Lord and find protection and safety.

- God has been a wonderful Refuge for me throughout my life. During one relationship when I felt battered, I could run to the Lord and find shelter. He was and is always a safe place for me to go.

- Ask the Lord to show you what your Refuge looks like. Are you encircled in His arms? Or is He some kind of fortress with thick walls that no enemy can penetrate? He appears to us in different ways at different times in our lives. Take the time to see Him as your Refuge today.

**A Prayer for You:**

*Lord, thank You for being my Refuge, my Place of Safety from trouble. I know I can depend on You, because You never change. You are bigger than any enemy I might encounter. When I think I can find my own refuge, remind me that You are the best one there is.*

# God of Jacob, Who Turned the Rock
### into a Pool of Water

*Tremble, O earth, at the presence of the Lord, At the presence of*
*the **God of Jacob**, **Who turned the rock into a pool of water**,*
*The flint into a fountain of waters.*
Psalm 114:7-8 (NKJV)

**Steps on Your Journey to Know God More Intimately:**

- Last month we looked at The God of Jacob. Let's focus on the second part of this name. Do you remember the story of when Moses struck the rock and God made water flow from it? You can read about it in Exodus 17:1-7.

- Imagine being there when God turned a rock into a pool, a hard rock into fountains of water. Stop and think about what that would have been like.

- This name reminds us that the Lord can do anything, since He can turn a rock into a pool of water. He is all-powerful. He is the God who does miracles. What do you need Him to do for you today? Ask Him in faith, believing that nothing is impossible for Him (see Matthew 19:26).

- What areas of your life seem like a rock? Unchangeable. Dry. Hard.

- Ask the Lord to turn your rocky places into a refreshing, thirst-quenching pool of water (and whatever else you may need from that pool).

**A Prayer for You:**

*God, I praise You because You are such a strong, all-powerful God. Thank You that nothing is impossible for You. You know the rocky places in my life [stop and talk to the Lord about each one.] I give them to You and ask that You would change them into pools of water. I don't know how You'll do it, but I trust You.*

# My Righteous God

Elohim Tsedek (Hebrew)

*Answer me when I call to you, **my righteous God**.*
*Give me relief from my distress; have mercy on me and hear my prayer.*
Psalm 4:1

**Steps on Your Journey to Know God More Intimately:**

- *Tsedek* means righteousness or righteous. The definition of righteous is morally upright; without guilt or sin.

- As a righteous God, He expects us to be righteous and holy as He is holy. In what areas are you struggling to live a righteous life? God is forgiving and merciful if you come to Him and tell Him how you are struggling and ask for forgiveness. But we need to be careful that we don't sin, expecting Him to forgive us.

- What does it mean to you that God is *your* righteous God?

- This verse is David's prayer. What can you learn from it that will help you when you are feeling stressed and distressed? How can it help you manage your stress?

- Spend some time talking to the Righteous One, your Righteous God.

**A Prayer for You:**

*My Righteous God, I praise You for Your righteousness and holiness. Thank You that You are a personal God. Even though You know I am not perfect, You still love me and want to be my Righteous God. Thank You that what Jesus did on the cross made me righteous in Your eyes.*

September 12

*Ear-Maker*

*Do you think **Ear-Maker** doesn't hear, Eye-Shaper doesn't see?*
Psalm 94:9 (MSG)

**Steps on Your Journey to Know God More Intimately:**

- I love the way the Message translates some names, like this one.

- The New International Version says, "Does he who fashioned the ear not hear? Does he who formed the eye not see?"

- What does it mean to you that God is your Ear-Maker? Imagine if you couldn't hear.

- If you can't hear with your physical ears, talk to God about that. Ask Him to heal them. Just as Jesus healed many who can't hear, He is still healing ears today. If you want me to pray for your hearing, email me. I'd love to believe with you for total healing.

- Stop and listen to the sounds around you. What do you hear?

- Thank Ear-Maker that He made your ears so you can hear all kinds of sounds.

- I googled parts of the ear. It's incredible how many different parts our ears have. Each one has a purpose. Ear-Maker knew exactly what we needed.

- This verse says that God hears you. I'm so grateful that He hears my prayers, and yours.

- Consider this name today. What is God saying to you through it?

**A Prayer for You:**

*Ear-Maker, thank You for creating my ears to be able to hear all the sounds around me. I can't even imagine living in total quiet. You created my ears perfectly. Thank You for not only making my ears, but also for listening to me.*

## Eye-Shaper

*Do you think Ear-Maker doesn't hear, **Eye-Shaper** doesn't see?*
Psalm 94:9 (MSG)

**Steps on Your Journey to Know God More Intimately:**

- Think about this name. Yesterday we looked at God being our Ear-Maker, today we see Him shaping our eyes. What shape are your eyes?

- Consider all the parts of your eyes. Think about how intricate God made your eyes. They have at least twenty-eight different parts. Aren't you grateful that God made each element so you can see clearly?

- Thank the Lord that He made your eyes. Imagine if you couldn't see anything at all.

- Think about the end of this verse: "Do you think Eye-Shaper doesn't see?" How would you answer that question? How does that make you feel having God see you?

- What is God saying to you through this name?

**A Prayer for You:**

*Eye-Shaper, thank You for shaping my eyes just the way You did. Thank You for allowing me to see the beauty around me as well as being able to see my family and friends. Help me to remember to be grateful for my eyes.*

## September 14

### *Lord of Godless Nations*

*God is **Lord of godless nations**—*
*sovereign, he's King of the mountain.*
Psalm 47:7-8 (MSG)

**Steps on Your Journey to Know God More Intimately:**

- This is an interesting name. We think of God being Lord of believers. How is God the Lord of godless nations? If you're not sure, talk to Him and ask Him to show you.

- Is the country where you live godless? Whether it is or not, I encourage you to take the time to pray for your nation. Pray for the leadership on a national level, state level and local levels. I'm part of the National Day of Prayer task force, because the United States of America needs prayer, maybe more now than ever!

- Philippians 2:10 says that every knee will bow and every tongue confess that Jesus is Lord. Not only people who believe in God, but even those who don't believe in Him, will one day bow their knees to Him.

- I believe we need to be telling others about the Lord. There are so many who don't yet know Him. How can you share God's love with those around you who may be godless?

**A Prayer for You:**

*You are the Lord of Godless Nations as well as of those who know You. Show me more of what this name means and how it should affect my life.*

September 15

## *King of the Mountain*

*God is Lord of godless nations—*
*sovereign, he's **King of the mountain**.*
Psalm 47:7-8 (MSG)

**Steps on Your Journey to Know God More Intimately:**

- When I was a child, growing up in Guatemala, I went to a boarding school from the time I was six to thirteen. On Saturdays, we often got to play on ancient Mayan pyramids that were in ruins. The person who got to the top first would announce, "I'm the king of the mountain."

- How is God the King of the Mountain? What do you think that means?

- The ESV says, "God reigns over the nations; God sits on his holy throne." How does this change your view of this name?

- How does this name affect your life?

- Ask God to show you more about this name.

**A Prayer for You:**

*King of the Mountain, I praise You that You reign over the nations and that You sit on Your holy throne. You are the all-powerful God, the ruler of the whole earth. I want to learn to worship You more as my King.*

## September 16

## *Alpha and Omega*

*"I am the **Alpha and the Omega**," says the Lord God,*
*"who is, and who was, and who is to come, the Almighty."*
Revelation 1:8 (ESV)

**Steps on Your Journey to Know God More Intimately:**

- Today is Rosh Hashanah, the Jewish New Year (in 2012). It can be a day to start over. If you are reading this book a different year, the date will change.

- *Alpha* is the first letter in the Greek alphabet. *Omega* is the last one. God is the first and the last. He was before all things and He will be there to the very end—which, since He has no end, will be a very long time.

- Meditate on this name. Ask the Lord to reveal more about who He is.

- This name is only found three times in the Bible. Read and meditate on the other two verses:

  o Revelation 21:6: "He said to me: 'It is done. I am the Alpha and the Omega, the Beginning and the End. To him who is thirsty I will give to drink without cost from the spring of the water of life.'"

  o Revelation 22:13: "I am the Alpha and the Omega, the First and the Last, the Beginning and the End."

**A Prayer for You:**

*Lord, as today is the Jewish New Year, I choose to start over afresh with You. I want to know You in deeper ways. I want to grow in my love for You. Reveal to me more about this name, the Alpha and Omega.*

## September 17

### Abraham's God

*Princes from all over are gathered,*
*people of **Abraham's God**.*
Psalm 47:8 (MSG)

**Steps on Your Journey to Know God More Intimately:**

- Abraham is the father of the Jews, but he is also the father of anyone who believes, as Galatians 3:7 says, "Understand, then, that those who have faith are children of Abraham." So, whether you are a Jew or a Gentile, we have the same God, Abraham's God.

- Look at what God promised Abraham in Genesis 12:2-3: "I will make of you a great nation, and I will bless you and make your name great, so that you will be a blessing. I will bless those who bless you, and him who dishonors you I will curse, and in you all the families of the earth shall be blessed" (ESV).

- The God who made these promises to Abraham is also your God. Think about that. They are promises for you too.

- Ask the Lord to show you what it means to be the people of Abraham's God. Thank and praise Him for what He shows you.

**A Prayer for You:**

*God, show me more of what it means that You are Abraham's God. Reveal how that should affect my life. Thank You for all Your promises to Abraham that I can claim, since I am also one of Abraham's children.*

September 18

## *God Majestic*

**God majestic**, *praise abounds in our God-city!*
*His sacred mountain, breathtaking in its heights—earth's joy.*
Psalm 48:1 (MSG)

**Steps on Your Journey to Know God More Intimately:**

- Other translations say, "Great is the Lord and greatly to be praised."

- The definition of majestic is stately. It means having or showing impressive beauty or dignity. Synonyms of majestic include: classy, courtly, fine, graceful, handsome, elegant, refined and tasteful.

- Think about these definitions. What does it mean to you that God is majestic?

- Every day when I see the 14,000-foot Pikes Peak mountain looming outside my windows, I'm reminded of God's majesty. It seems that every time I look at it, it is different, depending on the lighting, clouds, etc. That's just like our Majestic God. He has so many different views. We are getting to see some of them through His names.

- Meditate on this name, God Majestic.

- Ask God to reveal more of Himself to you today through this name.

**A Prayer for You:**

*God, I praise You because You are so great and majestic. You are worthy of praise and adoration. Show me more of Yourself through this name.*

## September 19

### One Enthroned in Heaven

*The **One enthroned in heaven** laughs; he scoffs at them.*
Psalm 2:4

**Steps on Your Journey to Know God More Intimately:**

- Your God is the One who is enthroned in Heaven. Stop and consider what that means. Ask God to reveal Himself seated on His throne.

- Ephesians 2:6 says that we "are seated with Him in the heavenly realms." Ask Him to show you what that looks like. Since He is seated on a throne, that means that you must be too. What does it mean to you that you are seated with the Lord?

- The One who is on the throne has all power and authority. God has that, and you do too, since you are seated with Him. You have authority over your enemy, but you have a choice whether you'll use it or not. Doing spiritual warfare is using the authority God has given you.

- Look what God is doing in this verse. He is laughing at the people who are trying to fight against Him (see verses 1-3). Close your eyes and ask the Lord to show you His humorous side. If you're like me, you may think of Him as always being serious.

- God is on His throne right now. Worship the One who is enthroned in Heaven.

**A Prayer for You:**

*One Enthroned in Heaven, I worship You today, because You have all power and authority over Heaven and Earth. I give You power over my life. Thank You that because of Jesus, I am seated with You in the heavenly realms. Teach me to live in that place, using the authority I have from You.*

## Great High Priest

*Therefore, since we have a **great high priest***
*who has ascended into heaven,*
*Jesus the Son of God, let us hold firmly to the faith we profess.*
Hebrews 4:14

**Steps on Your Journey to Know God More Intimately:**

- *Megas* in Greek means great or loud. *Archiereus* means chief priest or high priest.

- A high priest represented the people to God and made atonement for their sins by offering sacrifices. The problem was that the priests had to keep on, year after year, making the sacrifices because they too were sinners.

- Jesus is our Great High Priest. He did the work once and for all to pay for our sins and then He went up to Heaven.

- It's like Jesus said to the Father, "Dad, I know _____ (fill in your name) is a sinner and doesn't deserve to have a relationship with us, but I died for him (her). I paid the price myself for his (her) sins, so he (she) can come right into Your presence."

- What does it mean to you today that Jesus paid the price for your sins and He is waiting in Heaven for you? Your loved ones who have gone ahead of you are there with Jesus waiting for you. Isn't that encouraging?! Someday I'll get to see my son and fiancé who are already enjoying Heaven!

**A Prayer for You:**

*Jesus, thank You that You came as my Great High Priest, representing me to the Father. Thank You that You paid for my sins with Your very own life. Thank You so much for what You did. And thank You that You are now in Heaven waiting for me.*

September 21

## High Priest Who Sat Down at the Right Hand
### of the Throne of the Majesty in Heaven

*We do have such a **high priest, who sat down at the right hand of the
throne of the Majesty in heaven**, and who serves in the sanctuary,
the true tabernacle set up by the Lord, not by a mere human being.*
Hebrews 8:1-2

**Steps on Your Journey to Know God More Intimately:**

- If we thought we looked at complicated names before, this one is even more involved. Meditate on each part of this name. Thank the Lord for what He shows you. Praise Him and worship Him for what a great God He is. Now let's look at each part:

  o High priest—how is Jesus your High Priest? What is He doing or did He do for you?

  o Who sat down—why did He sit? Why isn't He standing?

  o At the right hand—what is the significance of God's right hand? God's hand always refers to His power. It is also a place of honor.

  o Of the throne—close your eyes and imagine God's throne. Look at Isaiah 6:1-3 and Revelation 4 for a description.

  o Of the Majesty in Heaven    Close your eyes again and ask God to give you a glimpse of His Majesty. I don't think we can even begin to really grasp how awesome and amazing He is. Ask the Lord to show you what He wants you to see. I do know that whatever He shows you will be incredible! Look up Revelation 21:22-23 to learn more.

- What is God saying to you today through this name?

**A Prayer for You:**

*Jesus, thank You so much for being my High Priest who came to not only represent me before the Father, but also came to pay for my sins so I can have hope. Thank You that You are now seated at The Majesty's (God's) right hand in Heaven. Thank You that You are there praying for me as Hebrews 7:25 says.*

## September 22

# *Righteous God Who Probes Minds and Hearts*

*Bring to an end the violence of the wicked*
*and make the righteous secure—*
*you, the **righteous God who probes minds and hearts***.
Psalm 7:9

**Steps on Your Journey to Know God More Intimately:**

- Earlier we looked at God's name "My Righteous God." Today we see that this righteous God probes our minds and hearts.

- The Hebrew word for probing, *bakan*, means test, try, prove, investigate and examine.

- Think about this name and the meaning behind the words. What does it mean to you that the Righteous God tests and examines your mind and heart? For some people that might be scary. For me, most of the time, it is comforting.

- When I'm not sure what to think or how to feel, I can talk to the Lord. He knows my thoughts and heart better than I do. Think about that.

- Meditate on this name. What is the Lord showing you through it?

**A Prayer for You:**

*Righteous God, I praise You for Your holiness and righteousness. Thank You for testing and examining my mind and heart. Show me anything in me that needs to be purified so I can live a righteous life. When I'm not sure what I'm even thinking, thank You that I can go to You for understanding my own self.*

# God, Who Makes Things Right

*I'm thanking **God**, **who makes things right**.*
*I'm singing the fame of heaven-high God.*
Psalm 7:17 (MSG)

**Steps on Your Journey to Know God More Intimately:**

- Meditate on this name. What does it mean to you that God makes things right? Ask Him to show you.

- How have you seen God make things right in your life or your family's lives? If you don't think you have, ask the Lord to reveal ways He has been working, even when you can't see them.

- Are there any areas of your life that aren't right? Ask God to make them right. You can partner with Him in making them right. Ask Him what He wants you to do.

- When things are not right in our lives, we can start to feel very stressed. Talk to God about anything that is stressing you right now. Then listen for his answers.[6]

**A Prayer for You:**

*God, I'm so grateful that You are the One who makes things right for me. I don't have to fix everything in my life and in my family's lives. I can trust You to do that. And even when everything looks out of control, I choose to trust You to make everything right in Your own time.*

# Heaven-High God

*I'm thanking God, who makes things right.*
*I'm singing the fame of **heaven-high God**.*
Psalm 7:17 (MSG)

**Steps on Your Journey to Know God More Intimately:**

- Today let's meditate on the second name of God in this verse. Close your eyes and picture Heaven-High God. He lives in Heaven and He is also the way to Heaven.

- How high is Heaven? It's something to ponder, although I don't think we'll know the answer this side of Heaven.

- Ask the Lord to reveal more of Himself to you through this name.

- This verse says, "I'm singing the fame of Heaven-high God." Do you do that? How can you do a better job of singing God's fame?

**A Prayer for You:**

*Heaven-High God, I praise You that You are high and exalted. You are worthy of praise. I choose to sing of Your fame. I want to tell everyone I know, and even many people who I don't yet know, about You and Your fame. Show me how to do that better.*

September 25

## My (God's) Son

Ben (Hebrew) Huios (Greek)

*I will proclaim the Lord's decree: He said to me,*
*"You are **my son**; today I have become your father."*
Psalm 2:7

**Steps on Your Journey to Know God More Intimately:**

- *Ben* means son. *Huios* means son or Son of Man.

- Father God is talking here about His Son. Acts 13:32-33 affirms that Jesus fulfilled the promise in Psalm 2: "And we bring you the good news that what God promised to the fathers, this he has fulfilled to us their children by raising Jesus, as also it is written in the second Psalm, 'You are my Son, today I have begotten you'" (ESV).

- Because Jesus is God's Son, He opened the way for us to go directly into God's presence. Think about that. How exciting!

- What does it mean to you that Jesus is God's Son?

- If Jesus were not God's Son, how would that change your life?

- Ask the Lord to show you how it affects your life knowing that Jesus is God's Son.

**A Prayer for You:**

*Father God, thank You that You sent Your Son, Jesus to earth because You wanted to have a relationship with me. Thank You for writing promises for us in Your Word so long ago and then showing us their fulfillment. Help me to understand more about Your relationship—between the Father and the Son.*

# Chief Shepherd

## Arkipoimane (Greek)

*When the **Chief Shepherd** appears,
you will receive the unfading crown of glory.*
1 Peter 5:4

**Steps on Your Journey to Know God More Intimately:**

- *Arkipoimane* means head shepherd or chief shepherd. This is the only use of this word in the Bible. It comes from two Greek words: *arkay* meaning chief, beginning, magistrate, power or rule; and *poymane* meaning shepherd or pastor.

- Read 1 Peter 5:1-4. Peter told the elders to be "Shepherds of God's flock that is under you." They were to act as shepherds, but they were also under the Chief Shepherd.

- Sometimes the shepherds over us, our leaders in our churches, don't act the way they should. Remember, you have access to the Chief Shepherd. He will guide you and care for you

- Has a spiritual leader, shepherd or pastor, hurt you? If so, I encourage you to talk to your Chief Shepherd about it. Forgive that person. Then ask the Lord if there is anything else you may need to do.

- I was hurt deeply by a spiritual leader years ago, because he was jealous of my ministry. He began slandering me to many people I knew. Even years later, he continued to slander me. With God's help, I forgave him, although the Lord did lead me to a different church.

- What would you like to ask your Shepherd today?

**A Prayer for You:**

*Chief Shepherd, thank You that You always care for me, Your lamb, with love and tenderness. Thank You that I can run to You and find all I need, regardless of how any other shepherd may treat me.*

## Safe-House for the Battered

*God's a **safe-house for the battered**,*
*a sanctuary during bad times.*
Psalm 9:9 (MSG)

**Steps on Your Journey to Know God More Intimately:**

- The New International Version puts it this way, "The Lord is a refuge for the oppressed, a stronghold in times of trouble."

- Imagine you are in serious trouble. You are being abused by someone or maybe by life. God is your Safe-House. He is the One you can run to and find refuge and protection.

- Merriam-Webster states the meaning of oppression as "unjust or cruel exercise of authority or power; a sense of being weighed down in body or mind."

- There are many ways people can feel battered—physical, emotional, spiritual, religious, racial, etc. Do you ever feel battered or oppressed? If so, how? If you're like me, you have. I've been battered in many ways by people who I thought loved me. The emotional battering was worse than the physical, because physical bruises went away quicker than the hurts caused by words. I'm glad I can go to my Safe-House for refuge and protection.

- What does it mean to you that God is a Safe-House for the Battered?

- Thank the Lord that you can go to Him anytime you need a refuge or a safe house. You can find freedom from oppression.

**A Prayer for You:**

*God, thank You that You are a Safe-House for the Battered. You are the One I can run to when I am in trouble and afraid. I know You will always be there not only to protect me, but also to love me and care for me. Wow! Thank You.*

# Bread that Came Down from Heaven

*Jesus said, "I am the **bread that came down from heaven**."*
John 6:41

**Steps on Your Journey to Know God More Intimately:**

- You might want to read the whole chapter of John 6. Jesus had just fed 5000 men, not to mention all the women and children, with just five small loaves of bread and two fish. Can you imagine seeing Him do that miracle?

- Jesus was in Heaven with God, but He came down to earth because He wanted a relationship with us. If you don't yet have a relationship with God, He wants to know you, and you to know Him. Talk to Him now. If you would like to know more go to page 369.

- Think about why Jesus is called the Bread that Came from Heaven.

- Are you hungry? Is your soul hungry? In what ways? Let Jesus satisfy that hunger.

- Reading and studying the Word regularly is important to discover the satisfaction that comes from Jesus. My hunger for the Word started when I was thirteen. We had just moved to the United States from Guatemala. My entire world turned upside down. As I started to see all the world offered, I quickly realized that wasn't what I wanted. I was so hungry to know God that I couldn't ever get enough of Him. That hunger waned for several years, but it's back! I pray your hunger for the Lord increases.

- Meditate on this name and ask the Lord to reveal more of Himself to you through it.

**A Prayer for You:**

*Jesus, thank You that You are the Bread that Came Down from Heaven. Thank You that You came to satisfy my deepest needs. Show me what this name means.*

# Lord Our Lord

Yahweh Adon (Hebrew)

**Lord, our Lord**, *how majestic is your name in all the earth!*
*You have set your glory in the heavens.*
Psalm 8:1

**Steps on Your Journey to Know God More Intimately:**

- As we've seen before, this name has two different Hebrew words for Lord.

- LORD (in small caps) is *YHWH*, *Yahweh* or *Jehovah*. It reveals the intimate God, the Self-Existent One, the Covenant-Keeping God and the Unchangeable God. Most Jews will not even say this name because it is so holy. Do you treat God's name with the same reverence? So many people today see nothing wrong with taking God's name in vain.

- Lord (in lower case) is *adon* and *adonai* meaning master, owner, provider, and lord.

- What does it mean to you that *Yahweh* is your Lord and Master? How might this name change your life?

- This verse says that God's name is majestic in all the earth. His glory is seen in the heavens. Think about that. Ask God to show you more of His majestic name and His glory. Then don't forget to watch the sky. God loves to show off His glory.

**A Prayer for You:**

*O Lord, my Lord, Your name is so majestic. Thank You for revealing so much of Yourself through Your name—through all Your names. I want to know You in deeper ways and I want to see Your glory in the heavens.*

# Rabbi

*Then Judas, the one who would betray him, said, "Surely not I, Rabbi?"*
*Jesus answered, "Yes, it is you." Going at once to Jesus, Judas said,*
*"Greetings, **Rabbi**!" and kissed him.*

Matthew 26:25, 49

**Steps on Your Journey to Know God More Intimately:**

- *Rabbi* in Greek is a title of honor, meaning master, teacher or honorable sir. It comes from the Hebrew word *rab* meaning, master, captain, elder, mighty and much more.

- Judas used this name as he was betraying Jesus. How could he use a term meaning master and still betray Him?

- What does it mean in your life that Jesus is your Rabbi?

- How might you use this name of Jesus in your prayers?

- Ask the Rabbi to reveal Himself to you through this name today.

**A Prayer for You:**

*Rabbi, I want to honor You as my master. Teach me what that means and show me how to live like You are my Rabbi. Help me to never be disloyal to You in anyway. I want to know You so intimately that I would never even consider betraying You or dishonoring You in the way I live.*

October 1

## God in Heaven Who Reveals Mysteries

*There is a **God in heaven who reveals mysteries**.*
*He has shown King Nebuchadnezzar*
*what will happen in days to come.*
Daniel 2:28

**Steps on Your Journey to Know God More Intimately:**

- Think about each part of this name today. Ask the Lord to reveal more of Himself to you today as you focus on Him. Thank Him for what He shows you.

  o God in Heaven—our God is not like other gods. He is alive, living in Heaven (as well as living in you and me)!

  o Who reveals mysteries—what mysteries has God revealed to you? Think about that. He may have revealed mysteries to you, but you didn't recognize them, or seen Him in them. I wonder how often I've missed them, because I've been so focused on the natural realm that I fail to see in the spiritual realm.

- What mysteries or questions are you struggling to understand? Talk to the God who reveals mysteries. He has the answers.

- Ask God to open your eyes to what He is doing and has done in and around you.

**A Prayer for You:**

*God Who Reveals Mysteries, I praise You that You know everything. You have all wisdom. There is nothing that confuses You. Thank You that I can trust You with every area of my life. You know the mysteries and questions I have. Please reveal the answers to me.*

## Amen

*To the angel of the church in Laodicea write:*
*These are the words of the **Amen**, the faithful and true witness,*
*the beginning of God's creation.*
Revelation 3:14 (ESV)

**Steps on Your Journey to Know God More Intimately:**

- We'll look at this short verse for three days. I'd encourage you to read it several times a day and begin to memorize it.

- *Amane* in Greek means so be it, amen, surely, firm and trustworthy. It comes from the Hebrew word, *aman*, translated faithful, established, believe and much more.

- When Jesus said, "truly, truly" or "verily, verily," He was using the word Amen.

- Amen is used in Deuteronomy 7:9, where it says, "the faithful God." In other words, "the Amen God." See also Isaiah 49:7.

- Someone pointed out recently that this verse doesn't say "the angel of ________ (fill in the name of any specific church) Church." There was only one church in the city, even though they probably had many congregations. Churches today have become so splintered from each other. I believe God wants us to get back to unity with all our fellow followers of Jesus.

- Consider these definitions of Amen. What does it mean to you that Jesus is the Amen?

**A Prayer for You:**

*I praise You, Lord, that You are the Amen, that You are faithful, firm, established and trustworthy. Thank You that I can stake my life on You, knowing You will always be there for me and You will never change.*

# October 3

## Faithful and True Witness

Pistos kai Alethenos Martys (Greek)

*These are the words of the Amen, the **faithful and true witness**,
the beginning of God's creation.*
Revelation 3:14 (ESV)

**Steps on Your Journey to Know God More Intimately:**

- The Greek word for faithful, *pistos*, means reliable, trustworthy and sure. *Alethenos* means true, real and genuine. It also means that which has not only the name and resemblance, but the real nature corresponding to the name, in every aspect.

- *Martys* means witness or martyr. A witness is someone who has seen something and gives a testimony about it. He verifies that what He has seen is true.

- Jesus is the Faithful and True Witness. We know that whatever He tells us is true, in the written Word, as well as what He speaks to us, personally. We need to be careful to make sure we are hearing Him and not the enemy. We have the promise in John 10:27, "My sheep listen to my voice; I know them, and they follow me." As His sheep we can hear His voice. Learn it by spending time with Him through His Word. He will never lead you contrary to His Word, the Bible.

- Meditate on this name. What is the Lord saying to you?

**A Prayer for You:**

*Faithful and True Witness, I praise You for being so trustworthy, reliable and genuine. Thank You that I can trust whatever You tell me in Your Word as well as through Your Spirit. Thank You that You will never lie to me. Teach me to trust You and know You more.*

# Beginning of God's Creation

*These are the words of the Amen, the faithful and true witness,*
**the beginning of God's creation.**
Revelation 3:14 (ESV)

**Steps on Your Journey to Know God More Intimately:**

- This verse is talking about Jesus.

- Can you quote this verse yet? It's a great verse to know, because it is short and has three different names of the Lord in it.

- The Greek word for beginning is *arkay* and means origin, ruler, the person or thing that commences, the first person or thing in a series, the leader and the active cause. Consider the meanings of beginning. Jesus created everything in the world, in the universe. He is the ruler over all of it.

- Go outside today, right now, if you can, and thank Jesus for His creation. Be specific. What do you see? Thank Him for each thing you see outside. Birds, clouds, mountains, spiders. Spiders? Should I thank Him for them? Sure, why not. He created them too. For me it's easy to thank God for the mountains, but spiders aren't so easy. Next time I see one, I want to remember that it is part of God's creation too.

- What does it mean to you today that Jesus is the beginning of His creation? Ask the Lord to show you more of what it means.

**A Prayer for You:**

*Lord, thank You that You are the beginning of creation. You are the One who created everything I can see. You are the source of everything I see. Humans create things, but they can only create out of what You already created. I want to learn to worship You more through Your creation.*

## Branch of the Lord

*In that day the **Branch of the Lord** will be beautiful and glorious,
and the fruit of the land will be
the pride and glory of the survivors in Israel.*
Isaiah 4:2

**Steps on Your Journey to Know God More Intimately:**

- *Tsemakh* means a sprout, branch or bud in Hebrew.

- Isaiah 11:1 says, "A shoot will come up from the stump of Jesse; from his roots a Branch will bear fruit." Isaiah is using a picture of a tree that is cut down, but from the root another tree grows. Jesus came from the line of Jesse, who was King David's father.

- These passages are referring to the Messiah, who was yet to come. How is the Messiah like a Branch?

- In what ways is the Branch of the Lord beautiful and glorious? Praise Him for what He shows you.

- In John 15, Jesus talks about Himself as the vine and we are the branches. Why do you think He is called a Branch in Isaiah, and a Vine in John? Ask the Lord to reveal it to you.

**A Prayer for You:**

*Branch of the Lord, I praise You that You are beautiful and glorious. I want to see Your glory and Your beauty. Show me Your glory, Lord. And teach more of what it means that You are the Branch of the Lord.*

# Root and the Offspring of David

*I, Jesus, have sent my angel to give you this testimony for the churches.*
*I am the **Root and the Offspring of David**,*
*and the bright Morning Star.*
Revelation 22:16

**Steps on Your Journey to Know God More Intimately:**

- In Isaiah 11:10, the Messiah is called the "Root of Jesse." Jesse was King David's father.

- Matthew 1 shows Jesus' genealogy, proving that He came from David's lineage.

- Ponder this name. Jesus is both the root (the first one, the one David came from) and He's David's offspring (He was born in David's lineage). How can He be both?

- Do you think this name could be anything like Him being both the beginning and the end?

- Ask God to reveal to you what He wants you to know today from this name.

**A Prayer for You:**

*Lord, I praise You that You are both the root and the offspring of David. Show me more of what this name means and how You want me to relate to You because of it. I long to know all about every aspect of who You are (even though I realize I won't know everything this side of Heaven).*

## *Anointed One*

*Herod and Pontius Pilate met together with the Gentiles and the people of Israel in this city to conspire against your holy servant Jesus, whom you anointed. The kings of the earth take their stand and the rulers gather together against the Lord and against his **Anointed One**.*
Acts 4:26-27

**Steps on Your Journey to Know God More Intimately:**

- This is a direct quote from Psalm 2:2. It is a prophecy that the rulers of the earth (Herod and Pontius Pilate) would conspire against the Anointed One, Jesus.

- The Greek word for Anointed One is *Christos,* Christ, meaning the Messiah. It shows Jesus' deity—that He is God. The Hebrew word in Psalm 2 is *Mashiyah,* meaning Messiah.

- In the Old Testament, people were anointed to be kings and priests. In the same way, Jesus was anointed by God to be both a king and a priest (See Hebrews 7).

- Meditate on what it means that Jesus is God's Anointed One.

**A Prayer for You:**

*Jesus, I praise You that You are the Anointed One. You are the Messiah, the One God promised to bring me salvation. Thank You, Anointed One, for coming to earth to give me hope. Show me more of Yourself through this name.*

## Divine Power

*By his **divine power**, God has given us everything we need for living a godly life. We have received all of this by coming to know him, the one who called us to himself by means of his marvelous glory and excellence.*
2 Peter 1:3 (NLT)

**Steps on Your Journey to Know God More Intimately:**

- Merriam-Webster defines divine as "of, relating to, or proceeding directly from God or a god." The Greek word for power here is *dunamis,* from which we get the word for dynamite. *Theios* means godlike or divine.

- God's power is not like any human power. It's not of the earth. It's beyond our understanding. Take some time to think about God's divine power.

- First Corinthians 1:24 calls Christ "the Power of God." What does it mean to you that Christ is the Power of God?

- Consider what God has done with His great power. To begin with: He created the universe *and* He raised Jesus from the dead. That's amazing power. What else?

- When I was a missionary in Guatemala as an adult, I lived in a little village on the side of an active volcano. It was constantly spouting smoke. However, occasionally we'd hear a very loud rumble, like a train going right through our tiny, one-room house. Outside we'd see huge flames and billowing smoke. God showed His divine power in that volcano, in a very small way.

- How have you seen God's Divine Power in your life? Meditate on and thank God for what this verse says: God has already given us His divine power. I've meditated on this verse a lot and I am continually amazed at what God shows me through it. I pray God will bless you through it too.

**A Prayer for You:**

*Lord, I praise You for Your Divine Power that has given me everything I need for life and godliness. Thank You. And it's through my knowing You that You do it all. Pour out Your power in my life today.*

October 9

## Him Who Called Us
### to His Own Glory and Excellence

*His divine power has granted to us all things that pertain*
*to life and godliness, through the knowledge of*
***him who called us to his own glory and excellence.***

2 Peter 1:3 (ESV)

**Steps on Your Journey to Know God More Intimately:**

- We often hear people say, "I found God." We only find Him because He first called us. Thank Him that He called you to be His child, His friend and so much more.

- It wasn't because of anything we did that He called us. It was only because of His glory and His goodness. God wants to show His glory and excellence through you. Think about that.

- Ponder this name today. God chose you because of His great love for you. How does it affect you knowing that He called you?

- What do you think it means that He called you to His own glory and excellence? What might that look like? Ask Him.

- Notice that it's through our knowledge of God that we have everything we need for life and godliness. That's why it is so important to continue growing in our knowledge of God through ongoing Bible study and conversation with Him.

- I love this verse and all that it says God does for us.

**A Prayer for You:**

*Lord, thank You for calling me out of my sin by and because of Your own glory and excellence. Teach me more of what this means. I want to know You in new ways.*

## Everlasting Light

*The sun will no more be your light by day, nor will the brightness of the moon shine on you, for the Lord will be your **everlasting light**, and your God will be your glory. The Lord will be your **everlasting light**, and your days of sorrow will end.*
Isaiah 60:19-20

**Steps on Your Journey to Know God More Intimately:**

- This name in Hebrew is *Olam Or. Olam* means ever, everlasting, perpetual and old. *Or* means light, shine or to be luminous.

- These verses are talking about when we are face to face with God. It's exciting to think about Heaven and what it will be like. No pain, no sorrow and no crying. There will be no need for the sun or the moon, because the Lord will be our Light that will last forever.

- In John 8:12 Jesus says, "I am the light of the world. Whoever follows me will never walk in darkness, but will have the light of life." Jesus is our light right now, to guide us along our path. His Light will never be extinguished. It is comforting knowing we never have to be in darkness again.

- Ask the Lord to show you how He is your Everlasting Light.

- In what ways do you need the Lord to bring light into your life? Ask Him to be your Light today.

**A Prayer for You:**

*Everlasting Light, I praise You for Your plan to be my Light that will never go out. Thank You that You are my Light right now. I need Your radiance to reveal the path I am to follow. Show me more about how You are my Everlasting Light.*

# Fragrant Offering and Sacrifice to God

*Therefore be imitators of God, as beloved children.*
*And walk in love, as Christ loved us and gave himself up for us,*
*a **fragrant offering and sacrifice to God**.*
Ephesians 5:1-2 (ESV)

**Steps on Your Journey to Know God More Intimately:**

- Some other translations of fragrant offering include: sweet-smelling aroma, a pleasing fragrance and a pleasing aroma to God.

- In the Old Testament, the fragrant offerings were always voluntary, while the sacrifices were not. Sacrifices were given to pay for sins, to remove the people's guilt. The priest offered sacrifices to God on a regular basis. Jesus, our High Priest, gave Himself to pay for our sins once and for all. How could He be both a voluntary offering and an involuntary sacrifice?

- Think about this: Christ was both an offering and a sacrifice. Ask the Lord to show you why He used both terms.

- Christ's offering is fragrant; it has a sweet smell to it, because it is the smell of life and hope for us.

- Notice why these verses said Christ gave Himself as an offering and a sacrifice. How does that affect you today?

- Meditate on this name. Thank Him for what He shows you.

**A Prayer for You:**

*Lord, I'm so grateful You were willing to come to earth to be both a fragrant offering and a sacrifice for my sins. That is such incredible love. I can't begin to understand how much You love me. Reveal to me more of Your love for me.*

## Friend of Tax Collectors and Sinners

*The Son of Man came eating and drinking, and you say,*
*"Here is a glutton and a drunkard,*
*a **friend of tax collectors and 'sinners.'"***
Luke 7:34

**Steps on Your Journey to Know God More Intimately:**

- Tax collectors were considered to be the scum of the earth. They were the lowest people in their society. Yet Jesus was willing to associate with them, even though He was the King of kings and the Lord of lords. He didn't just come to be with the wealthy and the religious leaders.

- Think about this name. What does it mean to you?

- I'm so glad that Jesus was willing to be a friend of sinners. That's me! That's who I was. Now I've been declared righteous because of what Jesus did for me. The same is true for you. I'm grateful I don't have to be perfect for Him to want to be my friend.

- Consider what it means to you that Jesus is your friend, regardless of what others think about you or how low your earthly position is.

- How does this name affect you today?

**A Prayer for You:**

*Jesus, thank You for being willing to come to earth for the lowly people, the regular people, like me. I'm so glad that I don't have to be wealthy or powerful or anything else for You to accept me and be my friend. Teach me how to be Your friend.*

October 13

## *Angel of His Presence*

*In all their affliction He was afflicted,*
*And the **Angel of His Presence** saved them;*
*In His love and in His pity He redeemed them;*
*And He bore them and carried them all the days of old.*
Isaiah 63:9 (NKJV)

**Steps on Your Journey to Know God More Intimately:**

- *Malak* in Hebrew means angel, messenger or ambassador. *Panim* means presence.

- I'd encourage you to read all of Isaiah 63. It is talking about God. We will look at other names of God from this chapter in the coming days.

- Why do you think the Lord might be referred to as the Angel of His Presence, rather than as God or the Lord? Ask Him to show you.

- Exodus 14:19 calls the Lord the "angel of God."

- Read Isaiah 63:9 again. Notice the beginning of this verse, "In all their affliction He was afflicted." The word for afflicted in Hebrew is *tsar* and means distressed, anguished and troubled. What does it mean to you that God is distressed or in anguish when you are distressed and troubled?

- Then look at what He did for them, and us. This verse talks about four different things the Angel of His Presence does for us.

- Meditate on this name. What does it mean to you today?

- Praise God that He comes as an angel to protect us and save us.

**A Prayer for You:**

*Angel of God's Presence, I worship You today. Thank You for all the things You do for me: You are distressed when I am, You save me, love me, redeem me, lift me up and carry me all the days of my life. I don't deserve all You do for me, but I'm so thankful.*

# He Who Brought Them through the Sea

*Then his people recalled the days of old, the days of Moses
and his people—where is **he who brought them through the sea**,
with the shepherd of his flock?
Where is he who set his Holy Spirit among them?*
Isaiah 63:11

**Steps on Your Journey to Know God More Intimately:**

- This refers to when God miraculously led the His people safely through the Red Sea. If you remember, the Israelites had just left Egypt after being enslaved for years. The Egyptians followed them. When they got to the Red Sea, there was no way out—the huge army to their rear and an overflowing sea in front of them. God dried up the Red Sea so they walked through on dry land. When their enemies followed them, they were all drowned. You can read about it in Exodus 14.

- In the same way, God brings us safely through situations that would be impossible without His powerful concern for us.

- Can you remember a "Red Sea" experience that you thought was impossible, but God brought you through? Thank Him again for His loving care.

- Are you in a "Red Sea" experience that looks impossible? Remember nothing is too hard for the Lord and He'll bring you through it.

**A Prayer for You:**

*Lord, thank You that just as You brought your people safely through the Red Sea, so You have brought me—and will bring me—through difficult times in my life. Help me to remember what You've done in the past and trust You more in the future.*

# He Who Set His Holy Spirit among Them

*Then his people recalled the days of old, the days of Moses and his people—*
*where is he who brought them through the sea,*
*with the shepherd of his flock?*
*Where is **he who set his Holy Spirit among them**,*
Isaiah 63:11

**Steps on Your Journey to Know God More Intimately:**

- God set His Holy Spirit among His people back then, but today He actually puts His Spirit *in* us, as Jesus promised to all who believe in Him.

- In John 14:17, Jesus said, "And I will ask the Father, and he will give you another advocate to help you and be with you forever— the Spirit of truth. The world cannot accept him, because it neither sees him nor knows him. But you know him, for he lives with you and will be in you."

- It's only been in recent years that I have begun to recognize and rely on the Holy Spirit's power, wisdom, etc. He has over fifty different names. Each one shows a different facet of who He is. I challenge you to find out more about the Holy Spirit.

- Think about the reality of God's Spirit living in you. How does that affect you?

- How does the Holy Spirit help you? Thank Him.

- What would you like to receive from the Holy Spirit? Ask Him. He loves to answer our prayers.

**A Prayer for You:**

*Father God, who set Your Spirit among us and in me, I praise You for your presence. Thank You for knowing what I need and providing it for me. Teach me how to allow You to work in great ways in my life. I want to learn to find my power, wisdom and truth from Your Holy Spirit.*

## Glorious Arm of Power

*Where is he who set his Holy Spirit among them,
who sent his **glorious arm of power** to be at Moses' right hand,
who divided the waters before them,
to gain for himself everlasting renown.*
Isaiah 63:11-12

**Steps on Your Journey to Know God More Intimately:**

- In Hebrew this name is *Tifara Zeroa*. *Tifara* means beauty, glory and beautiful. *Zeroa* means arm, power and strength. These verses are referring to when God used Moses to part the Red Sea. You can read about it in Exodus 14. (See October 14.)

- How can God's arm be glorious? Ask the Lord to show you what that might look like.

- Meditate on God's Glorious Arm of Power that was with Moses, but is also with you.

- Recently I saw God Glorious Arm of Power at work. Within a minute, a few lazy raindrops turned into a gale-force, tornado-like wind, lashing out against everything in its path. When it was done, the outside of my house was destroyed. My insurance company paid for a new roof, all new screens, damages inside my house and all new paint on my house, deck and fence. The amazing thing—I needed new paint and a new roof, but didn't have the money to pay for it. But an even more amazing thing—my next-door neighbors' house didn't have any damage—their house is about ten feet from mine. It seemed God targeted my house with the fury of the storm, just to bless me, to provide in a very unexpected way. The next time you are faced with a storm—whether physical or anything else—stop and look for God's Glorious Arm of Power at work in it.

- In what ways have you seen God's Arm of Power at work in your life? It's not always as we want or would plan.

**A Prayer for You:**

*Lord, I praise You for Your Glorious Arm of Power that You display in unexpected ways. Teach me to see You at work in my life, rather than complaining when things seem to go wrong.*

## Desire of Our Hearts

*Yes, Lord, walking in the way of your laws, we wait for you;*
*your name and renown are the **desire of our hearts**.*
*My soul yearns for you in the night; in the morning my spirit longs for you.*
Isaiah 26:8-9

**Steps on Your Journey to Know God More Intimately:**

- *Tahava* means desire, longing and delight in Hebrew. *Nefesh* is translated soul, heart, mind and life.

- Read the following verses. What do they say to you about God being the desire of your heart? These verses make great prayers.

    o Psalm 42:2: "My soul thirsts for God, for the living God. When can I go and meet with God?"

    o Psalm 63:1: "O God, you are my God, earnestly I seek you; my soul thirsts for you, my body longs for you, in a dry and weary land where there is no water."

    o Psalm 73:25: "Whom have I in heaven but you? And earth has nothing I desire besides you."

- Meditate on this name: the Desire of Our Hearts. How does it affect you?

- The more I get to know the Lord, the greater the longing I have to spend time with Him and to know Him more intimately. I pray the same for you.

- Is the Lord as important to you as He was to Isaiah and the psalmist? If not, what do you need to do to make Him a greater priority? What will you do today?

- Ask yourself, "Do I fellowship with the Lord in prayer and in Scripture because of duty or because He is the desire of my heart?

**A Prayer for You:**

*Desire of My Heart, I long for You. I long to know You and to spend more time with You. Create in me a deeper thirst for You. I don't want to satisfy that longing with anything or anyone else.*

# Great God

*For the Lord your God is God of gods and Lord of lords,*
*the **great God**, mighty and awesome,*
*who shows no partiality nor takes a bribe.*
Deuteronomy 10:17 NKJV

**Steps on Your Journey to Know God More Intimately:**

- *Gadol* means great, high and greater in Hebrew. *El* means God. Titus 2:13 says, "We look forward with hope to that wonderful day when the glory of our great God and Savior, Jesus Christ, will be revealed (NLT).

- Creation reveals how great and awesome our God really is. Think about the human body, everything on the earth, planets, stars, angels, Heaven and so much more. Last night I heard Louie Giglio speak about God's greatness shown in creation. All creation is praising God audibly. I love going out into creation to enjoy what an incredibly great God we have.

- Think about God's greatness. In what ways do you see His greatness around you? Talk to the Lord about how you see Him.

- Give yourself time to revel in all that God is. Share with a friend. Often when we share with others, we gain more than we share, because we have the opportunity to see God through the other person's eyes.

- Look at all the names of God in Deuteronomy 10:17. Meditate on them today.

- Titus 2 reminds us to look forward to the day our Great God is revealed. In what ways are you looking forward to Jesus' return?

**A Prayer for You:**

*Great God, You are so immense, so much greater than my human mind can even begin to comprehend. Show me Your greatness in new ways. I want to see You more clearly. I want to praise You along with all creation.*

October 19

## *Spirit of Adoption*

*For you did not receive the spirit of slavery to fall back into fear,*
*but you have received the **Spirit of adoption** as sons,*
*by whom we cry, "Abba! Father!"*
Romans 8:15 (ESV)

**Steps on Your Journey to Know God More Intimately:**

- *Pneuma* means spirit, breath or wind in Greek. *Huiothesia* means adoption.

- This name is one manifestation of the Holy Spirit, who is in you.

- The King of the Universe chose you. He picked you and adopted you to be His precious child. That makes you a prince or a princess! God gave you His Spirit of Adoption to remind you that He loves you and you're precious to Him. Do you act like a prince or princess? If not, why not?

- Think about this: when you give birth to a child, he may be ugly, but you still have to keep him and love him (well, at least most people do). But when you adopt a child, you can pick the one you want. God picked you because He wanted to have a relationship with you. He wanted *you*. He *wants* you. He loves you more than you'll ever know.

- This name means so much to me, because I often need reminders that God does love me. The Spirit reminds me that I am a daughter of the King of kings. And, so are you (well, if you're a male, then you are His son)!

- Thank God today that He gave you His Spirit of Adoption—making you His child, but also reminding you how much He loves you.

- If you're not convinced that God loves you, ask Him to show you.

**A Prayer for You:**

*Father God, thank You for giving me Your Spirit of Adoption, making me Your child. I know I don't deserve it, but I'm grateful You picked me to be a child of the King of kings. Spirit of Adoption, show me more of who I am because of what You've done and how You see me.*

293

# *Abba! Father!*

*For you did not receive the spirit of slavery to fall back into fear,*
*but you have received the Spirit of adoption as sons,*
*by whom we cry, "**Abba! Father!**"*
Romans 8:15 (ESV)

**Steps on Your Journey to Know God More Intimately:**

- There are only three references for the word, *abba*, in the New Testament. Jesus used it once and Paul twice. Look at the others:

  o In Mark 14:36, Jesus said, "Abba, Father, everything is possible for you. Take this cup from me. Yet not what I will, but what you will."

  o Galatians 4:6: "Because you are his sons, God sent the Spirit of his Son into our hearts, the Spirit who calls out, "Abba, Father."

- *Abba* is Aramaic. It comes from the Hebrew word *ab*, meaning Father. *Abba* is a personal, intimate term for the Father, like Dad or Daddy. *Pater* means father. Meditate on what it means that God is not like an absent, overstressed, abusive or preoccupied father. Your Abba always has time for you.

- I love spending time sitting on my heavenly Daddy's lap, talking and listening to Him. When I slow down enough to hear Him, He has amazing things to say. Many times when I am sad or hurting, Abba picks me up and holds me close.

- Take some time to talk to Abba, your Daddy. In what ways do you struggle with God being your Father? Talk to Him about your questions.

- I pray Abba will draw you closer to Himself today, as you take time to be with Him.

**A Prayer for You:**

*Abba, Father, thank You for being my Daddy. Thank You that I can come to You anytime, knowing You are never too busy to spend time with me. You're never absent, abusive or preoccupied. Thank You for Your great love for me. Help me understand the depths of Your love in new ways.*

October 21

## *My Loving God*

Elohim Khesed (Hebrew)

*O my Strength, I sing praise to you;*
*you, O God, are my fortress, **my loving God**.*
Psalm 59:17

**Steps on Your Journey to Know God More Intimately:**

- *Khesed* is translated loving kindness, mercy, goodness and kindness.

- How do you normally see God? Is He a loving God or is He angry? Or do you see Him some other way? If so, how?

- God loves you and me unconditionally. His love is not dependent on who you are or what you do. Think about what that means.

- The Bible has so much to say about God's love. The Word, especially the New Testament, is the story of His love for you and me. Regardless of what else is going on in your life, take time everyday to look at God's love letter, the Bible, to you.

- I spend time regularly meditating on how much God loves me and the ways He shows it. I also take time alone with Him daily to grow in my love relationship with Him. If this isn't your practice, I encourage you to develop the habit.

- Take some time today to rest in the Lord's love for you. If you're not sure what that looks like, ask Him to show you. Study God's love for you. The more you get to know His love, the more it will transform your life.

**A Prayer for You:**

*My Loving God, I'm so blessed to know You love me unconditionally. Thank You that Your love for me is not based on anything I can do. Instead it is based on who You are and what You've done for me. Show me more of Your love today, Lord.*

# A Very Present Help in Trouble

*God is our refuge and strength, **a very present help in trouble***.
Psalms 46:1 (ESV)

**Steps on Your Journey to Know God More Intimately:**

- The New Living Translation translates this verse, "God is our refuge and strength, always ready to help in times of trouble."

- Do you ever wish someone was there to help you when you are in a predicament? The Lord is always there to help.

- There were many times during the years raising my sons alone that I cried out to God for help. It was too much for me to take care of them by myself. I only had sisters, so I didn't understand boys very well. Whenever I called out to Him, He was always there to help me. And He still is.

- Meditate on how God Is a very present help in trouble.

- What kind of troubles are you having right now?

- How do you need the Lord to be your help in trouble? Ask Him. If you're not sure, you can ask Him that too.

- Thank Him for always being there for you, no matter what you are going through or where you are.

**A Prayer for You:**

*Lord, I'm so grateful You are my Very Present Help in Trouble. Thank You that You are the One I can turn to when problems arise. Thank You that I'm never, ever alone, because You are always here. That is so comforting. Help me to see You and Your work in my life more clearly.*

## Advocate

*My dear children, I am writing this to you so that you will not sin.*
*But if anyone does sin, we have an **advocate***
*who pleads our case before the Father.*
*He is Jesus Christ, the one who is truly righteous.*
1 John 2:1 (NLT)

**Steps on Your Journey to Know God More Intimately:**

- The Greek word for advocate is *parakletos*. It is used in court for someone who pleads another's cause.

- Think about why we need an advocate before the Father: We are sinners. God is holy. Because He is holy, He cannot and will not tolerate sin. So the only way we can have a relationship with God is for us to be made righteous. We couldn't do that on our own, so Jesus came to earth to do it for us.

- Jesus is the One who pleads our case before the Father. Remember, it's like we are in a court room, being tried for what we did wrong. Jesus stands up and says, "Dad, I already paid for _____'s penalty when I died on the cross." At that Father God says, "Not guilty."

- It's comforting to know Jesus is representing me before the Father. What does it mean to you knowing that Jesus is your Advocate?

**A Prayer for You:**

*Advocate, thank You for coming to earth to die for my sins to make me righteous. Thank You that You are my Advocate before the Father, pleading my case, asking the Father to accept me because of what You did.*

## Bridegroom

Khathan (Hebrew)

*As the **bridegroom** rejoices over the bride,
so shall your God rejoice over you.*
Isaiah 62:5 (ESV)

**Steps on Your Journey to Know God More Intimately:**

- *Khathan* means a bridegroom or a husband.

- Consider what it means to you today that God is your Bridegroom. Close your eyes and imagine it's your wedding day. You are marrying the King of kings. What are your feelings and thoughts?

- And guess what? Your Bridegroom rejoices over you. You're His precious bride. What do you think it looks like when God rejoices over you? Stop and enjoy this thought.

- Zephaniah 3:17 adds, "The Lord your God is with you, he is mighty to save. He will take great delight in you, he will quiet you with his love, he will rejoice over you with singing." Spend some time meditating on each phrase of this verse separately. Do you believe this verse? If not, why not? If you are not convinced of any part of it, ask the Lord to show you what is holding you back.

- Wow! I trust this thought, that God is your Bridegroom and that He rejoices over you, is as amazing to you as it is to me!

**A Prayer for You:**

*Lord, thank You for being my Bridegroom. What a privilege to be Your bride. And to think that You rejoice over me with singing. Help me to see how You rejoice over me. I want to hear You singing over me. But I also want to bring You joy in the ways I act toward You. Teach me, Lord.*

# Faithful God

*Know therefore that the Lord your God is God;*
*he is the **faithful God**, keeping his covenant of love*
*to a thousand generations of those who love him*
*and keep his commands.*
Deuteronomy 7:9

**Steps on Your Journey to Know God More Intimately:**

- *El* means God in Hebrew. *Aman* means to be firm, sure, established and steady. It is translated with the following words: believe, assurance, faithful, sure, established, trust, verified, steadfast and several other words. Which of those words stand out to you today?

- Meditate on how you've seen God's faithfulness in your life. It's important to remember what God has done for us in the past. It gives us strength and courage to face new challenges.

- Earlier this month was my son Daniel's birthday. As I look back on his life, I can see God's amazing faithfulness. The Faithful God was always there, even when I couldn't see Him—even though my son only lived six months. I want to challenge you to look for and remember God's faithfulness in your life—even when everything looks bleak.

- Notice what this verse says: the Faithful God keeps his covenant of love to a thousand generations. That is a very long time.

- In what areas of your life do you need Him to be the Faithful God to you? Talk to Him about that.

**A Prayer for You:**

*Faithful God, thank You for being dependable, firm, true and steady, so I can trust You and build my life on You. Thank You for Your incredible love that lasts a thousand generations. Wow! My mind can't even comprehend how long that is and how much love You have for me.*

October 26

## He Who Has Compassion

*They will neither hunger nor thirst,*
*nor will the desert heat or the sun beat upon them.*
***He who has compassion*** *on them will guide them*
*and lead them beside springs of water.*
Isaiah 49:10

**Steps on Your Journey to Know God More Intimately:**

- Other translations of this name include: Compassionate One, He who has mercy on them and He who has pity on them. The Hebrew word for compassion, *rakham,* means to love deeply, be compassionate and to have mercy or pity.

- Think about compassion, with its various translations and meanings. What stands out to you?

- The Lord cares about you. He has compassion on you. You can talk to Him about anything and everything that bothers you. He wants to hear you share with Him—even though He already knows what is happening. He's a patient listener, not getting angry with what you share and not interrupting you.

- Tell the One Who Has Compassion on you what's happening in your life right now. Then thank Him for caring about you.

- This verse says that He Who Has Compassion on You will guide you and lead you beside springs of water. Think about that. How does that encourage you today?

**A Prayer for You:**

*Lord, I praise You that You are the One Who Has Compassion on me. Thank You for caring about me and all the details of my life. I'm glad when I run to You for comfort, You will never turn me away or think that my problem isn't as important as other people's problems.*

## Our Mighty One

*The Lord will be **our Mighty One**. He will be like a wide river of
protection that no enemy can cross, that no enemy ship can sail upon.
For the Lord is our judge, our lawgiver, and our king.
He will care for us and save us.*
Isaiah 33:21-22 (NLT)

**Steps on Your Journey to Know God More Intimately:**

- In the coming days we'll look at three of God's names in these two verses. I want to encourage you to memorize them, or at least read them every day.

- When I was at boarding school in Guatemala from ages six to thirteen, we had to memorize verses every week. At the time, I learned them because I had to, but now I'm so glad I know those verses. The Lord brings them back to me when I most need them.

- *Adeer* is the Greek word translated Our Mighty One. It means mighty, power, strength, excellent and glorious. Our God is all powerful. He is not just a powerful, impersonal God. He is *your* Mighty One. His strength and power are personal for each of us.

- Meditate on how God is not just powerful out in the universe, but He is *your* powerful God. What does that mean to you today?

- In what ways do you want to see God's power in your life?

- How do you need Him to be your Mighty One?

**A Prayer for You:**

*Lord, I praise You that You are my Mighty One. You are all-powerful. Thank You that You are a personal God whose power is available to me. Show me more of how You are my Mighty One. Help me to trust in You and Your strength more than my own or other humans.*

October 28

*Our Judge*

Shafat (Hebrew)

*For the Lord is **our judge**, our lawgiver, and our king.*
*He will care for us and save us.*
Isaiah 33:22 (NLT)

**Steps on Your Journey to Know God More Intimately:**

- *Shafat* means to judge, to pronounce sentence and to vindicate or punish. 1 Peter 4:4-5 says God is the judge of the living and the dead.

- God is the righteous judge. Because He is holy, he has to judge our sin. However, for all who have a relationship with His Son, Jesus, we have an Advocate. We looked at Jesus as the Advocate a few days ago. Remember, when Jesus stands before the Judge (His Father) to defend us, He says, "I already paid for that sin."

- If you don't yet have a relationship with the Lord, I'd encourage you to continue to get to know Him. He really does love you and wants a relationship with you.

- Our Judge will bring judgment against our enemy, Satan, and all the demons of hell. How does that affect you?

- In what ways have you seen God as your Judge?

- How do you need Him to be your Judge? Ask Him.

- I pray God's greatest blessings on you this day as you continue to seek to know Him better.

**A Prayer for You:**

*Father, I'm so glad that You are my Judge, because I know You are always just and fair. Teach me to honor and reverence You as my Judge.*

302

## Our Lawgiver

### Khakak (Hebrew)

*For the Lord is our Judge, The Lord is **our Lawgiver**,*
*The Lord is our King; He will save us.*
Isaiah 33:22 (NKJV)

**Steps on Your Journey to Know God More Intimately:**

- *Khakak* is translated lawgiver, governor and decree.

- The Old Testament is filled with God's laws that He gave His people. I can't imagine trying to obey all of them. How could anyone even keep them all in mind?

- James 4:12 says, "There is only one Lawgiver and Judge, the one who is able to save and destroy. But you—who are you to judge your neighbor?"

- In Matthew 5:17 Jesus said, "Do not think that I have come to abolish the Law or the Prophets; I have not come to abolish them but to fulfill them." What does it mean that Jesus came to fulfill the Law? How did He fulfill it?

- What do these verses say to you about God being our Lawgiver?

- Look what these verses say our Lawgiver does. How does that affect you?

**A Prayer for You:**

*Lord, thank You that You are the Lawgiver, but You also came to fulfill the Law. I'm so grateful that I don't have to keep every one of the laws in the Old Testament. Since You are the Lawgiver, remind me that it's not my place to judge others.*

# King For Ever and Ever

*The Lord is **King forever and ever**.*
Psalm 10:16 (ESV)

**Steps on Your Journey to Know God More Intimately:**

- *Melek* means king or royal.

- Think about what it means to you today that the Lord is your King. He's not just the King of the universe. He is also your King. He's my King.

- How is God your King? How is your life different because He is your King?

- What does it mean to you that the Lord is King forever and ever? Think about how long that is.

- How does your life reveal that He is your King? If it doesn't, you might want to talk to God about that and ask Him how you can honor Him as your King.

- Consider your life today. Are there any attitudes, actions, habits or ways of relating to others that are not in submission to your King? If so, what will you do about them?

**A Prayer for You:**

*God, I praise You for being my King forever and ever. It's encouraging to know that You will always be my King. I honor You and worship You as my King. Teach me how You want me to honor You.*

# He Who Will Save Us

## Hu Yasha (Hebrew)

*For the Lord is our judge, the Lord is our lawgiver,
the Lord is our king; it is **he who will save us**.*
Isaiah 33:22

**Steps on Your Journey to Know God More Intimately:**

- *Hu* is he. The Hebrew word for save is *yasha* meaning to save, deliver, defend, preserve, avenge, rescue and much more. Consider all the meanings for this word. God does so much more for us than just save us from our sins. Which meanings stand out to you today?

- How has God saved you? Think about all the meanings in the Hebrew. Think about all that Jesus did for you when He came to earth to save you.

- I constantly stand in amazement as I think about all Jesus did for me. I try to take time every day to meditate on what He did for me on the cross.

- Take some time to thank the Lord for saving you.

- In what ways do you need the Lord to save you now?

**A Prayer for You:**

*Lord, I praise You that You are the One who has saved me and will save me. Thank You for delivering me, defending me, preserving me and so much more. Teach me more about what You did and do for me.*

## Ancient of Days

*As I looked, thrones were set in place,*
*and the **Ancient of Days** took his seat. His clothing was as white as snow;*
*the hair of his head was white like wool.*
*His throne was flaming with fire, and its wheels were all ablaze.*
*Daniel 7:9*

**Steps on Your Journey to Know God More Intimately:**

- *Ateek* means ancient or antique in Aramaic. *Yom* means day or time.

- There are only three references to the Ancient of Days in the Bible. The other references are Daniel 7:13 and 22.

- *Ateek* refers to God's eternity. He has been around for a very long time. Why do you think Daniel refers to God as the Ancient of Days, rather than some other name?

- Meditate on the descriptions of God in these verses. What is the Lord showing you through them?

- Our God is so amazing. Worship Him today as the Ancient of Days.

**A Prayer for You:**

*Ancient of Days, I praise You because You are so awesome. Teach me about Yourself through this name. I want to know You more, Lord.*

# God Who Richly Provides Us
## with Everything for Our Enjoyment

*Command those who are rich in this present world not to be arrogant nor to put their hope in wealth, which is so uncertain, but to put their hope in **God, who richly provides us with everything for our enjoyment**.*
1 Timothy 6:17

**Steps on Your Journey to Know God More Intimately:**

- There is so much in this name! Take some time to meditate on each of the main words or phrases in this name and thank Him for everything He shows you:

  o God—what does it mean to you that He is God?

  o Richly provides—He doesn't just give us a little bit (although sometimes it may feel like it). How have you seen God provide for you? Think about how God has *richly* provided for you. Thank Him.

  o Everything—how much is that?

  o For our enjoyment—consider what He has provided for your enjoyment.

- This verse says "to put our hope" in this God Who Richly Provides us with Everything for Our Enjoyment. Where is your hope today? If you're struggling to trust the Lord, talk to Him about that. You can tell Him. He knows how you're feeling anyway. Ask Him to help you find hope in Him.

- You might want to write this name on a card or sticky note and put it somewhere that you'll be reminded what a great God we have.

**A Prayer for You:**

*God, You have richly provided me everything I need. Thank You so much for all the things You do for me. Help me to recognize Your provision and thank You more.*

# Spirit of Power, Love and Self-Discipline

*For God did not give us a spirit of timidity,*
*but a **spirit of power, of love and of self-discipline.***
2 Timothy 1:7

**Steps on Your Journey to Know God More Intimately:**

- This name has three parts to it. Take some time to meditate on each part of it.

    o Spirit of Power—We looked at this name earlier in the year, but take some time to meditate on the Spirit who is power and gives you power. In what areas do you want to see His power in your life?

    o Spirit of Love—If you are struggling with feeling loved by God or others, ask the Spirit of Love to reveal His love to you in new ways. If you have a hard time loving those around you, ask the Spirit to fill you with His love for them.

    o Spirit of Self-Discipline—Does the Holy Spirit need self-discipline? Or does He give us self-discipline? Think about that. Ask Him to show you what He wants you to know today through this name.

- I love it that God shows us new and different things each time we focus on Him. Our God is so amazing. He is so multi-faceted. No matter how much we get to know Him, there is always more that we will learn. Yay God!

**A Prayer for You:**

*Holy Spirit, I praise You for Your power, love and self-discipline. Here is my life. I allow You to work in me and fill me with each of these qualities. Thank You for how You work in my life. I don't want to ever hold You back in anyway.*

## Father in Heaven

Pater Ho En Uranos (Greek)

*Pray like this: Our **Father in heaven**,
may your name be kept holy.*
Matthew 6:9 (NLT)

**Steps on Your Journey to Know God More Intimately:**

- *Pater* is father. *Ho* is which or who. *En* is in, by or with. *Uranos* is translated Heaven, air or sky.

- Meditate on this name. What does it mean to you that you have a Father in Heaven? What is He like? If you don't have a very good earthly Father, ask the Lord to show you how He is different.

- It's easy for us to see our Father in Heaven the same as our earthly fathers. That couldn't be further from the truth for most of us. For me it's easy to picture my Heavenly Father as loving and kind, because my earthly father is that way. Even still, I know that my Dad in Heaven is so much more loving and caring and always, always, *always* available for me.

- Take some time today to thank the Lord that He is your Father. Ask Him to reveal Himself to you in greater ways.

- Ask the Lord to open the eyes of your heart to see more of what Heaven is like. One time when I asked the Lord to show me Heaven, I could see my heavenly Daddy and Jesus playing games with my son Daniel. They were running around, having fun! And surprisingly, I saw Ian, my fiancé who was killed, playing with them. Isn't God good!

**A Prayer for You:**

*Father in Heaven, thank You that I am Your child. Thank You for loving me so completely. I want to learn to understand Your love more. As Matthew 6:9 says, I want to always keep Your name holy.*

# November 5

## *Banner for the Peoples*

### Nace Am (Hebrew)

*In that day the Root of Jesse will stand as a **banner for the peoples**;
the nations will rally to him, and his place of rest will be glorious.*
Isaiah 11:10

**Steps on Your Journey to Know God More Intimately:**

- *Nace* means flag, banner, standard or signal. *Am* means people, nation or tribe.

- In the Old Testament when nations were at war, they would fly their own flags or banners on their front lines. This gave their soldiers hope and a focal point. Jesus is our banner of encouragement to give us hope and a focal point.

- How has Jesus brought you hope and courage during your struggles?

- First Timothy 6:12 says, "Fight the good fight of the faith. Take hold of the eternal life to which you were called when you made your good confession in the presence of many witnesses." What does this say to you today?

- In John 12:32 Jesus says, "But I, when I am lifted up from the earth, will draw all men to myself." Jesus fulfilled Isaiah 11:10 when He was lifted up on the cross, just as the banner was lifted up.

- Praise and thank Jesus that He was willing to be a Banner for you. He was willing to go to the cross for you to pay for your sins. Thank Him that as you look to Him you can find hope and courage.

**A Prayer for You:**

*Jesus, thank You for coming to earth to be a Banner for me. You came to bring me hope and encouragement, so that I can keep fighting the good fight. Help me to keep my eyes focused on You, especially when I'm in the midst of the hardest battles.*

# Branch of Righteousness

*In those days, and at that time, will I cause
the **Branch of righteousness** to grow up unto David;
and he shall execute judgment and righteousness in the land.*
Jeremiah 33:15 (KJV)

**Steps on Your Journey to Know God More Intimately:**

- *Tsemakh* in Hebrew means branch, sprout, bud or that which grew up. *Tsedaka* means righteousness, justice and righteous acts.

- This verse and name are referring to Jesus. Isaiah 4:2 and 11:1 also refer to the Messiah as the Branch.

- Ask the Lord to show you what it means that He is the Branch of Righteousness.

- Second Corinthians 5:21 says Jesus became sin for you and me. He didn't just take your sin on Himself. He *became* sin. He became sin for you so you might become God's righteousness. Wow! Think about that! Jesus is righteous and He made you the righteousness of God! That amazing thought brings me to my knees.

- Thank the Branch of Righteousness that He will bring justice and righteousness to you. What does that mean to you today?

**A Prayer for You:**

*Lord, thank You that You are the Branch of Righteousness. Teach me more of what this name means. Thank You that You traded my sin for Your righteousness, so I can have a relationship with You. I choose to live my life in right ways that will honor You.*

## Gate for the Sheep

Thura Probaton (Greek)

*Jesus said, I am the **gate for the sheep**.*
John 10:7 (NLT)

**Steps on Your Journey to Know God More Intimately:**

- *Thura* means gate, door or portal. *Probaton* means sheep or sheepfold.

- Think about this: Jesus is both the Shepherd (as we'll look at tomorrow) and the Gate. He's also the Lamb (see John 1:36) as we saw earlier.

- How can Jesus have all those roles? Do you think it has something to do with Him being everything we need?

- In a sheepfold, the shepherd would stretch out to sleep across the opening. He became the "gate" to the sheepfold. The sheep could not get out or predators get in without the shepherd knowing.

- Jesus protects us by being our Gate. He protects us from the enemy who comes to steal, kill and destroy (John 10:10). How have you seen the Lord protect you? Thank Him.

- When we wander away from the fold and the Gate for the Sheep, we may not have his protection. Do you need to return to the Shepherd today? If so, He's waiting for you and eager for your return.

**A Prayer for You:**

*Jesus, thank You that You are the Gate for the sheep. You are the One who provides the way to the Father. You are also the One who protects me from the enemy. Help me to always remember to stay within Your protection.*

## Good Shepherd

*I am the good shepherd.*
*The **good shepherd** lays down his life for the sheep.*
*I am the **good shepherd**; I know my sheep and my sheep know me.*
John 10:11 and 14

**Steps on Your Journey to Know God More Intimately:**

- *Kalos* in Greek means good, better or honest. *Poimane* is a shepherd or a pastor.

- Think about how a shepherd takes care of his sheep. Psalm 23 talks about some of the things the Lord does for us as our Shepherd. You might want to read that Psalm today.

- Our Good Shepherd laid His life down for us when He died on the cross, because He loves us so much. Think about that. Thank Him.

- Our Shepherd knows us and wants us to know Him. Are you satisfied with where your relationship with the Lord is right now? If not, talk to Him about it.

- Throughout the last seventeen years as I raised my sons alone, I relied on the Lord as my Good Shepherd. He was and is always there to lead me, protect, provide, give me rest and so much more.

- How has Jesus been a Good Shepherd to you?

- In what ways do you need to let Jesus be your Shepherd? Maybe you need to snuggle into His arms and let Him carry you. Maybe you need to slow down and get to know Him better. If you're not sure, ask Him to show you.

**A Prayer for You:**

*Good Shepherd, thank You for all the ways You lead me, protect me and provide for me. I want to get to know Your voice, so that I can distinguish it from the voice of the enemy. Thank You for being willing to lay down Your life for me.*

## Gift of God

*Jesus answered her, "If you knew the **gift of God***
*and who it is that asks you for a drink, you would have asked him and*
*he would have given you living water."*
John 4:10

**Steps on Your Journey to Know God More Intimately:**

- *Dorea* in Greek means gift. *Theos* is the Supreme Deity.

- My birthday was just a couple of days ago and I received some great gifts. However, none can begin to compare with the gift I've received through Jesus and all He did for me and for you.

- Jesus is the most precious gift you and I can ever receive.

- How is Jesus God's gift to you?

- What has He done for you?

- Talk to Jesus about what this name means.

- Thank Him for what He shows you.

- I trust you are getting to know the Lord better each day. I'd love to hear what you're learning. You can go to our website and post your comments.

**A Prayer for You:**

*Jesus, thank You for being the Gift of God to me. You bring me joy, peace, comfort, strength, hope and so much more. I want to understand You as the Gift of God. Open my eyes to see You clearly.*

## God of Gods

*Give thanks to the Lord, for he is good! His faithful love endures forever.*
*Give thanks to the **God of gods**. His faithful love endures forever.*
Psalm 136:1-2 (NLT)

**Steps on Your Journey to Know God More Intimately:**

* *Elohim* is the plural name of God, pointing toward the Godhead—
Father, Son and Spirit. This name is *Elohim elohim*.

* Today we're going to start preparing our hearts for Thanksgiving (in
the United States. We'll look at God's names from Psalm 136. This
whole chapter is about giving thanks. I'd encourage you to read it
several times this week. Let's use it to help us focus on the great
things God has done in the past as well as in our own lives.

* Our God is the God of gods. What are some gods people worship?
Often we think of other gods as idols sitting on a table or the floor.
However we can make anything into a god or an idol, such as money,
people, success, prestige and things. A god is anything that you
worship in place of the Only True God.

* Take some time to talk to the Lord. Ask Him if there is anything or
anyone that you are putting in place of Him.

* Close your eyes and imagine the God of gods. Imagine all the various
gods people worship—all on their faces before the God of gods.
I see all the gods as lifeless, broken images placed in front of our
great God.

* This verse says, "Give thanks to the God of gods. His faithful love
endures forever." What does it mean to you that His faithful love
endures forever?

**A Prayer for You:**

*God of gods, thank You for Your love that endures forever. Thank You that it's
not dependent on what I do. I praise You that You are so high above any other
god. None can even begin to compare with You. Show me if I have anything
or anyone that I worship in place of You. If so, forgive me, Lord.*

# Him Who Alone Does Mighty Miracles

Asa Gadol Pala (Hebrew)

*Give thanks to **him who alone does mighty miracles**.*
*His faithful love endures forever.*
Psalm 136:4 (NLT)

**Steps on Your Journey to Know God More Intimately:**

- *Asa* means to do or make. *Gadol* means great or high. *Pala* is translated wonders, marvelous and wonderful. Our God is the One who does mighty miracles. What are some of the mighty miracles God did in the Bible? If you can't think of any, I want to encourage you to take some time to look for them. The Bible is filled with amazing miracles.

- When my sons were four and ten, we had just moved with our dog, Barkley, to Colorado to start a new life. Soon after, Barkley ate a whole bag of chocolate chips (it's a long story). By the time we found him, he was so shaky he could hardly stand up. When I called the vet, she said there was nothing they could do. He would die very soon. The boys and I laid hands on him and prayed. Within *one* hour he was completely healed. God did a mighty miracle that day for us.

- The New International Version says, "Him who alone does great wonders." What wonders has God done in your life? There are probably many more than you realize. Think about this all day.

- If you think you haven't seen any miracles in your life, ask the Lord to show you. I would be surprised if there haven't been some. The problem is that often we don't recognize the miracles God does. Often we give a person the credit or we say it was a coincidence.

- Share what God has done for you with a friend or family member.

- This verse, as well as each verse in this chapter, reminds us that God's faithful love endures forever. Think about that.

**A Prayer for You:**

*Lord, I praise You that You are the One who does mighty miracles. Thank You that You still do them today. Open my eyes to see miracles You have done in my life. Increase my faith so I can trust You to see more miracles around me.*

# Him Who Made the Heavens so Skillfully

Asa Shamayim Tabun (Hebrew)

*Give thanks to **him who made the heavens so skillfully**.*
*His faithful love endures forever.*
Psalm 136:5 (NLT)

**Steps on Your Journey to Know God More Intimately:**

- *Asa* means to do or make. *Shamayim* refers to both the visible sky as well as the higher heavens where the celestial bodies are. *Tabun* means understanding, skill, discernment and reasoning.

- Consider all God created in the heavens—the stars, moons, suns, planets, galaxies, black holes, etc. Earth can't even begin to compare with a few of the stars, because some are so massive. The largest known star is Canis Majoris, located about 5,000 light-years from Earth. A University of Minnesota professor recently calculated its size at more than 2,100 times the size of the Sun. That's amazing.

- The New International Version says, "him who by his understanding made the heavens." He not only has understanding to make the heavens, He understands you. I've felt very alone sometimes, feeling like no one (human) understands me. How precious to know He cares and understands me—and you. His faithful love for us will never end.

- Since God is so great and big, don't you think He is big enough to handle whatever situations may come into your life?

**A Prayer for You:**

*God, my mind can't even begin to comprehend how great and awesome You are. Thank You for making the heavens so skillfully. And thank You once again for Your faithful love for me that will never end.*

# Him Who Placed the Earth among the Waters

## Raka Erets Al Mayim (Hebrew)

*Give thanks to **him who placed the earth among the waters**.*
*His faithful love endures forever.*
Psalm 136:6 (NLT)

**Steps on Your Journey to Know God More Intimately:**

- *Raka* means to spread or stretch. *Erets* is land or earth. *Al* is above, over or among. *Mayim* means water.

- The Message translates this verse, "The God who laid out earth on ocean foundations, His love never quits."

- God's love never quits. Do you believe that? If not, ask the Lord to show you His great love today.

- Think about God laying the earth on ocean foundations. How might that show you His faithful love?

- Meditate on this name. Ask the Lord to show you what He wants you to see through it.

- This verse says to thank the God who placed the earth among the waters. Take some time to thank the Lord for what He did when He created the earth.

**A Prayer for You:**

*God, thank You for how You laid the earth on the ocean foundations. You created everything perfectly. Thank You for Your faithful love that endures forever. I want to understand Your love more. And I want to learn to give thanks to You for everything.*

# Him Who Made the Heavenly Lights

*Give thanks to **him who made the heavenly lights**—*
*His faithful love endures forever.*
*the sun to rule the day, His faithful love endures forever.*
*and the moon and stars to rule the night. His faithful love endures forever.*
Psalm 136:7-9 (NLT)

**Steps on Your Journey to Know God More Intimately:**

- *Asa* means do or make in Hebrew. *Gadol* is great or high. *Or* means light or lights.

- The Message translates Psalm 136:7: "The God who filled the skies with light, His love never quits."

- I used to read Psalm 136 skipping over the last part of each verse, "His faithful love endures forever." It just seemed so repetitive. Why do you think God repeated Himself so many times in this Psalm? If you're anything like me, you probably need to be reminded over and over about how much God loves you. Think about that.

- There was a time I gave up on God, because I started to focus on all the hard times in my life up to that point. I felt like God must not really love me, otherwise He would protect me from so much pain and loss. I desperately needed to understand that He really did love me. It's a long story how I made the slow journey back, but it was because of His love.

- Have you ever struggled with knowing God loves you? Are you struggling with that now? Ask God to reveal to you how much He really does love you.

- The heavenly lights include the sun, moon and stars. Go outside sometime today and look at the lights in the sky. How do they reveal God's love for you? If you're not sure, ask God to show you.

**A Prayer for You:**

*Lord, thank You for making the heavenly lights for me to enjoy, but also to provide light and warmth for me. Thank You that Your love never quits. Open my heart to understand more of what that means.*

# Him Who Killed the Firstborn of Egypt

*Give thanks to **him who killed the firstborn of Egypt**.*
*His faithful love endures forever.*
Psalm 136:10 (NLT)

**Steps on Your Journey to Know God More Intimately:**

- How can God killing the firstborn of Egypt possibly show you and me His faithful love? Think about that.

- God killed all the firstborn to save His people, to rescue them. It was the only way the Egyptians would let the Israelites leave, because they were slaves there. You can read the story in Exodus 12 through 14.

- Think about this name. Ask God what He wants to show you through it.

- Thank God He loves you enough to do whatever needs to be done to save you. Remember, the enemy God protects us from most of the time is Satan and his demons (Ephesians 6:12).

- Take some time to read all of Psalm 136 again. It is a great reminder to be thankful.

**A Prayer for You:**

*Lord, sometimes You work in ways I don't understand. Teach me more about Yourself through this name. Thank You for saving me from the enemy. I'm so blessed by Your faithful love and care for me.*

# Him Who Led His People through the Wilderness

Yalak Am Midbar (Hebrew)

*Give thanks to **him who led his people through the wilderness**.*
*His faithful love endures forever.*
Psalm 136:16 (NLT)

**Steps on Your Journey to Know God More Intimately:**

- *Yalak* means go, walk, come or lead. *Am* is people or nation. *Midbar* is wilderness or desert.

- Do you ever feel like you're wandering around in a wilderness? Have you ever thought that God might be there leading you, like He led the children of Israel?

- God shows His love to us when He leads us through the dry and hard times in our lives, although often it may not feel like it. Think about some of those periods in your life. How did God show you His love during those times?

- God has shown me His love during the hard times of my life, like after my fiancé was killed on his motorcycle. I could hear the Lord reminding me of Bible verses about His love and care for me, as I lay curled in my bed sobbing. He led me through those dark days.[6]

- Thank Him for how He has led you. If you can't see His love in the hard situations, ask Him to show you.

- Wilderness times can be very stressful. During those times, knowing God's faithful love can help you manage your stress. Ask God to show you how His love can help with your stress management.[7]

**A Prayer for You:**

*Lord, thank You that You are always there to lead me through the wilderness times of my life. Remind me that You are there when I have a hard time seeing You. I want to know Your love more in the hard times of life.*

# Him Who Struck Down Mighty Kings

*Give thanks **to him who struck down mighty kings**.*
*His faithful love endures forever....*
*God gave the land of these kings as an inheritance—*
*His faithful love endures forever.*
Psalm 136:17, 21 (NLT)

**Steps on Your Journey to Know God More Intimately:**

- Once again we see God's faithful love in the middle of Him killing off people. Those don't seem to go together, do they? However, God was protecting and taking care of His people, dealing with those who hated and wanted to destroy them. His love for them was unconditional. He didn't just take care of them when they were acting right and loving Him. He cared for them, even when they sinned.

- How have you seen God protect you and take care of you?

- How have you seen Him strike down your enemy (Satan and his demonic forces)?

- How have you seen God stand up for you with humans?

- Thank God again today for His faithful love for you that endures forever. It will never, ever end.

**A Prayer for You:**

*Lord, I don't understand Your ways, but I'm so grateful that You are always there to protect me and stand up for me. I'm amazed at Your love that never ends.*

# He Who Remembered Us in Our Low Estate

## Shayfel Zakar (Hebrew)

*It is **he who remembered us in our low estate**,*
*for his steadfast love endures forever.*
Psalm 136:23 (ESV)

**Steps on Your Journey to Know God More Intimately:**

- This name in Hebrew is *Zakar Shayfel. Zakar* means remember and mention. *Shayfel* is a low estate or humble rank.

- The Message translates this verse, "God remembered us when we were down, His love never quits."

- God isn't just the God of the rich and powerful. He is also the God of those who feel like they are at the bottom of society.

- When I first became a single parent, I felt like I was "less than" others around me. I didn't have status, success, wealth or a spouse. But during those years, God was always there taking care of me. He remembered me in my low estate. He did miracles in my finances. Most months I didn't have enough to pay my bills, but they were always covered. No one else paid them. God just multiplied what I had. I felt like the widow who kept pouring oil into the jars (2 Kings 4).

- How have you seen God remember you when you were down?

- Thank the Lord that He remembers you no matter where you are or what you are experiencing. Everything He does is because He loves you.

**A Prayer for You:**

*God, thank You that You remember me when I'm down and feeling like I'm not important. Thank You that You don't look down on me when I am at my lowest points. I'm so grateful that You reveal Your steadfast love to me in this way.*

## November 19

## One Who Freed Us from Our Enemies

*To the **One who ... freed us from our enemies**,*
*His love endures forever.*
Psalm 136:23-24

**Steps on Your Journey to Know God More Intimately:**

- Sometimes we think people are our enemies. Ephesians 6:12 says our enemy is not flesh and blood—either within ourselves or others. Have you ever felt like you are your own worst enemy?

- Who does Ephesians 6:12 say is our enemy? "For our struggle is not against flesh and blood, but against the rulers, against the authorities, against the powers of this dark world and against the spiritual forces of evil in the heavenly realms." What does this say to you?

- Jesus died to free us from Satan's power. Thank Him. What a gift!

- Every day I try to take the time to remember who my great God is and who my enemy is. I put on the armor in Ephesians 6:10-18. I'd encourage you to get in that habit too. Our God is so much bigger than the enemy and He has already freed us from him. However, often people live as though the enemy is stronger.

- How might God freeing you from your enemies help you to see that His love endures forever?

**A Prayer for You:**

*Jesus, thank You that You came to bring me freedom from Satan. He has no power over me, because You already overcame him. I want to know and understand Your great love for me in fresh ways. Teach me, Lord.*

# He Who Gives Food to All Flesh

**He who gives food to all flesh**,
*for his steadfast love endures forever.*
Psalm 136:25 (ESV)

**Steps on Your Journey to Know God More Intimately:**

- The New International Version says, "He who gives food to all creatures."

- If the Lord gives food to every creature, how much more will He provide for you and me!

- How has God provided for you in the past?

- Thank Him for His provision of food (and other things He gives you) whether you're eating steak and lobster or beans and rice. When I was a missionary in a Mayan village in Guatemala, I ate mostly beans, rice and tortillas. I was grateful to have "normal" food! I ate some interesting things in Guatemala, including katydids, dragonflies and the claw on an iguana (they gave us the best part)!

- In what ways do you need Him to provide for you now? Ask Him.

- Can you thank God for what He gives you, even if it isn't what you might have wanted?

**A Prayer for You:**

*Lord, thank You so much for all the ways You have provided for me in the past and in the present. And thank You for how I know You will provide for me throughout my entire life. I know You give me my food, because You love me.*

# God of Heaven

El Shamayim (Hebrew)

*Give thanks to the **God of heaven**. His love endures forever.*
Psalm 136:26

**Steps on Your Journey to Know God More Intimately:**

- *Shamayim* refers to Heaven and the sky. *El* is God.

- The Bible has so much to say about Heaven. I found 454 references to Heaven. I'd encourage you to read Revelation 4 and 5 to learn more about what it will be like when we get there.

- Philippians 3:20 says, "But our citizenship is in heaven, and from it we await a Savior, the Lord Jesus Christ."

- First Peter 3:21-22 says, "Jesus Christ, who has gone into heaven and is at the right hand of God, with angels, authorities, and powers having been subjected to him."

- Think about Heaven. What does it mean to you today that your God is the God of Heaven?

- Meditate on this name. Then thank Him and praise Him for what He shows you.

- If He's big enough to manage all of Heaven, don't you think He's big enough to handle your issues and problems?

- When my son Timothy was four years old, we were driving to church one evening when the sun was shining through a little hole in the clouds. I said, "It looks like Jesus could come back to take us to Heaven." Without missing a beat, Timothy said, "Yeah, to pick up a load of dead dudes." His theology was great. His vocabulary was interesting!

**A Prayer for You:**

*God of Heaven, I praise You that You are such a big God who is over all of Heaven and Earth. Thank You that You are there preparing a place for me. That reminds me that Your love endures forever. I'm blessed knowing I'll always be with You in Heaven.*

## Son

*Therefore go and make disciples of all nations,*
*baptizing them in the name of the Father and of the **Son***
*and of the Holy Spirit.*
Matthew 28:19

**Steps on Your Journey to Know God More Intimately:**

- *Huios* means son in Greek. Think about how Jesus is God's Son—the Son. What does that mean to you?

- If you have children, think about how important they are to you. Consider how important Jesus is to the Father.

- Luke 10:22 says, "No one truly knows the Father except the Son and those to whom the Son chooses to reveal him." Because of what Jesus did for us on the cross, Jesus chooses to reveal the Father to us. In what ways has Jesus revealed the Father to you?

- Spend some time talking to the Son today. Don't forget to listen to what He wants to say to you.

**A Prayer for You***:*

*Jesus, I praise You for being the Son of God. Thank You for being willing to come to earth to live and die for me because of Your great love for me. I want to know You more intimately. Open my mind and heart to understand You in deeper ways.*

## Great and Awesome God

*I prayed to the Lord my God and made confession, saying,
"O Lord, the **great and awesome God**, who keeps covenant and
steadfast love with those who love him and keep his commandments."*
Daniel 9:4 (ESV)

**Steps on Your Journey to Know God More Intimately:**

- This name in Hebrew is *Gadol Yaray El. Gadol* means great, high and greater. *Yaray,* means awesome, the One to be feared or reverenced.

- The King James Version calls him "the great and dreadful God."

- Meditate on each word in this name. Ask the Lord to show you what they mean.

  o Great

  o Awesome God

- How can you show reverence for God today?

- This verse says this Great and Awesome God keeps His covenant and His steadfast love with those who love Him and keep His commands. Meditate on this. What is the Lord showing you?

**A Prayer for You:**

*Lord, I praise You that You are such a Great and Awesome God. You not only created the heavens and the earth—which is absolutely incredible—but You also care about me. You keep all Your promises to me and Your love will never quit. Thank You so much.*

# God of All the Earth

*For your Creator will be your husband;*
*the Lord of Heaven's Armies is his name!*
*He is your Redeemer, the Holy One of Israel,*
*the **God of all the earth**.*
Isaiah 54:5 (NLT)

**Steps on Your Journey to Know God More Intimately:**

- This name in Hebrew is *Elohim Erets*. *Erets* is earth or land.

- Earlier this year we looked at the other names of God in this verse.

- Meditate on this name and this verse.

- Your creator, your husband, is the God of All the Earth. He is the One who created the earth and He is over it. Think about what the earth is like, all its diversity: hills, mountains, oceans, rivers, plants, animals, bugs, trees, lakes and so much more. Our God is so creative.

- I've been privileged to travel around the United States and the world speaking and training churches and mission groups. I love seeing all the diversity of God's handiwork.

- What is God showing you about yourself and Himself through this name?

- How can you thank, praise or worship God today through this name?

**A Prayer for You:**

*God of All the Earth, I worship You for Your greatness and power. I need to be reminded of how great You really are. Forgive me for putting You in a little box and forgetting how creative and awesome You are.*

# Lord Who Has Compassion on You

*"For the mountains may depart and the hills be removed,*
*but my steadfast love shall not depart from you,*
*and my covenant of peace shall not be removed,"*
*says the* **Lord, who has compassion on you.**
Isaiah 54:10 (ESV)

**Steps on Your Journey to Know God More Intimately:**

- This name in Hebrew is *Yahweh Rakham. Rakham* means to have compassion, love or pity. One definition of compassion is "sympathy and concern for the sufferings or misfortunes of others."

- How have you seen God have compassion on you?

- In what areas do you need God's compassion?

- I've experienced God's compassion so many times in my life. One time was when I was at boarding school when I was about seven years old. I got a whole series of childhood illnesses including measles, mumps, chicken pox and scarlet fever. I was in the infirmary all alone for most of two months. God showed His compassion with the infirmary being next to Aunt Margaret's room. She was one person who really loved us and showed compassion.

- Read this verse again. It is what the Lord Who Has Compassion on You is saying to you. Even if the mountains could go away, God's steadfast love will never, ever leave you.

- Did you know God has a covenant of peace with you? This verse says He does and it will never be taken away from you. Ask Him to show you what that looks like.

- What does it mean to you that the Lord has compassion on you?

**A Prayer for You:**

*Thank You, Lord, that You have compassion on me. Sometimes it seems like no one around me has compassion or cares about how I'm feeling. Yet You always do. Thank You that I can run to You when I need compassion and kindness. And thank You for Your steadfast love for me and Your covenant of peace.*

## Architect

Teknitace (Greek)

*For he was looking forward to the city with foundations,*
*whose **architect** and builder is God.*
Hebrews 11:10

**Steps on Your Journey to Know God More Intimately:**

- *Teknitace* means craftsman, builder, artisan or creator. This is the only time in the whole Bible that the word *teknitace* is used.

- The English Standard Version translates this word "designer."

- An architect designs buildings, cities, etc. God is the greatest architect. He designed the heavenly city.

- In John 14:1-2, Jesus says He is going to His Father's house to prepare a place for us.

- Think about what Heaven might be like. God did such a wonderful job creating the earth and the universe, I imagine He outdid Himself on designing Heaven. I don't know about you, but I'm eagerly waiting for the day I get there!

- Thank God that He is Heaven's architect, that He is preparing a place for your future.

**A Prayer for You:**

*God, thank You that You designed an incredible place for me to go when I leave this earth. I know it will be amazing, because everything else You've done is marvelous—here on earth and in the heavens. I'm looking forward to seeing the city You designed.*

November 27

## *Builder*

Demiorgous (Greek)

*For he was looking forward to the city that has foundations,*
*whose designer and **builder** is God.*
Hebrews 11:10 (ESV)

**Steps on Your Journey to Know God More Intimately:**

- *Demiorgous* means maker or builder.

- Hebrews 3:4 says, "For every house is built by someone, but God is the builder of everything."

- Consider that God built Heaven, but He also built everything else. There is nothing that He has not made. Yes, people make things, but everything is made out of materials God created.

- Think about what it means that God built the heavenly city. Why would He have to build it? Couldn't He just speak it into existence like He did the earth? Ask Him to show you more of what this name means.

- This verse is talking about Abraham looking forward to the city that has foundations. Why do you think this verse talks about the foundations, rather than about the mansions prepared for us (John 14:1-2) or the streets of gold (Revelation 21) or God's throne or anything else he could have mentioned?

**A Prayer for You:**

*God, I'm looking forward to getting to the city You built for my eternal home. Thank You for designing and building it. When life begins to get mundane, remind me about my future with You.*

## Author and Perfecter of Our Faith

*Let us fix our eyes on Jesus, the **author and perfecter of our faith**,
who for the joy set before him endured the cross, scorning its shame,
and sat down at the right hand of the throne of God.*
Hebrews 12:2

**Steps on Your Journey to Know God More Intimately:**

- Other versions use founder or pioneer for author. Some use finisher instead of perfecter. How does this name change how you see Jesus?

- I'm the author of books, but God is the author of *your* faith. Think about that. He is the One who began your faith, on whom it's founded and He is the One who will make your faith stronger, more perfect. Ask God to reveal what this name means to you.

- This verse says that we are to fix our eyes on Jesus, the Author and Perfecter of Our Faith. Once again, we are reminded to focus on Jesus. He is the perfect example of how to live this life and go through hard times. Read this verse again, meditating on each part of it.

- The Message translates this verse, "Keep your eyes on Jesus, who both began and finished this race we're in. Study how he did it. Because he never lost sight of where he was headed—that exhilarating finish in and with God—he could put up with anything along the way: Cross, shame, whatever. And now he's there, in the place of honor, right alongside God."

- Focusing on Jesus has helped me so many time throughout my life. When I focus on my problems, they seem to get bigger and bigger. But when I focus on Him, they seem to shrink in comparison with His greatness. What do you need to do today to fix your eyes on Jesus, Author and Perfecter of Your Faith?

**A Prayer for You:**

*Jesus, thank You that You are the One who both began my faith and You are perfecting it. I want to learn to keep my eyes on You, looking at how You went through Your terrible suffering. You kept your eyes on the joy set before You. Teach me how to imitate You in this area.*

November 29

## *Christ Jesus Our Lord*
### Who Has Given Me Strength

*I thank **Christ Jesus our Lord, who has given me strength** to do his work.*
*He considered me trustworthy and appointed me to serve him.*
1 Timothy 1:12 (NLT)

**Steps on Your Journey to Know God More Intimately:**

- Look at each part of this name. Think about what each part means to you.

    o Christ—meaning the Anointed One, the Messiah, revealing His deity.

    o Jesus—comes from the Hebrew word, *Yeshua,* or Joshua. It means "Jehovah is Salvation" or "the Lord saves." Jesus reveals his humanity.

    o Lord—meaning master or owner.

    o Who Has Given Me Strength—even though He is your Lord and Master, yet He gives you strength. As your Master, He could expect you to just serve Him, yet He *chooses* to give you strength.

- In what areas do you need God's strength today? Talk to Him about it. Then thank Him for the strength He does give you.

- When one of my sons made some very poor choices in his teens, the Lord gave me so much strength to keep going. I couldn't have done it without Him.

- There is amazing power in Jesus' name. Read John 14:12-14 and John 15:16 to discover more of the power in the name of Jesus. Ask the Lord to show you how you can tap into the power in Jesus' name in new ways.

**A Prayer for You:**

*Christ Jesus My Lord, I praise You today for who You are, both God and Man. You are both my Master as well as the One who gives me strength. Thank You. Teach me to rely more on Your strength and less on my own.*

334

# Crown of Glory

*Atara Tsebee* (Hebrew)

*In that day the Lord of hosts will be a **crown of glory**,
and a diadem of beauty, to the remnant of his people.*
Isaiah 28:5 (ESV)

**Steps on Your Journey to Know God More Intimately:**

- *Atara* means crown. I wonder if tiara comes from this word. *Tsebee* means glorious, beautiful and splendor.

- The New International Version translates this name "glorious crown."

- Isaiah 28:1-4 talks about the proud crown of the drunkards, which the Lord will cast down. But He will be the glorious crown of His people.

- Ask the Lord to show you how He is or can be your Crown of Glory. After you ask, don't forget to stop and listen to what He says. Often it helps me to close my eyes and ask the Lord to give me a picture of Him—in this case as a Crown of Glory. Thank Him for what He shows you.

- First Peter 5:4 says, "When the Chief Shepherd appears, you will receive the crown of glory that does not fade away." He'll give us a crown of glory and He is our Crown of Glory. Think about that!

**A Prayer for You:**

*Lord of Hosts, thank You that You will be a Crown of Glory for me. Show me how You will be my Glorious Crown, as well as giving me a crown of glory. Teach me. Open my mind and heart to know You more.*

December 1

*Diadem of Beauty*

Tsefeera Teefara (Hebrew)

*In that day the Lord of hosts will be a crown of glory,
and a **diadem of beauty**, to the remnant of his people.*
Isaiah 28:5 (ESV)

**Steps on Your Journey to Know God More Intimately:**

- *Tsefeera* is a diadem or a crown. *Teefara* means beauty, glory or honor.

- This name is also translated Beautiful Wreath. Dictionary.com says diadem is a "crown worn as a sign of royalty." It is an ornamental headband (a wreath around the head) that is worn as a badge of royalty, revealing royal power or dignity.

- Consider this name, either version of it—Beautiful Wreath or Diadem of Beauty. How is the Lord a beautiful crown for you?

- Isaiah 62:3 says to Israel, "You shall be a crown of beauty in the hand of the LORD, and a royal diadem in the hand of your God." I believe this was meant for us also (Galatians 3:7-9). Once again, not only is the Lord your beautiful crown, but you are also a crown of beauty and a royal diadem. Wow!

- I pray that God is blessing you as much as He blesses me in this study. I want to challenge you to study each of these names deeper. There is so much to learn about our Lord. His names are wonderful.

**A Prayer for You:**

*Lord, once again I am in awe of who You are and all Your many facets. Thank You that You are my Crown of Beauty, but I am also a royal diadem. Teach me to understand You and Your names in greater ways. I long to know You more intimately.*

December 2

*Heavenly Man*

*Adam, the first man, was made from the dust of the earth,*
*while Christ, the second man, came from heaven....*
*Just as we are now like the earthly man,*
*we will someday be like the **heavenly man**.*
1 Corinthians 15:47, 49 (NLT)

**Steps on Your Journey to Know God More Intimately:**

- This name is *epuranios* and means heavenly or celestial in Greek.

- This passage is comparing Adam, the first man, with Christ—the earthly versus the heavenly.

- Meditate on this name. It combines both Jesus' deity (being God) and His humanity.

- Ask the Lord to make this name real to you today, revealing Himself to you through it.

- Philippians 2:5-8 adds, "Have this mind among yourselves, which is yours in Christ Jesus, who, though he was in the form of God, did not count equality with God a thing to be grasped, but made himself nothing, taking the form of a servant, being born in the likeness of men. And being found in human form, he humbled himself by becoming obedient to the point of death, even death on a cross" (NLT).

- What do these verses say to you?

**A Prayer for You:**

*Jesus, thank You that though You are God, You were willing to come to earth to become a man. You became like us so that we could someday become like You, the Heavenly Man. Show me more of what this name means. I want to know You, Lord.*

December 3

## *Immanuel, God with Us*

*Therefore the Lord himself will give you a sign: The virgin will be with*
*child and will give birth to a son, and will call him **Immanuel**.*
Isaiah 7:14

**Steps on Your Journey to Know God More Intimately:**

- Matthew 1:23 quotes Isaiah 7:14: "'The virgin will be with child and will give birth to a son, and they will call him Immanuel'—which means, 'God with us.'"

- I encourage you to read Luke 2 and Matthew 2 as we begin to prepare ourselves to celebrate Jesus' birth.

- Consider what Jesus' name, Immanuel, means.

- What does it mean to you that God is with you?

- Isaiah prophesied hundreds of years before Jesus was born exactly what would happen. A virgin would be with child—that was a total miracle. Isaiah also said the virgin would have a son and call Him Immanuel.

- What is the chance of a virgin getting pregnant? It's impossible without God.

- God wanted people to know many years beforeexactly what He would do, so that people would believe in Him. What do you think about all this?

- I'm so grateful that God came as Immanuel, God with Us. He is still with me—and you—today. I love talking to him throughout the day and night. It's comforting knowing there is always someone to listen to and hold me.

**A Prayer for You:**

*Immanuel, thank You for Your impossible plan that You laid out hundreds of years before it happened. Thank You for performing miracles in how You came to earth. What comfort I find in knowing You are always with me.*

## *Wonderful Counselor*

*For to us a child is born, to us a son is given;*
*and the government shall be upon his shoulder,*
*and his name shall be called* **Wonderful Counselor***, Mighty God,*
*Everlasting Father, Prince of Peace.*
Isaiah 9:6 (ESV)

**Steps on Your Journey to Know God More Intimately:**

- We'll look at Jesus' names in this one verse for the next few days. I want to encourage you to begin to memorize Isaiah 9:6. If you prefer another version of the Bible, memorize it in that translation. Write it out and read it daily.

- This name is *Pele Yahats* in Hebrew. *Pele* means a miracle, a wonder or a marvelous thing. The Hebrew root for *yahats* means to advise, consult and guide. Think about these meanings. What does it mean to you that God sent us the Wonderful Counselor?

- In what areas do you need the Wonderful Counselor today?

- Read the verses, below to see more about God as our Counselor. What do they say to you?

  o John 14:16: "And I will ask the Father, and he will give you another Counselor to be with you forever."

  o John 14:26: "But the Counselor, the Holy Spirit, whom the Father will send in my name, will teach you all things and will remind you of everything I have said to you." See also John 15:26.

- Isaiah refers to the Messiah, Jesus, as the Counselor, whereas John refers to the Holy Spirit as the Counselor. I'm grateful I have two Counselors.

**A Prayer for You:**

*Wonderful Counselor, thank You for coming to earth to show me the truth and to guide me throughout my life. Help me to rely on You and Your wisdom more and less on my own understanding. I want to learn to go to You first when I need advice.*

## Mighty God

*For to us a child is born, to us a son is given;*
*and the government shall be upon his shoulder,*
*and his name shall be called Wonderful Counselor, **Mighty God**,*
*Everlasting Father, Prince of Peace.*
Isaiah 9:6 (ESV)

**Steps on Your Journey to Know God More Intimately:**

- This name is *Gibbor El* in Hebrew. The word for mighty, *gibbor*, in Hebrew means powerful, strong and valiant.

- Read the verses, below to see more about how mighty God is:

  o Jeremiah 32:18: "You show steadfast love to thousands, but you repay the guilt of fathers to their children after them, O great and mighty God, whose name is the LORD of hosts" (ESV).

  o Luke 22:69: "But from now on, the Son of Man will be seated at the right hand of the mighty God."

- What do these verses say to you about the Lord?

- In Isaiah 9:6, the Messiah is referred to as the Mighty God. In Luke 22:69, the Messiah will be seated at the right hand of the Mighty God. What does it mean to you today that both Jesus and Father God are called the Mighty God?

- In what ways do you want to see His might, His power? Ask Him.

- Continue to memorize Isaiah 9:6. Memorizing the Word isn't as hard as many people think it is. Simply reading it repeatedly and meditating on it will get it into your mind and heart.

**A Prayer for You:**

*Mighty God, I worship You today. Thank You that Your strength is not like any human's. You are all-powerful. There is absolutely nothing that is too hard for You. Thank You that I can lean on You and trust You for everything in my life.*

December 6

*Everlasting Father*

*For to us a child is born, to us a son is given;*
*and the government shall be upon his shoulder,*
*and his name shall be called Wonderful Counselor, Mighty God,*
***Everlasting Father***, *Prince of Peace.*
Isaiah 9:6 (ESV)

**Steps on Your Journey to Know God More Intimately:**

- The Hebrew word for Everlasting is *ad*, meaning eternal, perpetual, eternity and world without end. Father is *ab*, from which we see God called *abba* in the New Testament.

- Consider that your Father has no end. He will always be there, so you can depend on Him. How does knowing that affect you today?

- This verse is talking about the Messiah. Think about how Jesus is the Everlasting Father. How can He be the Father if he is the Son?

- What does it mean to you that Jesus is the Everlasting Father?

- Continue to read Isaiah 9:6 several times a day. Have you memorized it yet?

- In 1 Chronicles 29:10, David praised the Lord in the presence of the whole assembly, saying, "Praise be to you, O Lord, God of our father Israel, from everlasting to everlasting." Our Father deserves all praise forever and ever.

**A Prayer for You:**

*Everlasting Father, I praise You today, because You are not only everlasting, with no end, You are also my Father. You are the One who cares about me. Thank You that I can trust You to always be with me, because You have no end.*

## December 7

### *Prince of Peace*

*For to us a child is born, to us a son is given;*
*and the government shall be upon his shoulder,*
*and his name shall be called Wonderful Counselor, Mighty God,*
*Everlasting Father, **Prince of Peace**.*
Isaiah 9:6 (ESV)

**Steps on Your Journey to Know God More Intimately:**

- This name in Hebrew is *Sar Shalom. Sar* means chief, captain, head person, master and governor. *Shalom* means not only peace, but also well-being, prosperity, safety, good health and wellness.

- Read or quote Isaiah 9:6 to someone. Remember, it's talking about the Messiah, Jesus.

- Read and meditate on the verses, below. What do they say to you?

  o Philippians 4:9: "Whatever you have learned or received or heard from me, or seen in me—put it into practice. And the God of peace will be with you."

  o 2 Thessalonians 3:16: "Now may the Lord of peace himself give you peace at all times and in every way. The Lord be with all of you."

- What does it mean to you that Jesus is the Prince of Peace? How does that impact your life?

- How do you need Jesus to be your *Shalom*?

- I've seen how God has been my Peace numerous times. One example was when I was working in Guatemala during a war between the government and terrorists. At night I often went to sleep hearing bombs and gunshots. I couldn't stay in that situation without God's peace that is beyond understanding (Philippians 4:6-7).

- Ask the Lord to be your peace today, regardless of what you are facing.

**A Prayer for You:**

*Prince of Peace, thank You that You came to be my Shalom—peace, wellness, safety, prosperity, health and so much more. Show me how You are my peace. I want to learn to rest in You and trust You more.*

## Jesus Christ Our Lord

*To the only God our Savior be glory, majesty, power and authority,*
*through **Jesus Christ our Lord**, before all ages,*
*now and forevermore! Amen.*
Jude 1:25

**Steps on Your Journey to Know God More Intimately:**

- Consider each word in this name:

    o Jesus—His human name

    o Christ—the Messiah, the Anointed One

    o Our—He's not only the Lord of others, but He is your Lord

    o Lord—Master and Owner

- Jesus came to earth as God's Anointed One to be your Lord and Savior. What does that mean to you?

- First Corinthians 1:9 says, "God is faithful, who has called you into fellowship with His Son Jesus Jesus Christ our Lord." Think about that. The word faithful is *pistos* meaning trustworthy, sure and true. How does this affect your life?

- How does your life reflect that Jesus is your Lord and Master? Is there anything you may need to change?

**A Prayer for You:**

*Jesus Christ, thank You for coming to earth to be both my Messiah, the One who would save me from my sins, as well as my Lord and Master. I'm so grateful for all You did for me. I want to bring You glory, majesty, power and authority through my life.*

## Son of the Most High

*[The angel said to Mary,] "You will conceive and give birth to a son,*
*and you will name him Jesus.*
*He will be great and will be called the **Son of the Most High**.*
*The Lord God will give him the throne of his father David."*
Luke 1:31-32 (NLT)

**Steps on Your Journey to Know God More Intimately:**

- Imagine if you were Mary, a young virgin girl. Suddenly an angel came to you and told you that you were going to have a baby. And what's more, that baby was going to be God's Son. What might that have been like?

- Most High, *hupsistos*, in Greek is one word and means the highest or Supreme God. Son is *huios*. Jesus is the Son of the Supreme God.

- I'm sitting in a house of prayer. Two women are singing an appropriate song: "Consider this for a moment: *Yahweh* in the flesh. How can this be? The center of attention in Heaven is walking the streets of Jerusalem completely unnoticed." Remember, *Yahweh* was God's holy name in Hebrew.

- Stop and meditate on this: Jesus was the center of attention in Heaven, yet He was willing to give that all up and become an unknown on Earth. How does that affect you? I pray that impresses you, like it does me.

**A Prayer for You:**

*Jesus, thank You for being willing to leave Heaven with all the attention You received there to come to Earth, knowing You would be hated, betrayed, beaten, mocked and crucified. That is incredible love. I worship You, the Son of the Supreme God. I want to learn to know Your love in deeper ways.*

# Holy One to Be Born

*"How will this be," Mary asked the angel, "since I am a virgin?"*
*The angel answered, "The Holy Spirit will come upon you,*
*and the power of the Most High will overshadow you.*
*So the **holy one to be born** will be called the Son of God."*
Luke 1:34-35

**Steps on Your Journey to Know God More Intimately:**

- *Hagios* is holy. *Genao* means to be born, bring forth or conceive.

- This was Mary's response when the Angel told her she, a virgin, was going to have a baby. And this wouldn't be a normal baby. He would be the Son of God.

- Consider that the God of the universe was born as a helpless baby. The holy God came to earth as a tiny infant.

- Part of the song I shared yesterday said, "Consider this for a moment: Yahweh in the flesh." The Holy God in the flesh. God became human. Stop and think about this amazing thought today.

- Jesus is the holy, pure, righteous One, without fault, without sin. Think about why He would leave the glory of Heaven to come to Earth.

- Thank and worship the Holy One who was born.

- I pray God's blessings on you as you focus on Jesus this holiday season and worship Him. Make a choice this year to not get so caught up in all the trappings of the season that you forget about the One whose birthday we are celebrating.

**A Prayer for You:**

*Jesus, I worship You today as the Holy One who was born. Thank You that the Holy God came to Earth to be born as a tiny, helpless baby. I choose to focus on You this month and worship You.*

## Son of God

*The angel answered, The Holy Spirit will come upon you,*
*the power of the Highest hover over you;*
*Therefore, the child you bring to birth will be called Holy, **Son of God**.*
Luke 1:35 (MSG)

**Steps on Your Journey to Know God More Intimately:**

- Imagine how overwhelming and probably frightening it must have been to Mary to speak face to face with an angel. But more than that, to find out she is going to give birth to the Son of God. Think about that. Imagine if that was you. How would you react?

- In John 19:7, years later, the religious leaders wanted to kill Jesus because He claimed He was the Son of God.

- Many dispute the fact that Jesus is God's Son even today. Some people believe Jesus was a good man, a great prophet or a powerful teacher. But they don't believe He was actually the Son of God. Think about this: if Jesus was not God's Son, then He couldn't have been a good man or a great prophet. He would have been a liar or a lunatic, since He *claimed* to be God.

- What do you think about Jesus being the Son of God?

- Meditate on how Jesus can be both God and the Son of God. What is the Lord showing you?

**A Prayer for You:**

*Jesus, I acknowledge You as the Son of God. You are God come to earth in the flesh. I choose to worship You and bring You praise.*

# My Lord

## Mou Kurios (Greek)

*Elizabeth said, Why am I so honored,
that the mother of **my Lord** should visit me?*
Luke 1:43 (NLT)

**Steps on Your Journey to Know God More Intimately:**

- Read Luke 1:39-45 to see more of the story of Mary visiting her cousin, Elizabeth, who was pregnant with John (the Baptist). I'll give you portions to read in the coming days to see more of the story of Jesus' birth.

- Elizabeth recognized that Mary's unborn baby was the Lord. Verse 41 says that Elizabeth was filled with the Holy Spirit, who revealed to her that Mary's baby was not ordinary.

- The Greek word for Lord here is *Kurios*, meaning supreme in authority, controller, master or sir. Elizabeth recognized that Mary was pregnant with her Lord and Master, the Messiah. Do you treat Jesus as your Lord and Master?

- Other translations say, "Why am I so favored?" "Why am I so blessed?" Elizabeth said she was favored or blessed that the mother of her Lord had come to her. Your Lord has also come to you. Spend some time today with your Lord.

- Do you feel God's favor on you? If so, thank Him. If not, ask the Lord to open your eyes to see His favor (sometimes we miss it, because we're not looking for it).

- What does it mean to you that your Lord came to earth as a baby?

- In what ways does your life reveal that Jesus is your Lord?

**A Prayer for You:**

*My Lord, I worship You today for You are holy. You are the supreme authority over the universe, but also in my life. Show me how to honor and worship You more. Thank You that as I spend time with You, I am favored and honored.*

# God My Savior

Theos Mou Sotare (Greek)

*My spirit rejoices in **God my Savior**.*
Luke 1:47 (ESV)

**Steps on Your Journey to Know God More Intimately:**

- Read Luke 1:45-65. This is Mary's song of praise to the Lord after she got to Elizabeth's house and heard her greeting acknowledging Mary's baby as God's Son.

- Jesus came to earth to be our Savior. He didn't have to come. God didn't have to save us. He did it because He wants a relationship with you and me. Wow!

- The Greek word for Savior is *Sotare* from the root *sozo*, meaning to save, heal, deliver and make whole. We've looked at this before, but I believe it is so important for us to focus on all Jesus came to earth to do for us.

- Psalm 25:5 says, "Guide me in your truth and teach me, for you are God my Savior, and my hope is in you all day long."

- In recent years, I've enjoyed discovering all Jesus came to do for us. He didn't just come to save us from our sins. He cares about our spirits, souls and bodies.

- As Mary rejoiced, I want to encourage you to take some time to rejoice today in God your Savior. If you're not sure how to do that, ask the Lord to show you. One way is just spending time focusing on all He did for you.

**A Prayer for You:**

*Lord, I praise You that You are God My Savior. You came to earth to sozo me—to not only save me, but also to heal me, deliver me from the enemy and make me whole. I'm so grateful for all You did for me. Thank You.*

## December 14

### *Mighty Savior*

Keras Soteria (Greek)

*He has sent us a **mighty Savior** from the royal line of his servant David,*
*just as he promised through his holy prophets long ago.*
Luke 1:69-70 (NLT)

**Steps on Your Journey to Know God More Intimately:**

- *Keras* means strong, strength or horn. *Soteria* means salvation, health and deliverance.

- The next two days are names Zechariah, John the Baptist's father, called Jesus in His prayer. You can read it in Luke 1:67-79.

- Some translations use Horn of Salvation. Horn symbolizes strength, power or might. It comes from the image of battling animals. Horns are an emblem of power, dominion, glory and fierceness, as they are the chief means of attack and defense for the animals endowed with them.

- Zechariah recognized that Jesus' coming was a fulfillment of Scripture. God foretold hundreds of years before it happened that the Messiah, Jesus, would come to earth to bring salvation (Jeremiah 23:5-6).

- What does it mean to you today that Jesus is your Mighty Savior?

**A Prayer for You:**

*Mighty Savior, thank You for predicting everything that would happen, so many years before You came. Thank You for being my Mighty Savior. You are big enough and strong enough to save me from my sins as well as from any enemies I may face, especially Satan.*

December 15

*Sunrise*

*Because of the tender mercy of our God,*
*whereby the **sunrise** shall visit us from on high*
*to give light to those who sit in darkness and in the shadow of death,*
*to guide our feet into the way of peace.*
Luke 1:78-79 (ESV)

**Steps on Your Journey to Know God More Intimately:**

- This is a continuation of Zechariah's prayer.

- Other translations use Rising Sun for this name. *Anatolay* means a rising of light or dayspring.

- Think about what the rising sun is like—bright, giving hope, warmth, light and clarity. What else is a sunrise like? If possible, watch the sunrise sometime this week.

- How is Jesus like a sunrise?

- Luke says the Sunrise will come to us from Heaven. He came as a baby! Could it be that Jesus was called the Rising Sun because like a sunrise, He started small? As He grew He shone brighter and brighter. Think about that.

- Ask the Lord to reveal Himself through this name.

- Look at what Luke 1:78-79 says about the Sunrise. How has He given you light? In what ways has He guided your feet into the way of peace?

- Worship the Rising Sun who came to us.

**A Prayer for You:**

*Lord, I praise You that You came to us from Heaven as a Sunrise. Show me more of what this name means. I want to worship You in new ways. Thank You that You came to give me light, hope and peace.*

December 16

*Baby*

*While they were there, the time came for her **baby** to be born.*
Luke 2:6 (NLT)

**Steps on Your Journey to Know God More Intimately:**

- You can read about Jesus being born in Luke 2:1-7.

- Jesus came as a helpless baby—no power, no greatness, and totally dependent. Think about what a baby is like.

- I remember when my babies were born. They were so helpless and dependent on me. It's hard to think about God coming to earth as such a tiny infant.

- What can a baby do? At first, all they do is eat, sleep, cry and dirty their diapers. That doesn't seem like a very glorious way to bring the King of kings into the world. I'm so glad I wasn't the one who figured it all out!

- Why would the God of the universe come as a baby, when He could have come as a reigning King? Think about that.

- Ask the Lord to show you more about Himself and His love for you through this name.

**A Prayer for You:**

*Jesus, thank You that You were willing to come to earth as a tiny, helpless baby. You could have come as a King or as someone who was respected and honored, but You didn't. I want to understand Your plan more. Teach me, Lord.*

## Mary's Firstborn, a Son

*She gave birth to her **firstborn**, **a son**.*
*She wrapped him in cloths and placed him in a manger,*
*because there was no room for them in the inn.*
Luke 2:7

**Steps on Your Journey to Know God More Intimately:**

- *Prototokos* is firstborn in Greek. *Huios* is son.

- Jesus came to a young virgin in the humble town of Bethlehem. He was born in a stable or a cave. He wasn't even born in a palace, as a king should be. The Greek word for manger comes from the word "to eat." It means crib, manger or stall.

- This name reveals Jesus' humanity once again. He was the son of a young girl the community knew.

- One of my favorite Christmas songs is "Mary Did You Know?" by Mark Lowry. I encourage you to listen to the whole song. Here is part of the first verse:

  "Mary, did you know that your Baby Boy would one day walk on water? Did you know that your Baby Boy has come to make you new? This Child that you delivered will soon deliver you."

- Think about all that Mary's firstborn would later do.

- Jesus was born in a place where animals lived, because there wasn't any room for Him in the inn. Do you have room for this newborn King in your life? Or are you too busy with all your preparations for Christmas that you don't have time for Him? I encourage you to make Jesus a priority in your schedule this month and throughout the coming year.

**A Prayer for You:**

*Jesus, thank You for coming as a baby to a young girl. Show me more of Yourself through this name. I want to make time in my schedule this month to spend time with You every day. It's such a great privilege to be with You.*

# Christ the Lord

Christos Kurios (Greek)

*For unto you is born this day in the city of David
a Savior, who is **Christ the Lord**.*
Luke 2:11 (ESV)

**Steps on Your Journey to Know God More Intimately:**

- This is part of what the angel said to the shepherds the night Jesus was born. You can read the whole story in Luke 2:8-20.

- This name reveals Jesus' deity. Christ means Messiah or Anointed One. Lord means sir, owner or master, revealing His authority and supremacy.

- Jesus is not just Christ a lord. He's *the* Lord. Is He your Lord and Master? If not, what do you need to change?

- What might you need to do to focus on Christ the Lord more in the midst of all the chaos that often surrounds the Christmas season?

- In recent years, I have simplified how I celebrate the holidays, so I can focus on the reason for the season. I don't want to get so caught up with all the trappings of Christmas that I forget why we're celebrating.

- How can you help your family and others around you to focus on Christ the Lord as we approach Christmas?

- Worship the Messiah, your Lord, today.

**A Prayer for You:**

*Messiah, I praise You because You came to earth to be my Savior and Lord. I choose to make focusing on You a priority today and in the coming days. I want to honor You more this year. How do You want me to honor You?*

## Consolation

*Now there was a man in Jerusalem, whose name was Simeon,
and this man was righteous and devout,
waiting for the **consolation** of Israel, and the Holy Spirit was upon him.*
Luke 2:25 (ESV)

**Steps on Your Journey to Know God More Intimately:**

- Read Luke 2:21-35.

- Consolation is from the Greek word, *paraklaysis*, meaning comfort, encouragement and one called alongside to help. It comes from the same root word as comforter in Greek.

- Meditate on Jesus coming to be your Comforter, your Encourager and your Helper.

- The holidays can be a very difficult time for many people, especially if your life and family are not all that you had hoped they would be. Remember, Jesus came to bring you comfort and encouragement. Meditate on this today and the rest of the week. Rather than focusing on what you don't have, focus on what you do have.

- Thankfulness helps us to change our perspective. I know. I struggle sometimes with my life not being all I had hoped it would be. I never thought I'd have to raise my sons alone. I never imagined I would be single for so many years. But I choose not to focus on that. I have so much to be thankful for—and so do you!

- What can you thank the Lord for right now? Take time to do it.

- I pray God will fill you with joy during this holiday season as you focus on Jesus and all He has done and is doing for you!

**A Prayer for You:**

*Jesus, thank You for coming to be my Comforter and Encourager. I have so much for which I can be grateful. Help me to focus on Your blessings, especially the miracle of the newborn King who came to save me. Thank You.*

## *Lord's Christ*

*Kurios Christos* (Greek)

*It had been revealed to him by the Holy Spirit
that he would not see death before he had seen the **Lord's Christ**.*
Luke 2:26 (NKJV)

**Steps on Your Journey to Know God More Intimately:**

- This verse is talking about Simeon, a godly man, who was filled with the Holy Spirit.

- Meditate on this name for Jesus. Remember *Christos* means Anointed One. Jesus is God's anointed, chosen One. *Kurios* means master.

- Why do you think Luke calls Jesus "The Lord's Christ" rather than "the Messiah" or some other name?

- What is the Lord showing you about this name?

- As the Holy Spirit spoke to Simeon, He also speaks to us today. Are you listening? Are you filled with the Holy Spirit so you *can* hear Him?

- I'm sure there are so many times when God has tried to talk to me, but I haven't been listening. There have also been times when there was something that kept me from being able to hear God when I was trying to listen. Now, when I sense there is something keeping me from seeing or hearing Him, I ask Him to remove whatever it is. Sometimes He shows me the hindrance, because I need to do something myself to eliminate it. Other times He just removes it.

- If you can't hear the Lord speakng to you, ask Him to remove anything that keeps you from seeing Him or hearing Him clearly.

**A Prayer for You:**

*Jesus, I'm amazed at all the different names You have. Thank You for revealing so many various facets about Yourself through Your names. Help me to learn to know You more through each one.*

## Salvation

Soterion (Greek); Yeshua (Hebrew)

*With my own eyes I've seen your **salvation**;*
*it's now out in the open for everyone to see.*
Luke 2:30-31 (MSG)

**Steps on Your Journey to Know God More Intimately:**

- In Luke 2, Simeon praised God as He held the baby Jesus. He said that Jesus was God's salvation. Since God didn't need to be saved, it means that Jesus was God's plan of salvation for us.

- The Greek word for salvation, *soterion*, means defender, defense or that which brings salvation. The Hebrew word for salvation is *yeshua*, meaning deliverance, prosperity, health and victory. *Yeshua* is Jesus' Hebrew name. Think about these meanings. How do they affect how you see Jesus and what He did for you?

- As Simeon saw God's Salvation, we have also. We have experienced His Salvation. If you're not sure if you have experienced it, ask God to show you. You can also go to page 369 to learn more.

- What does it mean to you that Jesus came as your Salvation?

**A Prayer for You:**

*Yeshua, thank You that You came to earth over two thousand years ago because You wanted a relationship with us. Thank You for coming as my defender, bringing me deliverance, prosperity, health and victory. Show me what I need to do to have a better relationship with You. Please reveal more of Yourself to me.*

## Light for Revelation to the Gentiles

*My eyes have seen your salvation,*
*which you have prepared in the sight of all people,*
*a **light for revelation to the Gentiles***
*and for glory to your people Israel.*
Luke 2:30-32

**Steps on Your Journey to Know God More Intimately:**

- The Message translates this name as "a God-revealing light."

- Jesus came to reveal God and His Kingdom to us. He is the light shining on us, to bring us into relationship with Himself.

- The word for revelation is *apokalypsis*, meaning manifestation, appearing and revelation. Revelation is God revealing Himself and His message to the world, or to us. He gives revelation through the Bible, Jesus' nature and to us directly through the Holy Spirit.

- Thank the Lord that He didn't just come for Jews, but He also came for Gentiles (that's anyone who is not a Jew). He could have just come for His people, but He chose to include us. Being a Gentile myself, I'm so thrilled Jesus came for us too.

- Ask the Lord to show you today what else it means that Jesus came as a Light for Revelation.

- How has God been a Light for Revelation for you?

- In what ways do you need Him to be your light and to bring you revelation?

**A Prayer for You:**

*Jesus, thank You that You came to earth as a Light for Revelation. You came revealing the Father and what the Father wanted to say to us. Thank You for shining Your light into my life, to show me what Your plan is for me. Open my eyes and ears to see You and hear You more.*

## Glory of Your People Israel

*I have seen your salvation, which you have prepared for all people.*
*He is a light to reveal God to the nations,*
*and he is the **glory of your people Israel**!*
Luke 2:30-32 (NLT)

**Steps on Your Journey to Know God More Intimately:**

- This name is *Doxa Sou Laos* in Greek. *Doxa* means dignity, glory, honor, praise and worship. Glory in Hebrew is *nehtsak*, meaning strength, goal, splendor, truthfulness, confidence and victory.

- Simeon saw that this tiny baby would bring glory to the Jews. How did Jesus bring glory to the Jews?

- First Samuel 15:29 says, "He who is the Glory of Israel does not lie or change his mind; for he is not a man, that he should change his mind."

- Galatians 3:29 says, "If you belong to Christ, then you are Abraham's seed, and heirs according to the promise." That means that Gentiles receive the same promises as Jews (Abraham's seed), so Jesus is Glory to the Gentiles too. How does He bring glory to us?

- Ask the Lord to show you more of what this name means.

**A Prayer for You:**

*Jesus, I praise You that You are the Glory of Your People Israel. Show me more of what this means. Thank You that because I belong to Christ, I can claim any promises to the Jews (Galatians 3:29). Continue to prepare my heart to worship my newborn King.*

# Sign that Will Be Spoken Against

*Then Simeon blessed them and said to Mary, his mother:
"This child is destined to cause the falling and rising of many in Israel,
and to be a **sign that will be spoken against**."*
Luke 2:34

**Steps on Your Journey to Know God More Intimately:**

- This name is *Saymion Antilego* in Greek. *Saymion* is a sign or miracle. *Antilego* means spoken against.

- Today is Christmas Eve. Even though this was not the actual time of year that Jesus was born, it is the time we celebrate His birth.

- Why do you think Simeon said Jesus would be a sign that would be spoken against? Jesus was hated by the religious rulers. When else was Jesus spoken against?

- Thank Jesus that He was willing to come to earth, even knowing how people would treat Him. He did it because He loves us!

- Regardless of what else you have to do today, take some time to focus on Jesus and worship Him. If you have children or other family around, read the story of Jesus' birth in Luke 2 together.

- When my sons were young, on Christmas Eve we would camp out by our fireplace, roast marshmallows and read the story of Jesus' birth. We talked about the true meaning of Christmas.

**A Prayer for You:**

*Jesus, thank You that You were willing to come to earth, knowing how people would treat You, knowing they would speak against You. Today I want to focus on You, rather than all the things I feel like I have to do to make it a perfect Christmas. You are the One who makes Christmas perfect.*

# He Who Has Been Born King of the Jews

Tikto Basileus Ioudaios (Greek)

*The Magi asked, "Where is **he who has been born king of the Jews**?
For we saw his star when it rose and have come to worship him."*
Matthew 2:2 (ESV)

**Steps on Your Journey to Know God More Intimately:**

- *Tikto* means to be born. *Basileus* is a king or sovereign. *Ioudaios* means Jews.

- Today is the day we celebrate Jesus' birth. Take time to worship the newborn King.

- The Magi, wise men, were following a star searching for the One Who Was Born Kng of the Jews. How do you think they knew what the star meant?

- People believe it took them a long time (maybe years) to find where the star pointed, but they didn't give up. Are you searching for your King as diligently as the Magi? If not, why not? Is there anything you need to change?

- Spend some time today with family or friends remembering what Jesus did for you. He didn't have to come to earth. He chose to come, because He wanted a relationship with You.

**A Prayer for You:**

*Jesus, thank You for choosing to come to earth to be born the King of the Jews. I worship You because You are my King. You deserve worship and praise. Forgive me for making Christmas all about gifts, meals and parties, when it's all about You, Jesus. It's all about You.*

# Ruler

*O Bethlehem, in the land of Judah,*
*are by no means least among the rulers of Judah;*
*for from you shall come a **ruler** who will shepherd my people Israel.*
Matthew 2:6 (ESV)

**Steps on Your Journey to Know God More Intimately:**

- *Haygehomahee* in Greek means ruler, governor, chief or judge.

- Matthew 2:6 is a quote from Micah 5:2, which was a prophecy about the coming Messiah. Jesus fulfilled this prophecy and many, many others. There are about 350 prophecies Jesus fulfilled. It was absolutely impossible for one person to fulfill even a tiny portion of them, *but God…*

- Daniel 9:25 says, "Know and understand this: From the issuing of the decree to restore and rebuild Jerusalem until the Anointed One, the ruler, comes, there will be seven 'sevens,' and sixty-two 'sevens.'" This verse is also a prophecy about Jesus. The Anointed One is another way of saying the Messiah. Daniel is referring to when the Messiah returns a second time.

- What kind of ruler was and is Jesus? What kind will He be when He returns?

- How are you allowing Jesus to rule in your life? If you're not, what may you need to do?

**A Prayer for You:**

*Jesus, thank You for coming as a Ruler. I'm so glad You didn't come as a demanding dictator, but rather as a Shepherd, caring for Your sheep. I want to follow You and obey You completely. Show me any areas I'm not following You as my Ruler.*

## Shepherd for My People

*And you, O Bethlehem in the land of Judah,*
*are not least among the ruling cities of Judah,*
*for a ruler will come from you*
*who will be the **shepherd for my people** Israel.*
Matthew 2:6 (NLT)

**Steps on Your Journey to Know God More Intimately:**

- This is a quote from Micah 5:2 about the Messiah.

- John 10:11 says, "I am the good shepherd. The good shepherd lays down his life for the sheep."

- How is Jesus like a Shepherd?

- Think about how He shepherds His people.

- How has Jesus been your Shepherd?

- Read Psalm 23 to learn more about how God is your Shepherd.

- In what ways do you need the Lord to be your Shepherd today?

**A Prayer for You:**

*Shepherd, thank You for how You guide me, direct me, protect me, discipline me and provide for me. I choose to follow You without question, because I know You are a good Shepherd.*

# Child

*After they had heard the king, they went on their way,*
*and the star they had seen in the east went ahead of them*
*until it stopped over the place where the **child** was.*
Matthew 2:9

**Steps on Your Journey to Know God More Intimately:**

- *Paidion* in Greek means a young or little child.

- Repeatedly Jesus is called a "child" in Matthew 2. Often we think of Jesus as being an infant when the Magi got to Him. However, He is called a child here, not a baby.

- Think about what children are like. They are dependent on their parents, but they grow up, gaining more and more independence. Children skin their knees and get hurt. Jesus was a human child, so He probably skinned His knees and went running to His mom for comfort.

- When do you think Jesus began to realize He was not just an ordinary child? When do you think He realized He was God?

- He went through all the same stages of growing up as you and I did. How can you relate to Jesus, knowing He was a child?

- Ask the Lord to show you what He wants you to see through this name.

**A Prayer for You:**

*Jesus, thank You for going through childhood as a normal boy. You experienced pain, sadness and meanness from other children, just like I did. I'm so glad You can relate to me, because You understand what it's like being a human.*

## Nazarene

*And he went and lived in a city called Nazareth,*
*that what was spoken by the prophets might be fulfilled:*
*"He shall be called a **Nazarene**."*
Matthew 2:23 (ESV)

**Steps on Your Journey to Know God More Intimately:**

- The name, Nazarene, is *Nazoraios* in Greek. It reveals His humanity, because it says He was an inhabitant of the town of Nazareth. Nazareth is in the Northern part of Israel between the Sea of Galilee and the Mediterranean Sea.

- Nazareth was a small, unimportant town. Nathaniel asked in John 1:46, "Can anything good come out of Nazareth?"

- I remember going through Nazareth with my son Timothy, who was eleven at the time. It was fun seeing where Jesus grew up.

- Jesus was raised in Nazareth. The people knew him as Mary and Joseph's son, so they had a hard time believing He was the Messiah. In Mark 6:4, Jesus said, "A prophet is not without honor, except in his hometown and among his relatives and in his own household."

- Imagine how difficult it would have been for Jesus to begin His ministry, with people who couldn't believe He was anything special.

- What does it mean to you today that Jesus was human, just like you?

- What if He had only come to earth as God?

**A Prayer for You:**

*Jesus, even though You are God, You were willing to be a normal boy in Nazareth. I can't even imagine how hard it must have been once You started to understand who You were. It must have been frustrating that the people You knew didn't believe in You. I choose to trust You and believe in You.*

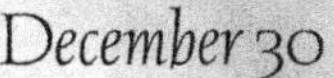

# Great Light

## Megas Foce (Greek)

*The people who sat in darkness have seen a **great light**. And for those who lived in the land where death casts its shadow, a **light** has shined.*
Matthew 4:16 (NLT)

**Steps on Your Journey to Know God More Intimately:**

- This is a quote from Isaiah 9:2, a prophecy about the Messiah.

- The very first thing God created was light (Genesis 1:3).

- Look at some other verses about light:

  o Psalm 4:6: "Many, Lord, are asking, 'Who will bring us prosperity?' Let the light of your face shine on us."

  o Psalm 36:9: "For with you is the fountain of life; in your light we see light."

  o Psalm 27:1: "The Lord is my light and my salvation—whom shall I fear? The Lord is the stronghold of my life—of whom shall I be afraid?"

  o John 8:12: Jesus said, "I am the light of the world. Whoever follows me will never walk in darkness, but will have the light of life."

- Meditate on the above verses. What can you learn from them about Jesus?

- How is Jesus a Light? A Great Light?

- How has Jesus been your Light?

- How do you need Him to be your Light today?

**A Prayer for You:**

*Thank You, Jesus, that You came to us as a Great Light in our dark world. Thank You for bringing me light and hope. Lord, let the light of Your face shine on me today. I want to know You and experience You in new and deeper ways.*

## The First and the Last

*I am the Alpha and the Omega, **the First and the Last**,*
*the Beginning and the End.*
Revelation 22:13

**Steps on Your Journey to Know God More Intimately:**

- *Protos kai Eskatos* is the Greek for this name. *Protos* means first, foremost, beginning or chief. *Eskatos* means last or final.

- Congratulations! You made it to the end of this book and to the end of another year.

- This verse has three names of God in it that are all very similar. If you went through this whole book, you studied the others already. If not, you can start at the beginning tomorrow

- Meditate on how Jesus is the First and the Last.

- He has always been with you and He always will be with you.

- Take some time to look back on this past year, focusing on all the good things God did in your life. If you don't already have a "Gratitude List," I'd encourage you to start one today. Write down everything for which you are thankful in this past year.

- Ask the Lord to reveal to you more of His character through this name.

- In what ways do you need the Lord to be your First and Last? Talk to Him about it. He loves you so much and loves talking to you and listening to you.

**A Prayer for You:**

*God, thank You for another year that You have been with me, even if things didn't turn out like I hoped they would. I praise You that You are the First and the Last. You were with me at the beginning of the year, as well as the beginning of my life. And You are still with me at the end of this year and will be throughout all time. Thank You.*

*Endnotes*

1. You can read more of my story in *Keys to Joy*. It is a Bible study on twelve keys to open the door to greater joy in our lives. You can get a copy on www.365NamesofGod.com.

2. What is meditation? Synonyms for mediate include: consider, think about, study, contemplate, ponder, deliberate and mull over. You can learn more at www.365NamesofGod.com.

3. All definitions labeled Merriam-Webster or Webster are from www.merriam-webster.com.

4. For ideas on how to memorize Scripture, go to www.365NamesofGod.com.

5. You can listen to this song, accompanied by pictures of nature, by going to www.RRbooks.org.

6. You can learn more about my stories in *All Stressed Up and Everywhere to Go!* Go to www.RRbooks.org.

7. You can learn some powerful, biblical stress management principles in my latest book, *All Stressed Up and Everywhere to Go! Solutions to De-Stressing Your Life and Recovering Your Sanity.* Go to www.RRbooks.org.

If you don't yet have a personal relationship with God, congratulations on taking a giant step in your search. I've had a relationship with God for many years. It has been the most exciting adventure of my life—and I have traveled all over the world and had some amazing adventures. I encourage you to get to know Him. It is well worth it.

**Consider the following:**

Romans 3:23 explains that we "all have sinned and fallen short of the glory of God." We can't have a relationship with God on our own.

Romans 6:23 tells us that as a result of sin in our lives there is price to be paid—death. But *instead* of death, God wants to give us a gift— "eternal life in Christ Jesus our Lord." He trades our sins for the gift of getting to live with Him forever. I say that's a very good trade for us!

John 3:16 sheds light on how much God loves us, how desperately He wants to give us this gift of living with Him forever. We see the sacrifice He made so He *could* give us this gift. "For God so loved the world that he gave his one and only Son, that whoever believes in him shall not perish but have eternal life."

Romans 10:9 explains there are two simple things you and I need to do in order to receive this gift: "If you confess with your mouth, 'Jesus is Lord,' and believe in your heart that God raised him from the dead, you will be saved." Confess just means to speak out that Jesus is Lord.

Do these truths resonate with you? If you haven't yet trusted Jesus as your Savior, you can do so right now, by praying a prayer like the following:

*Dear Lord, I realize I'm a sinner and need You. Thank You for dying on the cross for my sins and rising again the third day from the dead. I now confess all my sins and repent. I ask You to forgive me and cleanse me from all sin. Thank You for saving me and making me right with You. In Jesus' name. Amen.*

Look what happens in Heaven the moment we put our trust in Jesus. Luke 15:7 says, "I tell you that in the same way there will be more rejoicing in heaven over one sinner who repents than over ninety-nine righteous persons who do not need to repent."

How do you respond to that?

There's no pressure to trust God immediately. He's not in a hurry, although He would love to talk with you anytime.

**If you just trusted Jesus as your Savior, congratulations.** Now I'd encourage you to do some things:

- Get a modern Bible at a Christian bookstore (if you don't already have one) so you can read God's love-letters to you in familiar, contemporary language. As you read, you'll gain wonderful insights into who God is and the wonderful plans He has for you. A good place to start reading is in the book of John.

- Find a Bible-believing church where you can learn and grow.

Feel free to email me if you just trusted Jesus as your Savior, so I can pray for you and help you in any ways I can with starting your new life! Even if you're not sure about the whole concept, I'd love to hear from you. We can begin a dialog with no pressure at all.

**Email me at gaylyn@365NamesOfGod.com**

**Relationship Resources...**

- Facilitates growth for believers and not-yet-believers in their relationships with God, themselves and other people.

- Provides practical, biblical, interactive workshops and materials designed to empower and equip individuals and groups in their lives, work and ministries.

- Trains and mentors facilitators to provide their workshops for other groups.

- Gained IRS nonprofit status in 1999.

- Began as a concept in 1970 with Ken Williams training missionaries.

**For more information, go to www.RelationshipResources.org.**

## To get a free copy of the following books in PDF go to www.rrbooks.org/free-e-books:

- De-*Stress Your Life*
- *Reconcilable Differences*
- *Unlocking Your Joy*

*Gaylyn Williams and her incredible life story and spirit inspire all those who are fortunate enough to hear her speak or read her story. Gaylyn's humble, but powerful, style is laced with humor, grace, heartache and joy, while her story embodies adventure, courage, triumph and tragedy. By creatively sharing the lessons she learned along the way, Gaylyn helps the rest of us see how we too can apply those lessons to ease our own burdens.*

**—Kris Harty**, *Author and Speaker*

The author of seventeen books, Gaylyn is best known for her practical, biblical approach to self-help. She addresses the struggles, disappointments and challenges that are common to all, honestly sharing from personal experience, including: abandonment as a child, deaths of her six-month-old son and her fiancé, sixteen years as a single mom raising two rambunctious sons and major betrayals by a close friend.

Her titles include *The Keys to Joy* and *All Stressed Up and Everywhere to Go!* She has been published by traditional and nontraditional publishers including Readers Digest, B&H Publishing Group, Thomas Nelson Publishers, Wycliffe Bible Translators, International Training Partners, Outskirts Press, Success Books, Standard Publishing and Joshua Morris Publishing.

Raised as a missionary kid in Guatemala, Gaylyn went on to serve as a missionary with Wycliffe Bible Translators for fifteen years and The Navigators for three years. Since 1999, she has directed a nonprofit international ministry called Relationship Resources. To support the ministry, she started a real estate investment business in 2003. Gaylyn is the mother of two grown sons.

Today Gaylyn writes and speaks nationally and internationally. Dozens of radio and television programs have featured her. She taught as an adjunct professor at Dallas Theological Seminary, Wheaton College, and English Language Institute China. She has also served on many boards of directors.

Readers and students alike agree: Gaylyn is passionate about encouraging and equipping people in their relationship with God, themselves and others. Her writing and speaking are practical and biblical, empowering people to grow spiritually, personally, relationally, and professionally.

**Gaylyn can be contacted at Gaylyn@365NamesofGod.com**

# Where to Go When You Need Something from God

When you need something specific from God, you can check the following categories and go to the pages listed to see what Name of God will help you with that need.

**When you need or want... go to the following pages:**

## Go to the following pages when you feel:

Go to http://www.RRbooks.org to get a 25% discount on any of our products.

## All Stressed Up and Everywhere to Go!
*Solutions to De-Stressing Your Life and Recovering Your Sanity*

By Gaylyn R. Williams and Ken Williams, Ph.D.

From the daily hassles to the catastrophic events, this book will empower you to successfully de-stress your life and recover your sanity. You'll discover easy-to-use skills enabling you to gain greater freedom from life's ups and down.

In today's fast-paced, overworked world, stress is all around us: the economy, finances, raising children, health, job, school, family or lack of it, elderly parents, divorce, tragedy, debt, death and conflict.

### This is not an ordinary book about stress!

This unique workbook contains practical, biblical tools for attaining spiritual, emotional, physical and interpersonal balance. It is filled with powerful personal stories to illustrate principles, thought-provoking questions for individual or group study, Bible studies, self-assessments and easy-to-apply strategies to develop a balanced lifestyle.

As you explore the timeless connection between biblical principles and this practical, life-enhancing approach, you'll gain valuable solutions to cope with your own stress, as well as help friends and family.

These powerful strategies have been proven worldwide. Over twenty thousand pastors and ministry leaders in eighty countries have benefitted from these life-changing skills. Ken and Gaylyn first tested them in their own lives and continue to use them on a regular basis.

Rather than writing from a clinical perspective—although Dr. Williams, with his PhD in Human Behavior, could do that—they honestly share their personal experiences, having each dealt with numerous major and minor stresses. They have trained people in Christian organizations in these methods for twenty-five years. Now they are available to you.

# Keys to Joy

## *How to Unlock God's Gifts of Lasting Happiness*

**By Gaylyn R. Williams and Ken Williams, Ph.D.**


**Discover Thirteen Surprising, Proven Secrets To Unlock Your Joy!**
Experiencing joy is a natural—but often elusive—part of Christian living. The hurts of life, unhelpful habits and unhealthy attitudes all lock out joy for many believers. And it remains locked until they take action to open it up.

Keys to Joy not only shows you the door, but gives you the keys you need to usher yourself daily into the full, lasting joy God offers. You'll discover how to:

- Climb to new heights of joy in your relationships with God, family and others;

- Replace worry and fear with peace and contentment;

- Demolish unhappiness, misery and discouragement;

- Eradicate anything that locks joy out of your life;

- Transform trials into stepping stones.

In this practical, life-changing Bible study, you'll uncover strength and encouragement for your difficult times through the authors' powerful stories of God's joy in sufferings. Each daily study includes Scriptures with questions to contemplate and grow in your relationship with God. They are designed to empower you to experience the full joy God has for you.

Keys to Joy is for individuals, couples or small groups, and includes a leader's guide for group study. It provides the biblical understanding and life patterns you need to live joyfully regardless of your struggles. Once you've opened the door to joy, you'll know how to assure it's never shut again.

# Never Do Fundraising Again:

## A Paradigm Shift from Donors to Lifelong Partners

**In this practical, biblical book you will discover how to**

- Convert one-time gifts into lifetime support

- Experience the amazing power of gratitude to motivate people

- Employ effective communication skills—both written and verbal

- Transform the stress and drudgery of fundraising into a joyful ministry

- Utilize proven strategies to spend less time, effort and money to maintain full support

- Cultivate life-long ministry partners and close friends

- Inspire your partners to become your best recruiters for more support

- Enjoy freedom from worry about your financial needs

Never Do Fundraising Again contains over 200 pages of proven strategies and skills for building and maintaining your support. It is filled with powerful stories from the author's lives and others who are using the biblical principles.

This book is written by Ken and Gaylyn Williams, a father-daughter team with over 85 combined years' experience as supported missionaries. Gaylyn, as well as Ken and his wife Bobbie, served with Wycliffe Bible Translators.

# 2031 Names of God

## Transform Your Life As You Get to Know God in New Ways

By Gaylyn R. Williams

**Who is God? What is He like?**

**Discover how God describes Himself in the Bible.**

This rich treasury of God's names, with Scripture references and over 400 Greek and Hebrew names, will change your life forever as you

- Come into God's presence in deeper, more intimate ways
- Discover comfort, strength and hope from understanding God's character
- Expand your vision for God's power, majesty and greatness
- Enjoy a growing passion for God through praise and worship
- Transform your prayer life and strengthen your faith

"Gaylyn has compiled the powerful Names of God into a study guide for our spiritual growth. We need to know His Names to know His heart!"

**Camilla L. Seabolt, Exec. Dir. of Community Bible Study**

"We serve an amazing God! Gaylyn explores and uncovers who God is by examining 2031 Names given to the Lord."

**General David B. Warner, USAF (Ret.), Exec. Dir., Officers' Christian Fellowship**

"This wonderful collection will save you countless hours searching for these cherished expressions describing God's nature and character."

**Dick Eastman, International President of Every Home for Christ**

Made in the USA
Monee, IL
07 July 2026

56551141R00216